More Than Science ar

More Than Science and Sputnik

The National Defense Education Act of 1958

Wayne J. Urban

THE UNIVERSITY OF ALABAMA PRESS
Tuscaloosa

The University of Alabama Press
Tuscaloosa, Alabama 35487-0380
uapress.ua.edu

Copyright © 2010 by the University of Alabama Press
All rights reserved.

Hardcover edition published 2010.
Paperback edition published 2018.
eBook edition published 2015.

Inquiries about reproducing material from this work should be addressed to the University of Alabama Press.

Typeface: Caslon

Cover images: Courtesy of NASA
Cover design: Gary Gore

Paperback ISBN: 978-0-8173-5919-5
eBook ISBN: 978-0-8173-9026-6

A previous edition of this book has been catalogued by the Library of Congress as follows:

Library of Congress Cataloging-in-Publication Data

Urban, Wayne J.
More than science and Sputnik : the National Defense Education Act of 1958 / Wayne J. Urban.
p. cm.
Includes bibliographical references and index.
ISBN 978-0-8173-1691-4 (cloth : alk. paper) 1. Federal aid to education—United States—History. 2. National security—Law and legislation—United States—History. 3. United States. National Defense Education Act of 1958. 4. Federal aid to education—Government policy—United States. 5. Hill, Lister, 1894–1984. 6. Elliott, Carl, 1913–1999. I. Title.
KF4137.U73 2010
344.73'076—dc22 2009042197

To Mary Allen Jolley, aide to Carl Elliott during the passage of NDEA and long-time advocate of equalizing educational opportunity.

Contents

Preface and Acknowledgments

I came to The University of Alabama in January of 2006 to work in its newly revived Education Policy Center. What I sought to accomplish through this work was to show that history could be relevant to the world of education policy, not in any necessarily immediate sense but through the provision of a longer view of education policy issues and concerns that allows the present to be evaluated more judiciously than it could be without a historical perspective. Such a view allows policies to be seen as they evolve and in terms of their precedents and consequences, rather than in the cycle of immediacy and success or failure that seems to dominate the policy and policy analysis arena.

Shortly after I arrived in Tuscaloosa, the idea of pursuing a study of the National Defense Education Act (NDEA) surfaced as a possible Education Policy Center project. I was vaguely aware that Carl Elliott and Lister Hill, members of the United States House of Representatives and the United States Senate respectively, both Alabamians, were the two major congressional sponsors of NDEA, but knew nothing about how NDEA served their own political and ideological needs and how they interacted with the Eisenhower administration to pass NDEA. I subsequently learned that the papers of both Elliott and Hill were in the Special Collections division of The University of Alabama library, and that they were open for use with no restrictions. In reading biographies of Elliott and Hill, I learned that both were former student body presidents of the university. In researching both sets of papers, I discovered that the university itself was a major beneficiary of NDEA, an understanding that cannot be obtained from looking at the extant, and thin, institutional records for the period. Thus, this book was born, and has taken shape, as an integral part of my work as an educational historian in the Education Policy Center at The University of Alabama.

This book, especially in its first three chapters, is a fairly straightforward, though intentionally limited, political history of NDEA, passed by Congress in late August of 1958 and signed into law by President Dwight D. Eisenhower on September 2 of that year. It differs substantively from earlier works on NDEA in that it begins with the views of the two major congressional proponents of the legislation, Carl Elliott and Lister Hill. It concentrates on the liberal political ideology of Elliott and Hill and shows how their support of NDEA fit within their long-term pursuit of federal aid to education as a part of their liberal political agenda. Political liberalism characterized both of these southern legislators, as well as many of their colleagues in the Alabama congressional delegation in the middle of the twentieth century. Alabama political liberalism, as many historians of the state have described it, was propelled by the New Deal reaction to the Great Depression and shaped by World War II and its Cold War aftermath. In chapters 1 and 2 on Hill and Elliott respectively, I explore the contours of their liberalism and illustrate its relationship to the larger politics of the period, nationally and in the state of Alabama. Particularly, I indicate how these two Alabamians had to adjust their political philosophy in terms of two thorny issues in their state and their nation, race and religion. My interpretation of the actions of Elliott and Hill agrees with Wayne Flynt's characterization of their effort: "He [Elliott] and Lister Hill joined forces in 1958 to pass the National Defense Education Act, camouflaging their longtime desire for federal funding of education as a matter of national defense at a time when the Russian science and space programs created panic about the quality of America's public schools."[1]

After discussing Elliott and Hill in the first two chapters, I proceed to a consideration of NDEA from the perspective of the Eisenhower administration in chapter 3. The political ideology that characterized President Dwight D. Eisenhower, particularly in his support of NDEA, was moderation. This political moderation stands in stark contrast to the ideology of conservatism that characterized many, if not most, Republicans in the 1950s and Dwight D. Eisenhower himself on many issues, and came increasingly to characterize the GOP in the subsequent decades of the twentieth century. While political moderation underlay President Eisenhower's willingness to consider federal support for education, it clearly did not represent his views on every issue, or the views of many others in his administration on any issue at any time. Moderation was clearly also the political ideology that inspired all of the work of the Assistant Secretary for Legislation in the Department of Health Education and Welfare, Elliot Richardson, who became the administration point man in the development, consideration, and successful passage of NDEA. A self-acknowledged moderate Republican, Richardson's pursuit of NDEA represented that set of political beliefs, and it will be discussed in detail at the end of the chapter on the Eisenhower administration.

As Sputnik provided the spark for Elliott and Hill to pursue their long-held liberal advocacy of federal aid to education, it also empowered the Eisenhower administration to put forth its more moderate version of federal aid, one that conceived the problems it addressed, and the aid it offered, as temporary situations that were to be remedied, but not with a long-term solution. This is the first major theme of the book, namely that all participants in the NDEA campaigns used Sputnik to pursue educational agendas that ran far beyond the national defense scare it created. Elliott and Hill strategically used Sputnik and the Cold War for their own purpose of creating an extensive federal aid program for American education, while the administration also used the satellite and the political climate it created to pursue federal aid with more limited objectives and for a more limited time frame. Later description of the development of NDEA after passage will show that the congressmen were more prescient about the ultimate impact of the legislation than the administration.

After three chapters of discussion of the political genesis of NDEA in Congress and the administration, and the forces and factors that motivated and spurred its passage, I proceed to look at the two major interest groups that were involved in a consideration and evaluation of the substantive issues addressed in NDEA. These two groups were professional educators and academic scientists. In chapters 4 and 5, I discuss the political agendas of each group as they had evolved prior to 1957, and how those agendas were intensified, modified, and institutionalized by Sputnik and its immediate aftermath. A major theme in each of these two chapters is that NDEA was simultaneously about science education, and about much more than science education. Senator Hill, Congressman Elliott, and the Eisenhower administration also understood that science was a wedge to use to open the door to larger educational changes. My argument about the strategic use of science for nonscience educational reform distinguishes my analysis from earlier discussions of NDEA, which basically saw it as a science education measure that was part of a larger movement by which science was privileged in a variety of ways.

The argument that NDEA was science-oriented is not so much wrong, in my view, as it is incomplete. It ignores, or diminishes, issues in the internal politics of American education that were exceptionally important. I will name two of these issues here: the first is the ongoing debate over the place and limits of progressive education in the elementary and secondary schools as well as in the training of teachers. The second is the relationship of science to the social sciences and humanities, in schools but also, more importantly, in colleges and universities. The first issue is prominent in my discussion in chapter 4 of professional educators, and the second is more prominent in my treatment of scientists in chapter 5. Educators' lack of success in capitalizing on NDEA to help their own long-term occupational goals is another important focus in chapter 4, and the contrasting story of scientists' ability to use Sputnik for their purposes, is a theme of chapter 5.

In chapter 6, I supplement my political and educational ideological analysis of NDEA by considering how it developed for a decade after passage in 1958. In this chapter, I argue that NDEA broke the historic dam of resistance against federal aid to education, and document the amounts expended in various NDEA titles in the nation's schools and colleges. Also in chapter 6, I look at the loyalty oath that was attached at the last minute to NDEA prior to its approval, and the campaign against the oath waged by college and university leaders, abetted by officials in the Office of Education (OE), and ultimately, though not as zealously, supported by Congress.

In chapter 6, I also indicate how NDEA graduate fellowships undergirded the expansion of graduate education and the production of many new college and university teachers throughout the United States. The number of teachers needed in the context of an exploding college-age population could not have been produced by the small group of existing, prestigious graduate schools and departments then available. Using the state of Alabama and, particularly The University of Alabama as a case in point, I illustrate how the graduate school in Tuscaloosa was largely, if not directly, created by NDEA, through increasing the departments offering graduate degrees significantly and increasing even more the numbers of graduate students in many programs to the point that graduate education became a distinct, if minor, priority at this, and other, institutions. Finally in chapter 6, I discuss the growth of OE in the first decade after passage of NDEA. I show how the expansion of OE furthered the identification of the federal educational enterprise with the nation's prestigious colleges and universities, thereby facilitating an estrangement between OE on the one hand and the nation's public schools and their friends in education departments in the nation's colleges and universities, particularly the lesser public institutions in which large numbers of teachers were trained, on the other.

In chapter 7, I conclude the book with a long-term evaluation of NDEA, arguing again that it was the direct precursor of the much more generous federal educational programs such as the Elementary and Secondary Education Act (ESEA) and the Higher Education Acts that were passed in the next decade by the Johnson administration. Between NDEA in 1958 and ESEA in

1964, however, there was a lull in the tide toward more federal involvement in education, a lull that did not turn into a trend largely because of the successful reauthorizations of NDEA in those years. As NDEA itself diminished as an entity after ESEA, its programs did not disappear but rather were continued often through inclusion in other legislation. Further, the federal influence in education, which was enhanced substantially by NDEA, was also increased enormously by its successors such as ESEA, the Higher Education Acts, and Title VI of the U.S. Civil Rights Act of 1965.

In terms of the intellectual and political ideologies advocated, and sometimes embraced by, public schools and scholars who study education, NDEA had a distinct, and somewhat inconsistent, legacy. I discuss this legacy in chapter 7 and show that it helped create a significant expansion of educational opportunity, through its loans and its graduate fellowship programs, to allow the benefits of higher education to be more widely distributed. It also facilitated an excellence movement in the schools that allowed scientists and psychometrists, using the NDEA testing and guidance title, to try to ramp up academic studies in the schools, especially in the high schools. This movement developed in parallel with, and largely in support of, the narrowed educational agenda of the Reagan administration and that of all of his successors, including Bill Clinton. On balance, then, NDEA is probably best seen as playing an integral part in increasing educational opportunity offered through the expansion of the college and university enrollments in the second half of the twentieth century and in facilitating an educational excellence agenda that was in tension with, if not in opposition to, an educational opportunity focus.

One final, and pleasant, task in this preface is to thank those who have helped me in completing this work. First, I would mention my colleagues in the Education Policy Center at The University of Alabama, David Hardy, Research Director of the Center, and its Director, Steve Katsinas. I have enjoyed working with them over the past three years and look forward to future productive years in the Center. Mary (Allen) Jolley, who was introduced to me by Steve Katsinas, and who was a former member of Congressman Carl Elliott's staff, also responded generously to my questions and enthusiastically supported my entire effort. Similarly, Dean James McLean of the College of Education, who was instrumental in my coming to Tuscaloosa, deserves my sincere thanks for his support, both tangible and intangible. The director of The University of Alabama Press provided me with advice and support, especially at a crucial moment in preparing the manuscript.

The librarians and archivists who work in the places where historians do their research are always worthy of our gratitude. In terms of this project, I would mention specifically Helga Visscher and Benita Strnad of the McLure Education Library at The University of Alabama, as well as Clark Center, Donnelly Lancaster, and the rest of the staff at the Special Collections Division of the University Library. I also received substantial help from numerous staff members at the National Archives facility in College Park, Maryland, as well as from staff at the Eisenhower Library in Abilene, Kansas, particularly from Herb Pankratz.

I learned much from the work on NDEA of other historians. I would particularly like to acknowledge Carl Kaestle who has responded always to my questions and queries with good advice and wise counsel. Carl and I have been friends since the early 1970s when I visited him and his colleagues at the University of Wisconsin. Additionally, several historians who have published work on various aspects of federal educational policy and allied topics deserve my gratitude. Donald Warren of Indiana University is prominent in this regard, and as a reader of this manuscript for The University of Alabama Press was extremely helpful. Similarly, Robert Hampel of the University of Delaware read the manuscript and provided both extensive editorial guidance and substantive improvements. Other scholars whose company I have valued and with whom I have shared various aspects of this work include Marybeth Gasman, Roger Geiger, Philo Hutcheson, and Kate Rousmaniere. Jeffrey Mirel, of the University of Michigan, acquainted me with the work of two doctoral students at Michigan from whom I have learned a great deal. And of course, Mirel's colleague at Michigan, Maris Vinovskis, has taught me much about federal educational policy, from his scholarship and his practice in the federal government, over the years. I'm sure I have left out many who have helped me, both in this effort and throughout my career, and to them I offer both apologies and gratitude. Scholarship is a communal effort, and, if we do not learn from one another, our growth is indeed stunted.

Finally, I have a personal debt to my wife, Judy, that I can never repay. She has endured my packing us up, after thirty-five years in Atlanta, to move to Alabama to begin my scholarly life anew, with an enormous complication in her own life. I am immensely grateful to her for her support, always grateful.

More Than Science and Sputnik

Introduction

This book narrates the political development of the National Defense Education Act (NDEA) and takes a brief look at the impact of the measure for a decade after its passage. My purpose is not to provide a comprehensive account of the development of the legislation, or an exhaustive description of its supporters and opponents, their arguments and their objectives. That task has already been accomplished, and accomplished quite competently, by Barbara Barksdale Clowse.[1] That volume presents a comprehensive account of the impact of the launch of the Soviet Sputnik satellite on American politics and the adoption of NDEA largely in reaction to the satellite. Clowse also closely tracks the legislation as it was proposed, by the Eisenhower administration and in the Congress, and as it wended its way to passage. That entire process took eight months in 1958; it began in January of that year when the president spoke about education and suggested in broad strokes what the administration would propose to Congress, and when Carl Elliott and Lister Hill joined forces in a Birmingham hotel to develop separate but coordinated versions of their own education measure to be introduced in both houses of Congress. It ended in early September when the president finally signed the bill into law.

My work on NDEA is better described as an ideological history of the act rather than a comprehensively legislative, or purely procedural, political history. What I mean by ideological is that I choose to concentrate in my analysis on the political beliefs of several of the key actors in developing and passing the legislation. What Carl Elliott, Lister Hill, Dwight Eisenhower, and Elliot Richardson sought to accomplish through NDEA, how it fit into their political philosophies and their vision for education as a part of those philosophies, is the subject of my first three chapters. The fourth and the fifth chapters then discuss NDEA, as it was influenced by, and as it in turn exerted influence on, two major interest groups that were involved with the legislation. I deal in these chapters with elementary and secondary educators on the one hand, and with scientists on the other.

Because of my basically ideological approach, and the comprehensive work of Clowse, I have chosen in this introduction to describe briefly each title of the NDEA as it was passed in September of 1958. Additionally, I will discuss, also briefly, the relationship between what was finally passed and what the administration and the Congress had proposed. Having done this in the introduction, I will then only need to refer to various NDEA titles in the chapters as I stress the relationship of the legislation, in whole and in its parts, to the political convictions and agendas of the administration, Congress, and the two major interest groups involved. Finally, I will look briefly at some of the literature relating to NDEA and show how my account relates to it.

NDEA Essentials

The NDEA that Dwight D. Eisenhower signed into law on September 2, 1958 was made up of ten titles.[2] Title I contained two general provisions, the first of which acknowledged an educational emergency to which NDEA was addressed, without describing it, and the second of which assured that nothing in the act was to mean control over education by any federal agency.

Title II of NDEA dealt with student loans. It specified the amounts authorized for the loan program for the four-year duration of the act, from $47.5 million allocated for the first fiscal year (1959) to $90 million for fiscal 1962, the last year. Other parts of this title determined the allotment of loan funds to each state through a formula that compared the state's full-time enrollment to a national figure, provided that institutions must contribute 10 percent of the loan funds that they expended; allowed states to borrow their 10 percent contribution up to the amount of $25 million; established a ceiling for any state of $250,000 a year in loan funds and a ceiling of $1,000 per year for any student; and set an interest charge of 3 percent for repayment, a ten-year time within which repayment had to be made, and a provision that repayment begin after students end their studies or after three years of military service.

Title III dealt with the strengthening of science, mathematics, and foreign language instruction in secondary schools. It authorized $70 million per year for each of NDEA's four years to use for this purpose, specified grants to states for public schools and loans for private schools to achieve it, and authorized $5 million per year for supervisory services in science, mathematics, and foreign language. Funds were to be distributed to states on the basis of a formula similar to that for Title II and only after a plan was developed by a state, one-half the cost of which the federal government would pay.

Title IV established a national fellowship program containing 1,000 fellowships in the first fiscal year (1959) and 1,500 for the additional three years of the act. Fellowships were to be awarded to students enrolled in new or expanded graduate programs that were called for in an effort to seek a geographical distribution of graduate education in the nation and to give preference to those interested in becoming college teachers. Stipends were set at $2,000 for the first year of study, $2,200 for the second, and $2,400 for the third year, with an additional $2,500 per fellowship per year allotted to the institution for administrative purposes.

Title V was for testing, guidance, and counseling for the purpose of identifying and encouraging able students. It authorized $15 million per year for four years for state programs consisting of testing to identify student abilities and counseling and guidance to encourage their development. The $15 million was to go to states according to their proportion of the national school-age enrollment, and no state was to receive less than $20,000. Full support for programs in the first year of their operation was prescribed as well as half of their cost for the ensuing three years. Additionally, provision was made for contracts with universities for institutes for training high school guidance counselors, with public school personnel attending these institutes to receive a stipend.

Title VI on language development provided for Language Area Centers and for Language Institutes at colleges and universities that contracted with the government to offer them. The centers were authorized for use by people in government, private business, or education to teach modern foreign languages and also to offer understanding of a foreign region, including its history, economics, and geography, if deemed necessary. The institutes were for elementary and secondary school teacher training. The annual appropriation authorized for the centers was $8 million and for the institutes was $7.5 million.

Title VII was for research and experimentation in the effective use of educational media such as television, radio, and films. Grants or contracts for new audiovisual materials for education were to go to a variety of agencies for this purpose. Additionally, studies of the need for audiovisual media were permitted. The program was to be administered by the federal educational agency, the Office of Education, with oversight from a newly established committee that was to contain a representative from the National Science Foundation and other members chosen from elementary and secondary schools, from colleges and universities, and from the media areas.

Title VIII expanded the George-Barden Vocational Education Act of 1946 to meet the needs for technicians with science and technology training and to offer vocational training in underserved areas. The authorization was $15 million for each of the four years of the Act.

Title IX established a new Science Information Service operating under the National Science Foundation (NSF). The service was to be advised by a Science Information Council appointed by the NSF chair with members including representatives from other government agencies.

Title X contained grants to the states, which needed to be matched by them, for improving statistical services in the state educational agencies. No amount was specified but a limit of $50,000 for any state for any year was specified. The grants were for new or expanded programs to improve the reliability of statistics on education and the reporting of educational data.

Behind the Essentials

Much of the rest of this book deals with how and why certain things were, or were not, included in NDEA. The main point to be made about this jockeying over the particulars of NDEA is that all the participants used the Cold War climate that caused Sputnik to create a near panic about American education to proffer their own versions of educational improvement, many of which had little to do with national defense or the Cold War.

Especially important in terms of what was not included was a provision for federal scholarships for college attendance. NDEA was an amalgam of three bills, one introduced by the administration and two introduced by Congressman Carl Elliott and Senator Hill respectively. All three original bills contained a scholarship provision. The whittling down of scholarships and their eventual excision reveal much about the political maneuvering over the legislation. The student loan title that eventuated in NDEA was, in some sense, a replacement for scholarships. The loans originated in the House of Representatives and were expanded in the final version of the bill after scholarships were excised. Issues of merit and equity swirled around the debates over scholarships, and the eventual adoption of loans needs to be seen in relation to these debates.

The relations between intellectual merit and educational equity, or opportunity, were also a clear issue in Title IV of NDEA on graduate fellowships. The stipulation in that title that fellowships be at institutions with new or expanded programs and the further stipulation for geographical distribution marked this title as a clear victory for the equity emphasis. In contrast, Title V on testing, guidance, and counseling with its emphasis on able students marked it as clearly in evidence of an emphasis on intellectual merit and, by implication if nothing else, a de-emphasis on expanding opportunity.

The dominance of science and mathematics in NDEA is another issue of importance, since many scholarly and popular analyses of the legislation treat it as only that kind of measure. Science and mathematics are specifically mentioned in Title III, though foreign languages also appear in that title. The title on language development, Title VI, said nothing about science, and the broad language in that title allowed NDEA funds to flow to an enormous variety of fields. This is important for purposes of my analysis, since I argue that views of NDEA, both historically and in the present, as a science or mathematics measure are grossly oversimplified.

Finally, the issue of the place of private or religious schools in NDEA is worthy of mention in this introduction. The provision for loans to private schools, as opposed to grants for public schools, in Title III was a conscious compromise between those who wanted private schools included in the bill as eligible for all funds available and those who wanted funds to go only to public schools. This compromise was also present in a few other places in the bill. While it satisfied neither interest completely, it satisfied each interest enough to allow the bill to proceed to passage.

Generally speaking, the versions of NDEA from congressmen Hill and Elliott were more generous in their funding, for all of the titles, than the administration version. Notable also was that Title VIII, for vocational education, was in both congressional legislative proposals but not in the administration version of the legislation. Other minor differences existed in the three versions of the bill, but their commonalities were much more evident than these differences.

I will expand on the issues of merit versus equality, the provision for the sciences in relation to those for nonscience fields, and the issue of private religious schools, in the chapters that follow. Of course, things like merit/excellence in relation to equity/equality, the sciences versus the nonsciences, and private religious versus public schools are the core of any good ideological analysis of American education. Hopefully, they will be presented and discussed effectively in the pages that follow.

Historians and NDEA

Before ending this introduction, I would like to indicate the relationship of my work to a few noted studies of NDEA and related topics. I have already acknowledged that Clowse has provided a thorough analysis of the political maneuvering attendant to the passage of NDEA.[3] She meticulously covered the events taking place in Congress, and in the administration, as NDEA wound its way to passage under the spur of the near hysteria Sputnik created in the minds of the American public. Clowse's thoroughness has allowed me to revisit NDEA selectively, rather than comprehensively. My choices are just that, choices. But I think that focusing, as I do, on the political ideologies of Elliott and Hill, of the administration, and of educators and scientists, has allowed me to tell a complementary story that differs from that told by Clowse, but does not contradict the particulars of her account. Rather, I seek to amplify Clowse's work through a fresh interpretation of the forces and factors involved in the passage and early administration of NDEA.

Brief treatment of NDEA occurs in parts of two well-known works that cover late twentieth century educational history. Joel Spring, in *The Sorting Machine* (1989), made NDEA an integral part of his revisionist analysis of the creation of the educational program of a hegemonic political goliath in the United States of America, its federal government.[4] Spring was vehement in his condemnation of what he described, but his vehemence seemed to limit his ability to paint a comprehensive picture of NDEA and place it in the stream of federal educational policy development in the late twentieth, and the twenty-first, century. He was so intent on pursuing his thesis of a federal government leviathan that he neglected factors, such as the democratic emphasis I have stressed in the ideology of Carl Elliott and the fellowship and loan titles of NDEA, that might have minimized his indictment or otherwise called it into question. Diane Ravitch's *The Troubled Crusade: American Education, 1945–1980,* published in 1983, mentioned NDEA more briefly, seeing it mainly as one of many currents in a period of diverse movements in educational affairs.[5] One wonders if Ravitch, now some twenty-five years later, might be inclined to reinterpret NDEA in the light of her own subsequent critique of progressive education and advocacy of educational excellence. In contrast to Ravitch's picture of diverse ideological pluralism, I have tried to indicate the emphases that NDEA supported, however indirectly, in the educational battles over excellence and democracy, while also pursuing my interest in its larger political ramifications.

Carl Kaestle has provided several policy histories of federal educational activity after World War II. In the first, written with Marshall Smith and published in 1982, Kaestle and his colleague argued that NDEA was better seen as a result of the Cold War ideology that engulfed the United States in the 1950s than as a child of Sputnik. In "The Federal Role in Elementary and Secondary Education, 1940–1980," Kaestle and Smith argued first that it was alarm over Soviet educational accomplishment, in the sciences particularly, that predated Sputnik and was the fuel that fired the movement for NDEA. Sputnik may have provided the fuse, or the spark, but without the concern about the inferiority of American education compared to the Soviet system, the flame that ignited the passage of NDEA would likely not have been ignited.[6]

Kaestle and Smith illustrated how NDEA represented a foray by the subject matter forces, led by noted scientist and university president James Bryant Conant, into the secondary curriculum where the political and social needs concerns of progressive educationists were seen to hold sway. They then discussed some criticisms of NDEA offered soon after its passage, which noted too great a stress on science and technical studies. In considering some support for NDEA from school people who might have been expected to be sensitive to the criticism of overemphasis on science, however, as well as looking at concerns of those school people over federal control of state and local schooling, Kaestle and Smith argued that the school men and women were more swayed by the dollars that were sent into their systems by NDEA than by fear of what those dollars obligated them to do. Kaestle and Smith concluded their discussion of NDEA by offering cautious support for those who saw it as a questionable shift toward science and technology in American education on the part of the federal government, one that threatened the foundations of a free society, such as free expression, reflection, self-criticism, and diversity in perspective.

I agree with Kaestle and Smith, with two qualifications. The first is my argument that, from the beginning, in the minds of its two congressional sponsors from Alabama, emphasis in NDEA on any educational particulars was a strategic, not a substantive, priority. Further, as NDEA played out, especially in its title on graduate fellowships, many fields outside of the sciences were supported in development, just as Hill and Elliott had anticipated. Additionally, I would say that the defense of democracy that Kaestle and Smith described might have been more directly linked to progressive educators in the elementary and secondary schools than they chose to do, or at the least I would note that the progressive educators who feared NDEA thought that they were defending democracy in their own prescriptions for the schools.

Nearly three decades later, in 2001, Kaestle again undertook an explanation of the federal role in education since World War II, this time expanding his reach to the turn of the twenty-first century in "Federal Aid to Education since World War II: Purposes and Politics."[7] In addition to extending the time span of his earlier analysis with Marshall Smith, Kaestle in 2001 stressed a distinction that he had only discussed briefly in his earlier article on federal aid. Kaestle in the later essay argued extensively that NDEA represented a categorical approach to federal aid, that is, one that specified the particular categories or programs in which the money was to be spent. As categorical aid, NDEA was an alternative to the general aid approach that the National Education Association and other advocates of federal aid to education in much of the twentieth century had proposed. Kaestle noted that general aid, by not specifying categories in which the money was to be spent, was much less intrusive on states and local school systems, and, therefore, much less likely to raise the specter of federal control of local schools. However, at the same time, general aid by not specifying categories or programs meant, for Kaestle, that congressional and administration supporters of such aid had to argue for a vague, but expansive, principle rather than for specific gains to be achieved by its implementation. Thus, from the point of view of legislators, and federal administrators, general aid was much more difficult to accomplish, and less defensible politically.

After noting the similarity between NDEA and the Elementary and Secondary Education Act of 1965 (ESEA), which extended NDEA financially to serve the interests of the poor as representative pieces of categorical legislation, Kaestle went on to question the definitiveness of the distinction. He noted that the relatively subtle and supple regulatory mechanisms of NDEA meant that it functioned as much like general aid from the point of view of recipients such as local school systems or colleges and universities, and thus was embraced enthusiastically by those recipients, a point made in his earlier article with Smith. Kaestle also discussed the relationship between notions of crisis and the passage of federal aid to education legislation, pointing out that the perception of crisis was often, though not always, present when federal educational laws were considered and passed. And he also considered the tendency of federal educational policies to outlive the conditions that created them, buoyed by an administrative apparatus set up to implement the measures, and a group of clients that developed, and in turn sustained, the measures politically. For Kaestle, NDEA was better served by the first half of this conception than by the second. Thus, he noted NDEA's demise through incorporation into other laws and the eventual dismantling of many of its titles, in contrast to ESEA, which still lives in our time, though in much altered form.

My only criticism of Kaestle's argument on NDEA's demise is that it fits several of the NDEA titles, especially those dealing with elementary and secondary education, but not all of them. The student loan title and the graduate fellowship titles, for example, were not discussed by Kaestle. While NDEA loans and fellowships no longer exist, the enormous growth of federal loan policies for undergraduate students and various forms of aid for graduate students must be acknowledged, and attributed in large part, to momentum created by NDEA. My view leads to the conclusion that NDEA was much more productive, and long lasting, for higher education than it was for elementary and secondary schools.

1
Lister Hill, Federal Aid to Education, and Alabama Politics

Lister Hill was known nationally as a political liberal from Alabama, a phrase that has an air of unreality about it in the first decade of the twenty first century. In fact, Hill was but one of several liberals in the Alabama congressional delegation from the 1930s through the 1950s, with both senators and over half of the states' representatives, those representing various districts in the northern half of the state, proudly adhering to the label of liberal. The sources of their liberalism were economic and regional, residing in the mining and burgeoning industrial regions of the state and relying on organized labor as one of a group of liberal leaning interest groups for support.[1] Understanding the character of Hill's political liberalism, and that of his col-

Senator Lister Hill, proponent of the National Defense Education Act. Courtesy of the W. S. Hoole Special Collections Library, The University of Alabama.

leagues in Alabama's congressional delegation, allows one to see how such a philosophy took hold in this southern state, as well as elsewhere in the region, in the middle of the twentieth century. This chapter will discuss how Hill's political philosophy animated his pursuit of the National Defense Education Act (NDEA). It will also indicate briefly the circumstances attending the demise of Hill's liberalism as a significant force in Alabama politics.

For Lister Hill, as for many of his Alabama colleagues in Congress, the impetus for a generally liberal political philosophy was his devotion to the programs of Franklin Delano Roosevelt. Hill approved intervention in the economy and other areas by the federal government that Roosevelt employed in pursuing his New Deal and other programs. Roosevelt was popular among southerners for several reasons, most notably because he did not look on the region disdainfully as did many other politicians from outside the South. In fact, Roosevelt had a home in Warm Springs, Georgia, close to the Alabama border, and spent considerable time there and elsewhere in the South on many occasions. Also, Roosevelt's commitment to amelioration of the most drastic effects of poverty resonated with southerners (especially, but not only, white southerners) who struggled economically. Agricultural and other economic development programs that FDR initiated in the South were especially popular in Tennessee, Alabama, and Georgia, as well as in other southern states, for the opportunities they presented to the largely poor areas targeted for intervention. Roosevelt's Works Progress Administration (WPA) provided employment opportunities for southerners, and throughout the nation, that made it immensely popular regionally and nationally. Hill worked successfully for approval of Roosevelt's Farm Security Administration (FSA), believing that it would improve the living and working conditions of poor southern farmers.

More generally, the economic amelioration promised by various New Deal measures and agencies appealed directly to the political goals of Hill and other Alabama liberals. Hill's chief clerk in the Senate explained the agenda of Alabama's liberal congressmen during and immediately after the New Deal: "At the time they were elected, the issues in the South were economic, pulling themselves up, needing federal help, public works, and other things. These men knew how to get it and could work up here effectively."[2] Yet, as often has been the case with liberal politicians, Hill was a complicated person and personality. He came from a patrician Montgomery family, married into an equally distinguished family, and qualified as a member of the Alabama "aristocracy." In the Senate, in addition to his liberal goals he mastered the procedures and intricacies of that body to the point that he became a full-fledged member of its "inner club," a group not particularly known for its liberalism.[3] In short, Hill was liberal politically and conservative personally, grounded in the mores of the state that he served and devoted to the procedures of the legislative body in which he served. Again, according to his chief clerk, he "was a very complicated man. . . . He also was extremely intelligent and had had a good education and had read a great deal. His horizons were far wider than those of the typical Southerner, or even typical American."[4]

For Lister Hill, allegiance to the president and, to a lesser extent, to federal political activism waned somewhat with the ascent of Harry Truman to the White House. Truman made it clear in a variety of ways that he was at least somewhat partial to the desires of African Americans for voting rights and other civil rights. Hill, who seldom worked directly in favor of black rights of any kind, nevertheless was comparatively subdued in relation to other white state leaders in his political treatment of black Alabamians.[5] He did not reject Truman and the Democratic Party in the 1948 election, when the Democrats adopted a moderate civil rights plank in their party platform. While many Alabamians and other southerners defected to the Dixiecrat candidacy of Strom Thurmond, Hill stayed loyal to the Democrats and supported the Truman-Barkley ticket, though not with great enthusiasm. When Truman offered Hill a cabinet position as secretary of war, the Alabamian quickly turned it down, preferring his influential place in the U.S. Senate to the probable political wasteland of a peacetime War Department. Prior to that election, however, Hill stepped down as the Democratic whip in the Senate, fearing that the president might put the Senate leadership in the position of having to support policies such as civil rights advocacy.

Hill and other loyalists retained control of the Alabama Democratic Party well into the 1950s. Hill was easily reelected to the Senate in 1950; the Democrats carried the state of Alabama in the presidential election of 1952, with native son John Sparkman as the vice presidential candidate; and in 1954 elected the neopopulist liberal Jim Folsom as governor and reelected Sparkman to the Senate. Hill, Sparkman, and about one-half of the state's members in the House of Representatives were basically liberals in their political affiliation, advocating federal economic interventions and social programs of various kinds that promised to help Alabamians in their efforts to improve their lives.[6] The passage of the National Defense Education Act (NDEA) in 1958 culminated Hill's liberal accomplishments in the field of education. Before turning to education and the NDEA, however, a brief treatment of Hill's early career is in order.

Youth and Early Political Career

This section of the chapter lays out the essentials of Hill's background, and the next section discusses his political commitments to educational change, most particularly to the variety of federal funding measures for public schools he supported. Then, a brief look at NDEA shows Hill's proposed bill to be on the side of an expansive version of federal aid for defense education, as opposed to more confining interpretations of the measure by others. Finally, Hill's political actions on behalf of federal aid to education and NDEA are evaluated, with particular attention paid to the minefields of race and religion that he encountered in his home state of Alabama. For most of his career, he managed to maneuver his educational advocacy through the two minefields, with NDEA representing a triumph in relation to both of them.

Joseph Lister Hill, coauthor of the National Defense Education Act, was born and raised in Montgomery, Alabama. Lister's father, Luther L. Hill, was a physician who was politically aware and enormously influential. Known nationally and internationally for some pioneering work in heart surgery, he named his son after the famous English doctor, James Lister. Dr. Hill sent Lister to private schools in and around Montgomery and to The University of Alabama. While at Alabama, Lister joined a prestigious social fraternity and was active politically, participating in a popular prohibition campaign. He served as business manager of the student newspaper, *The Crimson and White,* and was elected as the first president of the student government association in the 1915–16 academic year.[7]

Luther Hill hoped that Lister would follow in his footsteps and become a doctor. Lister was not attracted to medicine, however, and chose instead another professional career, the law. After graduation from The University of Alabama, Lister studied law for a summer at the University of Michigan prior to his enrollment in the law school at Tuscaloosa. After finishing the law curriculum at Alabama in less than a year, he enrolled at the prestigious Columbia University law school in New York City and took a second law degree there. Upon returning to Montgomery in 1916, Lister Hill took a job in a leading Montgomery law firm. Lister's older brother, Will, had been elected to the Alabama state Senate. From that position Will, with his father Luther Hill, began Lister's political career by arranging his appointment to the school board in Montgomery, Alabama. Lister Hill had never been enrolled in the public schools for which he was now partially responsible, yet he quickly ascended to the position of president of the Montgomery board of education at the tender age of twenty-two. Lister Hill later used this early experience on a school board to illustrate what he called his life-long commitment to educational improvement. Hill's service on the school board was interrupted by military service during World War I. Although he did not see combat, Hill served as a lawyer in the military and thereby managed to earn the status of veteran. He also managed to make some contacts with other military lawyers that would prove profitable later in his political career.

Hill's mother was a Roman Catholic who also had Jewish immigrant ancestors. Both these aspects of Hill's background were problematic for an Alabama politician, since the state was clearly dominated by white Protestantism. Hill was always able to neutralize political opponents' negative use of his mother's religious background, often by concentrating on his father's Welsh Protestant ancestors, and the Methodist religion of his father and other paternal ancestors. Shortly before offering himself to an Alabama electorate in his first congressional election, Hill officially joined a prominent Methodist Church in Montgomery. He would retain his official status as a Methodist for the rest of his life. Hill's mother and sister were stunned by Lister's defection from the Catholicism in which he had been raised.[8]

The opportunity to begin a political career on a national stage presented itself to Lister Hill in 1922, when the incumbent member of the House of Representatives from the district that included Montgomery and several rural counties in south Alabama died unexpectedly. The Hill family was associated politically with the congressman and, when Lister was announced as a candidate for the seat, the son of the congressman signed on to his campaign. Lister Hill astutely used his relation to the congressman, his father's prominence as a physician, the influence of other physicians in the district, his military service, and a variety of familial and political connections, some forged as a student in Tuscaloosa, to win the election. Hill ran on a platform that advocated federal aid to education as a way to improve the schools in the district and that opposed the federal woman suffrage amendment. Hill was not opposed to women voting; in fact women had played an important role in his election to the presidency of the student government at the university. His opposition was to a federal amendment to enforce suffrage, a measure he saw as an imposition on the state's right to determine its electorate. A racial subtext was clearly involved here, as blacks had been removed from the Alabama electorate two decades earlier and federal supremacy in the electoral realm held the potential to reverse this policy. Hill's early political advocacy of federal aid to education, while simultaneously opposing federal electoral influence, could be seen as contradictory. Hill neutralized any suggestion of a contradiction, however, by noting that federal aid to education did not involve federal control, while a federal suffrage amendment was a clear imposition of federal power on the states. He added that the opposition to federal aid to education on the part of his most powerful opponent in the election was the same position that Catholics took on the issue.[9]

As a member of the House of Representatives in the 1920s, Hill concentrated on constituent support and populated his district with new post offices in the rural areas. He also concentrated on developing the Air Force presence at Maxwell field outside of Montgomery. In terms of national politics, Hill opposed the prominent progressive Senator George Norris of Nebraska, who fought for a strong federal role in the economic betterment of the Tennessee River valley, an area that included a large swath of northern Alabama. Hill played the role of loyal Democrat in the 1928 presidential election and successfully stumped the state on behalf of the Democratic nominee, the Roman Catholic governor of New York, Al Smith. Although one of Alabama's senators, the neopopulist Tom Heflin, had voiced opposition to Smith based on his religion, the New Yorker carried Alabama, narrowly, doing considerably less well than previous Democratic presidential nominees. Smith lost the election nationally, however. Hill contemplated running for a U.S. Senate seat in 1928, but deferred to the candidacy of another prominent Alabamian, John H. Bankhead. Hill thus amassed political capital as a devoted Democrat who chose not to oppose a rival he resembled in both party affiliation and social background.[10]

After the presidential election of 1932, Hill, like many southerners, became captivated by Franklin D. Roosevelt. Hill became an ardent New Dealer who idolized Roosevelt and supported his policies enthusiastically. He authored a bill in the House for economic development in the Tennessee River valley that ended up in a congressional conference committee with George Norris's Senate proposal. While Hill's bill called for less federal influence, he saw the handwriting on the wall and cooperated with Norris and other progressives in the establishment of the powerful Tennessee Valley Authority (TVA), which he had opposed for many years. In fact, in later years, Hill called himself a creator of the politically successful TVA, which provided substantial economic improvement in the northern regions of the state of Alabama. When FDR announced the nomination of Alabama senator Hugo Black to the U.S. Supreme Court in 1937, this set off a pitched battle for the Senate seat in Alabama that Hill chose this time to enter. With Tom Heflin as his major opponent, Hill wrapped himself in the mantle of Roosevelt, openly supporting Roosevelt's plan to increase the number of justices on the

Supreme Court and a proposed increase in the minimum wage. Using his father's political connections and his political networks, Hill won the Democratic primary, thus assuring his election in November in a state that had not elected a Republican to statewide office since the end of Reconstruction.

In the Senate, Hill was a strong New Dealer and rose quickly to a position of power in the Senate hierarchy. In 1940, he placed Roosevelt's name in nomination for a third term, after he had astutely outmaneuvered anti-Roosevelt Democrats in a struggle for primacy in the state's delegation to the Democratic convention. He vigorously supported Roosevelt's decision to enter World War II and the prosecution of that conflict. He also supported the establishment of the United Nations and most other Roosevelt initiatives. He maneuvered politically to keep his state in the Roosevelt fold, in the face of growing opposition based mainly on white fear of black restlessness.

Federal Aid to Education

Throughout those political developments, Hill never abandoned his commitment to federal aid to education. In a speech to the National Education Association (NEA) in 1941, Hill reaffirmed his belief that the federal government had a responsibility for the educational welfare of the nation and the success of its children.[11] Hill maintained a steady relationship with the NEA through his entire political career, as well as an even closer relationship with the NEA's affiliate in his home state, the Alabama Education Association. Federal aid to education was a long-standing goal of the NEA, and the group worked often with Hill for the cause, at times even writing speeches for the Alabama senator to give on the topic.[12] The senator and the educational organization agreed that general federal aid, that is, federal aid that was not for a specified purpose, was the desirable objective. For the Senator, general, or unspecified, aid protected the states that received it from control over their educational policies by the federal government. For the NEA, general aid protected the prerogatives that professional educators had earned in their states and communities from the designs of congressmen and federal bureaucrats often intent on forcing their will on professionals. Because of this conjunction of priorities, Hill was often called upon to speak before NEA groups, and he received the fervent thanks, and political support, of both the national organization and its Alabama affiliate for his pursuit of general federal aid. Hill remained a staunch advocate of federal aid to education throughout the 1940s and into the 1950s, though without significant success. It is to the contours of that advocacy that we now turn.

The attractiveness of a Cold War context for Lister Hill's support for federal aid to education after World War II was well illustrated in a speech he gave to the Alabama Education Association in 1947, which was read into the Congressional Record on March 28 of that year. In that speech, Hill talked of an educational crisis in a nation that spent only 1.5 percent of its income on education, while other nations such as Britain and Russia spent 3 percent and 7.5 percent respectively. Teachers' salaries were shockingly low, according to Hill, and state efforts alone could not make up for this situation. Even when states did all they could, differences between them were significant because of substantial differences in wealth, which in turn affected the revenues that could be generated for public education. Federal aid was needed primarily to overcome this inequality of educational opportunity. Alabama and other southern states suffered educationally because of their lack of wealth, especially when compared to states that had a much larger economic base from which to raise money for schools such as New York, Massachusetts, and others. The major obstacle to federal aid, according to Hill, was the fear of federal control. The specter of federal control of education was particularly powerful in Alabama, where states' rights advocates were viscerally vocal and guaranteed a hearing because of the state's and the South's political history. Hill was aware of this fear of federal control in his state and he always made sure that his support of federal aid never meant, or even implied, any form of federal control.

In 1947, Hill addressed the Alabama Education Association and told that body that fear of federal control of education because of federal aid was unwarranted. "The threat to States' rights in Federal aid is a bogeyman which frightens few people today." He added that those who invoked federal control as an argument against federal aid were the wealthy and the "powerful, those who oppose diffusion of knowledge, who believe in monopoly of power, who restrict the vote." Hill called these fearmongers "the reactionaries [who] still seek to keep tight the ranks of the educated."[13]

In the year before this speech was given, Hill had been named chair of a new Senate subcommittee on education and labor. This position gave him more power to push for federal aid and other educational changes. He became a named sponsor of a federal aid to education bill that would soon be the subject of hearings before his subcommittee. In support of his advocacy, Hill sent postcards to his Alabama constituents asking them for support for his pursuit of federal aid. Those who responded could be sure of a reply from their senator. In one such exchange, Hill put his advocacy of federal aid to education in the context of a several-pronged campaign to redress the conditions of Alabama farmers. He enclosed a copy of a speech he had recently given to the American Farm Bureau. In that speech, Hill noted that while three of ten children in the United States were farm children, farmers gained only one dollar out of every ten earned in the nation. Farmers were in desperate need of parity with others, Hill maintained. To attain this position, he had sponsored a fertilizer bill, an act to facilitate the construction of rural hospitals, and the Hill-Thomas federal aid to education bill.[14] Hill's advocacy of the interests of farmers, especially white tenant farmers, was consistent almost from the time he entered Congress. One of his notable accomplishments in the House of Representatives had been support for the establishment of the Farm Security Administration Act in 1937.[15]

The post–World War II era was a high point of agitation for federal aid to education, by Hill and the NEA, with the public schools and colleges facing the onslaught of returning veterans and the offspring that they were about to produce. In these years, Lister Hill corresponded, not just with Alabama supporters of federal aid, but also with constituents from other southern states who shared his advocacy of the policy. In January of 1946, Hill received a letter from a Mississippi school principal who was to take the affirmative position in a forthcoming debate over federal aid to education. To the request for arguments to use in the debate, Hill responded with copies of various bills that had been introduced, including one of Hill's, as well as copies of articles on the topic from newspapers and educational journals. No doubt, the prospective debater from Mississippi was well fortified for his task by his correspondence with the Alabama senator.[16]

Two months later, a woman from Sevierville, Tennessee, told him that good schools were beyond the means of the citizens of her community. She decried the prevalence of inferior one-room schools in rural areas especially, in which unqualified teachers provided inferior education to the students. Invoking a racial subtext that will be discussed later in this chapter, she added that the best school in the area was run by a Negro woman and noted that whites needed good schools too. She implored Hill to gain passage of federal aid that would improve the schools in her community. Hill responded that he was "leaving no stone unturned in my efforts to get Federal aid for Education."[17]

Hill explained to another constituent the difficulties that plagued his advocacy of federal aid to education. He noted that federal aid was a new thing, for which there were few precedents. Opponents included many powerful individuals who did not send their children to public schools and, thus, had no wish to pay taxes for those schools. Additionally, taxpayers in relatively wealthy states who might be persuaded to support public education in their own areas had no desire to support the children of citizens of poorer states. He added that large corporations that dreaded paying taxes for almost any purpose were even less inclined to support something as controversial as federal aid to education. Finally, Hill identified those who flat-footedly opposed progress in any dimension, especially if it would cost them in taxation, and those who simply were ignorant about the issues. Hill noted that he had never promised a successful federal aid campaign, but that he was trying hard to get one. He added that he was now a cosponsor with three Democrats and four Republicans of a federal aid bill, on which they were making substantial progress.[18]

Hill continued to fight for federal aid to education through the end of the 1940s and into the 1950s, and he let his constituents in Alabama, members of national educational organizations, and Alabama's educators know of his unrelenting pursuit of the objective. In February of 1948, an American Legion post in southwest Alabama sent Hill, and other members of the Alabama legislative delegation, a copy of a resolution they passed in support of federal aid. Hill responded by thanking the group for their support and added, "I am continuing to fight with every power at my command and am doing everything I can to get the bill enacted at the earliest possible date."[19] A few months earlier, Hill responded positively to a request from the National Education Association to help them convince President Harry Truman that federal aid to education was a dire necessity. Hill promised to reinforce that message with the president and to proceed vigorously with his efforts on behalf of the cause in Congress.[20]

Early in 1948, Hill heard from an Alabama high school principal who enclosed a petition signed by twenty or so educators in support of the campaign for federal aid to education. Hill responded that the support was gratifying to him personally, but also that it was important to the nation. Two months later the senator happily reported to forty-one radio stations in Alabama that the Senate had passed, by a 58 to 22 vote, a federal aid bill that meant $19.5 million for the state of Alabama and her teachers.[21]

Yet, in spite of progress in the U.S. Senate, a federal aid to education bill did not pass Congress in the 1940s, nor in the early or middle 1950s. Conservatives, mainly though not exclusively from the South, were firmly in control of the House of Representatives, especially of its all-powerful Rules Committee, and they kept close control of the agenda in the House, most often not even allowing federal aid bills to come to the floor. In early 1950, the Talladega County (Alabama) Teachers Association sent Hill a copy of their resolution seeking federal aid to education, which noted that the situation in their district was critical, including a severe shortage of teachers that could only be overcome by federal action. Responding positively to the resolution, and approving its provision that local control be protected, Hill noted that he had been advocating federal aid for over twenty years and that he was the author of a variety of measures other than general federal aid that would get federal funds into the public schools. He concluded his response by stating that "I am glad to send you this information as to my long and constant efforts for our schools, our teachers, and our children of Alabama."[22]

As he told the Talladega teachers, Hill's advocacy of federal aid had taken a variety of forms. While he, along with the National Education Association, sought general aid for education from the federal government, that is, aid that would be given to states and school districts to spend as they saw fit, he was willing to settle for more specific, or categorical, provisions of federal funds on numerous occasions. Thus, he was prominent in the movement for federal support for school construction, and for federal funds for other purposes for school districts impacted by military bases or other large federal installations. Hill's involvement in the passage of these two measures was acknowledged by the U.S. Office of Education in the federal Department of Health, Education, and Welfare, which kept him apprised of the progress in both arenas. Education commissioner Earl McGrath notified him in July of 1952 of a list of projects in the state of Alabama and the amount expended, in each case, of federal financial assistance to areas "overburdened as a result of federal activities." The assistance in these cases was for school construction in Alabama school districts with military installations within their boundaries, entities that meant a significant number of additional students in their public schools. School construction aid was a major source of substantial federal educational aid to Alabama and other states with military bases from the late 1940s on. A second federal program provided federal aid for educational purposes other than school construction for school districts impacted by federal military installations.[23]

Hill also supported the successful movement for a federal school lunch program that spoke both to his educational and his agricultural interests. In 1951, he informed a constituent that he had been able to head off a movement to cut school lunch funds in the last congressional session. Hill agreed with his constituent that this was a program that facilitated a meal for many poor students who would go hungry otherwise.[24] And Hill was a fervent advocate of the G.I. Bill, which granted assistance to World War II veterans who wished to further their educational opportunities. In addition to support for passage of the G.I. Bill, Hill advocated extending its reach to include those veterans who had served in the armed forces after World War II. He cooperated with the NEA's higher education advocacy group in this effort and engaged in a lengthy correspondence with supporters of extending the G.I. Bill throughout the 1950s and 1960s.[25]

In 1950, Hill tried to increase federal spending in education when he wrote a bill that designated a portion of federal money generated by offshore drilling of oil for education. A recent Supreme Court decision had provided that some of the rights from oil generated off the shores of coastal states belonged to the nation and the federal government. Hill skillfully headed a coalition of legislators that pushed hard for this measure and invited notable Senate Democrats from Missouri and Illinois to become cosponsors of the legislation. Although ultimately unsuccessful in getting this legislation passed, it represented one of a dazzling variety of paths that Hill was willing to follow in his quest for federal financial support of Alabama's schools. In all of these cases, he happily accepted what he could get on any occasion for the cause of federal aid to education, endured defeat with equanimity, and remained determined to come back, again and again if necessary, to attain his objective.[26]

Education was not the only public welfare area in which Hill was involved. In fact, when given his choice of which subcommittee within the larger Senate Labor and Welfare Committee to chair, Hill chose Health, perhaps in homage to his father, over Education and Labor as his bailiwick. Health turned out to be the arena in which Hill's most important legislation was passed. He was coauthor of the landmark Hill-Burton act that provided federal funds for the founding and expansion of hospitals, public and private, to meet the surging national need for health care.[27] Hill-Burton was not the most liberal legislation to be considered in the health field. It provided federal aid for hospitals and it passed with the support of the American Medical Association and the American Hospital Association in preference to a proposal from President Harry Truman for a much more radical overhaul of the nation's health care system, one that contemplated direct government involvement in health care.

Hill also was active in providing federal funds for public libraries, a move undertaken to combat illiteracy, especially in rural areas where the need was great and where many of his constituents resided. In pursuit of library expansion and support, Hill partnered with his Alabama colleague Carl Elliott, a representative from the rural northwest part of the state. Thus Lister Hill's advocacy of federal aid to education was only one of a variety of his legislative interests that involved federal financial support of various public welfare measures, though it is the one that is of direct interest to this analysis of NDEA. Another of Hill's efforts for federal involvement in the nation's educational welfare, his pursuit of federal aid for vocational education, is our next concern.

Federal Aid for Vocational Education

Lister Hill's campaign for general federal support for education was accompanied by his efforts for a more specific kind of federal aid, to vocational education. It was here, where Congress had begun support in the second decade of the twentieth century, that Hill experienced substantial success, in contrast to his failed efforts for general federal aid. There was a long tradition of southern congressional support of vocational education, starting with Senator Hoke Smith of Georgia and Representative Dudley Hughes of the same state, cosponsors of the landmark Smith-Hughes vocational education act of 1916.[28] Smith-Hughes put into law the recommendations of a commission appointed by President Woodrow Wilson that found that few of the 12 million Americans engaged in agriculture or the 14 million engaged in manufacturing had any training for their labor. Smith-Hughes authorized up to $7 million to be spent on vocational programs and set up a Federal Board of Vocational Education to administer the programs. Smith-Hughes also mandated the creation of state boards of vocational education that were to submit plans to the federal body for vocational programs and the training of teachers for these programs. This administrative apparatus at the federal and state levels quickly produced a vocational lobby that assiduously courted the Congress to maintain, and increase, the vocational appropriations. The original Smith-Hughes Act provided for programs in agricultural, manufacturing, and home economics education, as well as teacher training in each area. The emphasis on agriculture as well as the affinity that the law institutionalized for the interests of employers in need of a trained work force had much to do with its popularity with southern legislators who sought economic development.

Smith-Hughes remained intact as the federal education law until 1936 when the George-Deen Act, sponsored by Senator Walter F. George and Congressman Braswell Deen, both from the state of Georgia, doubled the appropriation from $7 million to $14 million and made the appropriation perpetual instead of subject to renewal. In 1946, the George-Barden Act, sponsored again by the Georgia senator but this time with a powerful House member from North Carolina, both of whom had reputations as conservatives, amended George-Deen by doubling its annual appropriation to $29 million. In the ensuing decade some vocational education funds were allotted for practical nursing.[29] These last three legislative accomplishments, George-Deen, George-Barden, and the health amendments, engaged the attention of Lister Hill and spurred his efforts in the Senate on their behalf.

Hill's papers are full of exchanges, entreaties, and assurances between the senator and his staff on behalf of vocational education, as well as between Hill and federal vocational education bureaucrats and their Alabama counterparts. While Hill was less immediately visible than the southerners whose names graced vocational education legislation in the 1930s and 1940s, he used his Senate committee assignments in those decades and in the 1950s, on the Education and Labor Committee and its Appropriations subcommittees, to make sure that the measures were treated generously when the time came for determining the exact amount of funds to be appropriated. In late 1951, for example, Hill corresponded with an Alabama vocational education official about a threat to reduce vocational education funding. The Alabama official warned Hill that pending cuts at the federal level would mean a 50 percent reduction in such funding for Alabama and, after stating that this was terribly threatening, asked Hill if he could do something. Hill replied that he would act when the bill calling for the reduction cleared the House and came to the Senate for consideration.[30]

Hill's efforts on behalf of vocational education funding became increasingly important after the election of Republican Dwight D. Eisenhower to the White House in 1952 threatened federal efforts in all education arenas, but particularly in vocational education where the amount of funding was large and the relationship to intellectual improvement was unclear. A memorandum from one of Eisenhower's staffers to Hill in April of 1953 provided Hill with a quote from Eisenhower's campaign for the presidency to be used in fighting a White House–initiated attempt to cut off 25 percent in vocational education funding under the George-Barden Act. The memo quoted an Eisenhower letter of September 27, 1952 that referred to the "magnificent system of vocational education" as one of the greatest parts of the mass education system of the United States. Eisenhower had added that vocational education was one policy arena in which much needed cooperation and understanding between state, local, and federal agencies was exhibited.[31] Hill and other supporters of vocational education could use these sentiments to show that the desires of the president as a candidate for vocational education were being contradicted by his move now to cut funds for the cause.

In the summer of 1954, vocational education funding was again threatened by a stunted appropriation recommendation from the White House. Congress, with considerable prodding from Hill and others, increased the appropriation substantially. Hill informed his constituents in Alabama that the victory over the president meant $5 million more for vocational education. He concluded his letter to constituents with the following: "I am sure that you and I agree that no program has contributed more to the building of the economic strength of Alabama and of the nation . . . than our vocational education program."[32]

One year later, Hill again made sure that all of his efforts on behalf of vocational education were well publicized in his home state. After Hill had sponsored an amendment increasing the amount of funds appropriated for vocational education, he sent a telegram to a long list of Alabamians regarding the adoption of the amendment and the amount appropriated.[33] And it was not just Alabamians who were aware of the benefits of Hill's efforts on behalf of vocational education. In March of 1956, Hill received a letter from the president of the American Home Economics Education Association seeking full appropriation for vocational education. She informed Hill that two years previously, after testifying successfully before Congress on behalf of full funding, she had been able to use the amount appropriated in her state for programs in Negro, white, and Indian schools. She added that thirty-nine home economics departments had been started nationally with the funds. She hoped that Hill would be as generous, and as effective, this time as he had been previously. Hill responded that, as in the past, he would do his best to assure the maximum appropriation.[34]

Still another national contact from Hill on behalf of vocational education occurred in the summer of 1956, after Hill had introduced a bill to extend the George-Barden vocational education legislation. One of his Senate staff members, John E. Campbell, corresponded with the president of the National Council of Parents and Teachers, who requested copies of the bill. The staff member assured the national parent-teacher leader that the senator would be made aware of her interest in vocational education, and reassured her about the senator's efforts on behalf of the cause.[35] And in 1957, Hill acted once again to protect vocational education. When vocational education funds were cut by action of the House of Representatives, Hill told the executive director of the American Vocational Association, the national lobby for vocational education, that the Senate was working hard to restore the funds. Hill vowed to do "everything in my power" to redress the situation. A few days later, the secretary of the Senate of the State of Alabama sent Hill a resolution that had been passed by that body in support of vocational education funding. Hill responded that the Senate Appropriations Subcommittee of the Senate Committee on Labor and Public Welfare, which he chaired, had authorized the full amount appropriated to be spent on vocational education. He also informed the head of vocational education in Alabama that he had held the line on vocational education appropriations.[36]

In January of 1958, when Hill and Representative Carl Elliott were beginning work on their versions of the National Defense Education Act, the Alabama director of vocational education quickly moved to make sure his area was being included, since it was not in the administration version of the bill. Writing to Hill about a possible college scholarship provision in the bill, R. E. Cammack promised support from the American Vocational Association for NDEA and encouraged Hill to include technical schools as places where scholarship students could attend, in addition to colleges and universities. Hill replied that the scholarship suggestion would receive careful consideration in his committee.[37] Several months later, in the midst of congressional consideration of NDEA, Hill received a flurry of letters from national and state vocational educational leaders, imploring him to save a recently added vocational education title. Hill replied to all that he would do his best to achieve that objective. And Hill's best was more than enough to save vocational training. Hill's Senate subcommittee on appropriations, in fact, added $20 million earmarked for vocational training to the amount of NDEA funding. An editorial in the Montgomery *Advertiser* acknowledged the importance to the state of Alabama, and the nation, of the NDEA, but questioned the amount of money going to vocational training. For the newspaper, vocational training was "clearly a boondoggle violating the purpose and intent of the act, which was to revitalize learning in the areas important to the nation's survival."[38]

While the topic of what areas should be included in NDEA will be addressed in the next section of this chapter, the criticism of vocational education in the newspaper was a reaction that had been encouraged by the nature of the vocational education effort since its inception in the early twentieth century. Establishing a federal bureaucracy devoted to vocational education and a parallel bureaucracy in each state for the same purpose resulted in institutionalizing a permanent lobby for the subject that was unmatched in effectiveness by any other curricular area of education. The existing vocational apparatus meant that, after passage of NDEA, the vocational educators were the first ones who were able to access the funds, much sooner than educators in any other field covered in the legislation. One of Hill's staff members reported to him in December of 1958 that Alabama should be getting its share of the vocational education appropriation from NDEA before the end of the year, a scant three months after the signing of the bill. The reason for this was that vocational education in Alabama and other states already had in place the machinery to use to request and to receive aid.[39]

Because of the effectiveness of its formidable bureaucracy and its relative separation from the other subjects in the school curriculum, vocational education was often seen to be a substitute for, or an opponent of, academic subjects. Hill seemed at times to lean far in the direction of vocational education. For example, in May of 1963 he reassured the Alabama director of vocational education that "I share your interest in the expansion and improvement of vocational education." Yet later in that same month he told a classics professor at The University of Alabama that "I am mindful of the value of the study of Latin and the need for strengthening and improving the teaching of Latin in our schools."[40] While there is no necessary contradiction between these two positions, the former, support for vocational education, is represented countless numbers of times in Hill's correspondence, while the latter appears sporadically at best. Given that Hill never took any vocational courses, nor expressed interest in them as appropriate for others in his family, one can, at the least, suggest that the alliance with vocational educators was much more political than substantive. Of course, for a politician politics is substance, and the political power of the vocational education lobby, and its ties to many of the business and agricultural leaders in Alabama and throughout the nation, were formidable.

Hill maintained his advocacy of federal aid for vocational education, and his ties to the vocational education lobby, to the end of his political career. In 1966, for example, two years before he retired from the U.S. Senate, Hill again reassured the Alabama director of vocational education of his interest in "the expansion and improvement of vocational education."[41] That interest was a constant focus throughout Hill's congressional career, as was his devotion to federal aid to areas other than vocational education. The two interests were combined in the National Defense Education Act, although vocational education was only one of several titles in that legislation. The curricular interests that were fed by the National Defense Education Act, and Hill's participation in the feeding and care of those various interests, are considered in the next section of this chapter.

Education and National Defense

The notion of education for national defense had been a major part of American political and educational discourse at least since the early 1940s. In that era, the National Education Association (NEA) had tied the successful prosecution of World War II, and any subsequent international conflicts, to improvement of the educational programs of the public schools. Lister Hill extended this line of argument even further in his speech to the NEA in 1941 when he told the group that any strong nation needed a combination of educational attainment in academic areas, in vocational fields, and in training for the professions.[42] Twelve years later, and five years before the passage of NDEA, when Hill introduced his latest version of a federal aid to education bill in the Senate, he called it "A Bill to assist in the provision of facilities for free public education required in connection with the national defense."[43] Substantial support for this approach to enhancing public education for purposes of national defense could be counted on whenever statistics surfaced on the number of Americans rejected for military service because of illiteracy or some other educational deficiency. Such statistics were influential in congressional discourse in 1953, in the midst of the Korean conflict, when Hill introduced his federal aid measure. Additionally, the entire period from shortly after World War II through the 1980s was characterized by an ideological Cold War between the United States and its allies and the Soviet Union and its allies that could be, and was, used to promote educational improvement deemed necessary to the waging of that conflict.

There was a much more limited counterinterpretation of national defense education in the 1940s and 1950s that competed with the general federal aid approach supported by Hill and the NEA. This orientation confined national defense education to subjects directly and indirectly related to international competition in armaments such as science, engineering, and mathematics. Alabamians were introduced directly to the economic benefits associated with this approach when the federal government installed Wernher von Braun and other German scientists in Huntsville, Alabama, before the end of World War II to conduct research on a variety of military topics, including the atomic bomb.

The dean of the engineering school at The University of Alabama invoked this narrowly explicit defense rationale when he sought Hill's help in gaining passage of an engineering education measure before the Congress in 1956. Dean J. R. Cudworth told Hill that the engineering educational crisis "affects the lives and well-being of every citizen in this country." Hill responded by generally agreeing with Cudworth, though pointing out that the problem was acute at the elementary and secondary levels of education as well. He added that the National Science Foundation, created by Congress in 1950, had just received its largest appropriation to date. Thus, two years before NDEA Hill offered his more general version of national defense education as a modification of the narrower version favored by the engineering dean.[44]

The launch of the Sputnik satellite into orbit by the Soviet Union in November of 1957 thrust the idea of education for defense into the forefront of the consciousness of the popular press and of Congress. Although Hill was in Europe at the time that Sputnik was launched, other senators immediately responded to what was deemed politically as a cataclysmic setback for the United States. For example, within days of the launch, George Smathers, Democratic senator from Florida, sent Hill a proposed bill for scholarships in science and technical fields. Smathers argued that Sputnik meant that the Soviets were ahead of the United States scientifically, and his bill sought the use of liquidated alien assets to fund the scholarships.[45] A handwritten note at the top of the letter, written by a staff member, posed the possibility of cosponsorship. There is no record of any reply by Hill. One reason for not signing on was the greater breadth of Hill's desires for federal educational involvement than the limited proposal championed by Smathers.

In December of 1957, one of Hill's staff members reported to the senator on an evening meeting during which Edward Teller, a German physicist who had come to work for the United States at the end of World War II and quickly acquired a reputation as a leading spokesman for scientific improvement, discussed the post-Sputnik situation. According to the staff member, Teller was both pompous and pessimistic to the point of almost embarrassing himself. Yet, the evening was, for the staff member, a "chilling" event. Teller claimed that the United States was ten years behind the Russians scientifically. He made additional criticisms of spelling instruction in the elementary schools and of dubious spending by American automakers on model changes every year, with no concern for the quality of their cars. Teller concluded that any catching up with the Russians would require a drastic change of attitude in the highest levels of the government and a commitment to shore up the nation's scientific education and research.[46]

Teller was quite likely disturbed at the timidity of the response of the Eisenhower administration to Sputnik. The president, reflecting his Republican Party's orientation, was not likely to prescribe extensive legislation to redress what many called the nation's severe educational deficit in science and technology in relation to Soviet achievements. In fact, Eisenhower had information that the Soviets were not really ahead of Americans in the space race, or in any other technological competition. To reveal that information, however, was to compromise intelligence gathering, so the administration sought to temporize. This strategy proved exceedingly troublesome when the Soviets launched a second satellite before any American response and, when the response came, the American attempt to launch a satellite resulted in a flaming failure on the launching pad.[47] Eisenhower ultimately relented to pleas for action from his scientific advisors, and his political brain trust, who pointed to, among other things, the large numbers of scientists produced in the Soviet Union and the paltry output in the United States. The Eisenhower administration began work in earnest on drafting a bill for temporary support for education in science and technology.

Hill was fortified by the furor over Sputnik and began to move to put into place his cherished vision of massive federal support for education. He was facile in employing the Cold War rhetoric that swirled around the nation as it contemplated the consequences of the Russian accomplishment. For example, he told an Alabama educator who wrote to him about the educational crisis that "I recognize, of course, that in this dark hour in our nation's history, we must pool our thinking and ideas that we may come up with the very best program in our battle for survival."[48] The objective that Hill sought involved much more than improvement in scientific and technical education, however. In pursuit of his objective of federal aid to large areas of the educational enterprise, Hill worked with Representative Carl Elliott from Alabama through the month of January 1958 to draft aid to education bills that would take advantage of the political opportunity presented by Sputnik.

Hill and Elliott were determined to produce a much broader and more expensive bill than anything that would emerge from the Eisenhower administration. Prominent Alabamians were aware of what Hill and Elliott were working on, and encouraged them in their efforts. The editor of the influential Anniston paper the *Star*, for example, wrote in support of the approach taken by Hill and Elliott. In February of 1958, George Land sent a copy of his editorial to Hill in which he specified his hope that Hill and Elliott would lead nationally. The editorial called the administration response being discussed a puny proposal for help for science only, noting that the international competition was for the minds of all people, not just for a few scientists. Hill told Land that he thought the editorial was "splendid" and added that the bill he and Elliott were working on sought $1.2 billion for elementary and secondary schools and a scholarship provision that would improve the preparation of elementary and high school teachers.[49] Many other letters in this period echoed the sentiments of the Anniston editor and encouraged Hill and Elliott to be expansive in planning their legislation to make it a powerful response to the challenge presented by the Soviet Union.[50]

The interaction between Hill and Elliott on the one hand, and the administration on the other, as well as the responses to the legislation by both educators and scientists are the subject of later chapters in this volume. My argument here, and later, is that the NDEA that passed into law, and its successor measures, spoke as much or more to the designs of Lister Hill and Carl Elliott for a broad program of federal aid to education than it did to the administration desires for a temporary, and more narrowly conceived, measure.[51]

As noted in the introduction to this book, the NDEA that was signed into law in September of 1958 had ten titles encompassing a variety of subsidies for elementary and secondary education, for vocational education, and for higher education, including undergraduate and graduate studies. Some titles spoke to the narrower vision of educational change favored by many in the administration and by some scientists: Title III provided federal funds to the states for laboratory and other equipment for high schools in science and mathematics. Even here, however, the field of modern foreign languages was added. Other titles such as Title IV spoke to the more general desires of Hill and others by providing federal funds for graduate fellowships to fulfill the acute need for college teachers. Title IV provided that the field of study for fellows be open, adding that because "college teachers are needed in every subject, the law puts no restrictions on fields of study." Still other titles provided for aid for training programs for high school guidance counselors, for language development programs, and for programs in communication studies. Title VII provided for language institutes in European and other foreign languages, and for area studies institutes and programs that would use social scientific approaches to study non-English-speaking cultures. Another title provided for federal aid and subsidy for loans to students—undergraduate, graduate, or professional—authorizing approximately $400 million for that purpose for four years. And another title provided funding for an educational research program that supported the other purposes of the legislation.[52] In short, the NDEA that was enacted in the fall of 1958 was much closer to the massive aid program desired by Hill and Elliott than to the tailored, limited objectives of President Eisenhower. In the words of one eminent historian of Alabama, NDEA camouflaged Hill's and Elliott's "longtime desire for federal funding of education as a matter of national defense at a time when the Russian science and space program created panic about the quality of America's public schools."[53] While Hill and Elliott did not get everything they asked for, they got an unprecedented infusion of federal financial support for a wide variety of programs.

And the amendments and renewals of NDEA enacted by Congress in the next decade, as I will show in chapter 6, broadened the reach of the law even more significantly. For example, in June of 1959, a supplemental allocation for Title IV, fellowships for college teachers, amounted to $4.5 million for nearly nine hundred fellowships in over two hundred new or expanded doctoral programs. The programs in this allocation included "far Eastern and Slavic Language and Literature, Child Development, American Studies, Quantitative Economic, Biochemistry and Solid State Physics." "Twenty percent of the fellowships" were in the "humanities, 23 percent in the social sciences, 5 percent in Education," in addition to those in the sciences, engineering, and mathematics, meaning that almost one-half of the fellowships granted were in areas other than science and technology.[54]

One year later a panel of prestigious educational consultants was chosen by the Commissioner of the U.S. Office of Education to advise him on the provisions that might be added or changed in the coming renewal of NDEA. Not surprisingly, the consultants recommended even more expansion of the areas to be included and the amounts to be appropriated. The consultants noted the great amount of waste in the educational system, that is, the large numbers of capable students who did not finish high school and the equally large number that did not go on to college. One necessary response to this situation was "to increase the supply of qualified teachers for all subjects at all levels—elementary, secondary, and higher education." Another response was to double the allotment of college student loans. Another recommendation expanded grants for high school equipment to include the fields of English and school library resources. Doctoral fellowships were increased both in number and in the scope of fields covered, and fellowships were expanded to postdoctoral programs and other graduate programs for training elementary and high school teachers. Recommendations advocated increases in support for almost every aspect of the original NDEA, as well as for reinstituting the scholarship program that had been eliminated from the bill in 1958. While the scholarship program was not part of the renewal of NDEA this time, the general approach of the consultants recommending more money for students and for the expansion of existing programs and the introduction of new programs was clearly the pattern that was followed.[55]

By 1964, for example, library media, reading, history, geography, civics, and education for the disadvantaged were added to the subject areas that were deemed critical and thereby qualified for financial support for institutes for high school teachers. Institutes for high school guidance counselors were expanded in their reach to include elementary, junior college, and technical institute personnel. The Office of Education summarized the 1964 changes as efforts similar to those of past congresses to "broaden the coverage to more learners, more teachers, and more programs."[56]

Copies of various reports from the Office of Education about the increases in NDEA funds grace the files of Senator Lister Hill, testifying to his continued interest in the expansion of the law he had cosponsored. He also had other evidence of the positive results of his efforts, both from his home state and elsewhere. In September of 1959 Hill told an Alabama Education Association official that the boost that NDEA had given to Alabama's teachers "was very much in our minds when Congressman Elliott and I proposed NDEA." The senator added that the political climate was not yet ready for the direct federal aid to teachers' salaries sought by both the Alabama and the National Education Association, because of the recalcitrance of the leadership of the House of Representatives. In place of this measure, Hill remarked that he and his allies had opted for passing a school construction measure, so at least they secured something.[57] In 1964, Hill corresponded with two English faculty members from Auburn University who thanked him for including English in the provisions of the expanded NDEA. In that same year, he received many letters from librarians, in Alabama and other states, thanking him for the inclusion of their subject in NDEA.[58] Two years later, Hill received several letters from several physical educators from Alabama educational institutions intent on getting their subject supported by NDEA.[59]

Hill's interactions with supporters of NDEA were not confined to Alabama. In March of 1967, Senator Mike Mansfield from Montana forwarded a letter to Hill from the state superintendent of schools in Montana praising NDEA as a law that had regulations that were easy to interpret and administer and simple application procedures that allowed schools to get the materials and equipment they need. The superintendent wanted extension of NDEA and sought to make sure that NDEA support would continue for the many subject areas currently encompassed by the law.[60] Early in 1968, Hill corresponded with supporters of language and area studies centers supported by NDEA, including the president of American University in Washington, DC. He assured that official that his interest in these centers was undiminished and that he would support them strongly in upcoming deliberations, though the Vietnam War meant considerable pressure on the federal budget.[61]

Hill left the Senate in 1968, choosing not to face an election in Alabama that he deemed unwinnable, not because of Vietnam but because of the rising influence of George Wallace and his inflammation of the race issue. Hill's Alabama political problems are discussed in the next section of this chapter. What remains here is to summarize Hill's contributions to NDEA. One way to do that is to look at the tributes to Hill, and to NDEA, from the National Education Association. In March of 1967, two articles appeared in the NEA newsletter, one on Hill and one on NDEA. Together, they testified to the accomplishments of this legislator, and to their wide impact. In one article, called "Meet Mr. NDEA," the newsletter talked of how federal "aid to education has snowballed since 1958, when Congress passed the landmark National Defense Education Act." The article added that Hill was the Senate sponsor and coauthor of the legislation, and that he currently served as chairman of the Senate Labor and Public Welfare Committee as well as its crucial Appropriations Subcommittee. Hill was described as a longtime supporter of federal aid to education, an advocate of the nation's health, and a firm friend of the NEA and of the nation's public schools.[62] The second article discussed NDEA more specifically, noting that its immediate aim of improving science, mathematics, and foreign language education had been extended to virtually all areas of education and that students at all levels of education had benefited from its provisions.[63] The efforts of Lister Hill were certainly prominent, if not dominant, in facilitating the extension.

Lister Hill, Educational Advocacy, and Alabama Politics

Two political issues complicated Hill's advocacy of federal aid to education in the 1940s, 1950s, and 1960s—religion and race. The latter would lead ultimately to Hill's political demise in 1968. The former, however, was finessed by the Alabama senator as he pursued his educational campaigns. Let us turn first to the religious issue, more particularly to the parochial schools of the Roman Catholic Church, and their impact on Hill's educational platform.

As indicated earlier in this chapter, Hill's mother's Roman Catholic faith was prominent in his early life, and he was raised in that faith. As an Alabamian with political ambitions, however, Hill realized that a Catholic would at the least be severely handicapped in winning the allegiance of a majority of citizens in the state. Hill thus became a Methodist and professed that faith throughout the rest of his life. His former Catholicism was controversial politically for a time, but Hill always was able to neutralize any political charges of Catholicism by pointing to his formal membership in a prominent Montgomery Methodist Church.

The issue of Catholicism intersected with several of Hill's campaigns for federal support of education discussed above. Worthy of attention here are the federal aid campaign of the late 1940s and the passage of the National Defense Education Act in 1958. In the late 1940s, as Hill optimistically offered his own bill for federal aid to education, the issue of Catholicism arose, especially in the eyes of the large non-Catholic majority of citizens in Alabama. Hill needed to get support for his federal aid to education bill from senators from northern and midwestern industrial states that had considerable working-class populations that were largely Roman Catholic. Those states also featured substantial numbers of Roman Catholic parochial (parish) schools. The Catholic Church in the late 1940s had changed its position from opposition to federal aid to education to support for the policy if it would provide funds for Catholic, as well as for public, schools. This shift was due in large part to Catholic schools experiencing some of the same enrollment pressures that public schools were facing from the coming baby boom. Hill thought he had the issue of parochial schools mastered politically in his federal aid bill in the late 1940s, as it provided that federal aid dollars would be spent in the same way that state dollars were. That is, in states that permitted public funds for parochial schools, federal funds could also be allotted for that purpose. This allowed Hill to tell Alabamians that he was firmly for separation of church and state, but that he was also firmly for states' rights. In Alabama, where the state constitution expressly forbade aid to religious schools, this meant that federal aid would also be withheld and no public funds, federal or state, would go to support Catholic schools. This strategy seemed to work for Hill, but his position was not completely free of controversy in the minds of some Alabama citizens.[64]

In late 1946, the Supreme Court had heard a case from the state of New Jersey where a public school system had paid for the transportation of students to both public and parochial schools. This was challenged as a violation of the First Amendment separation of church and state provision. The Court permitted the expenditures, however, reasoning that the transportation subsidies benefited the child who was transported to school, not the church that sponsored the school.[65] This "child benefit" theory grew increasingly important in the late 1940s and 1950s and funds were approved for textbooks in parochial schools, as long as the books were for nonreligious subjects. Hill explained to the superintendent of the Montgomery, Alabama, schools that the trend begun with the ruling in the New Jersey (*Everson*) case meant that the First Amendment was harder to interpret now than it had been earlier when a flat prohibition against aid of any kind was in place. The issue now was where to draw the line of separation. Federally supported school lunches in parochial schools, transportation of parochial students, textbooks, and support from the G.I. Bill for attendance by veterans at private religious colleges were now permitted. Hill told the Alabama education official that separation of church and state was a good principle, but one that was becoming increasingly difficult to apply to specific situations.[66]

Hill and the senators considering his federal aid to education bill heard from public school leaders in states that had a large number of parochial schools and permitted using state funds for those schools. These public school people bitterly opposed the provision in his bill allowing federal funds for the same purpose. Hill tended not to worry too much about these views, though he was not unsympathetic to them.[67] The political reality for Hill was that he needed the support of industrial state senators for his bill. Allowing states to adjudicate the situation of federal aid to Catholic schools in the same way that they appropriated state educational funds meant that constituents with students in parochial schools would look favorably on senators who voted to permit federal aid to those schools. Things got more complicated for Hill politically, however, when Alabama citizens opposed his bill because of its permissiveness in granting states the right to use federal funds for religious schools. The Alabama state superintendent of schools sent a letter to public school officials in the state supporting Hill's position. He argued that the provision allowing states to decide about the use of federal funds for parochial schools, though problematic, was not enough of a reason to oppose Hill's legislation. The state superintendent reminded his colleagues that the Alabama constitution expressly forbade any aid to religious or other private schools, and added that since Alabama would get a larger proportion of federal funds for schools than its taxpayers contributed to that effort, no Alabama tax dollars would be spent on parochial schools anywhere.[68]

Hill heard from citizens in his state with decidedly partisan, even passionate, opinions on both sides of the church-state issue. Throughout 1948, 1949, and into 1950, Hill heard from Alabama Catholics, mostly from Mobile, who opposed his bill because it meant their schools would get no federal funds. The Roman Catholic superintendent of schools in Mobile, for example, said that his schools, which educated 14,000 children, would get no money, even though Catholics had fought for the nation in World War II, and religion was certainly not an issue in that situation. Why was it an issue now, the Roman

Catholic leader asked, when Catholics sought support for their educational needs? Hill's response was easy in this case; he noted that the constitutions of the United States and of Alabama prohibited such aid.[69]

Hill heard a more sophisticated rationale for aid to Catholic schools from the Bishop of Mobile, who invoked the child benefit theory to justify his support of a federal aid bill with a more generous alternative provision for Catholic schools than Hill's own, one that would expressly allow federal aid to religious schools for purposes such as health services, transportation, and textbooks.[70] Hill was not inflexible and, if pushed, might well have gone along with that procedure. He almost always responded to letters from Catholics politely, choosing either to acknowledge their sentiments without making any commitment or to indicate ways in which he could offer some support. For example, in 1949 Rose Mary Norville wrote to Hill on behalf of one hundred Catholic girls at St. Joan of Arc Church and School in Mobile about the unfairness of a House of Representatives sponsored federal aid to education proposal that excluded Catholics explicitly. Norville argued that Catholics paid taxes for public schools and therefore should not be shut out completely from federal support for education. Hill responded that he had sponsored a Senate bill on school health that provided for "dental and medical examination . . . to all children, regardless of the school they attend" and added that his federal aid bill did not disturb the transportation or textbook decisions of the Supreme Court.[71] In 1950, he received a letter from a Catholic priest in Birmingham, with whom he was acquainted, that appealed to Hill for fairness in the matter of aid to Catholic schools. Hill responded that he was for what was fair, but also for what was constitutional. He reiterated his support for health services for Catholic schoolchildren and for school lunches and transportation in states that allowed it. He added that his successful hospital legislation had provided federal funds for the construction and improvement of Catholic hospitals. His tone in this letter was cordial and he sought the same fairness for his views that the priest had sought for his position.[72]

For every letter Hill received from Catholics feeling that they were being treated unfairly, he heard from many more Protestants, most often Baptists, from all over Alabama standing strongly against any aid to Catholics and their schools on the grounds that such aid violated the First Amendment. In February of 1950, Hill received a letter from a Montgomery Baptist pastor concerned about the possibility of allowing federal aid for Catholic schools in states that permitted state aid. The Baptist leader chastised Hill mildly for his hospital bill, arguing that by allowing federal aid for construction of Catholic hospitals, the measure unwittingly violated separation of church and state. Catholics, according to the Baptist clergyman, trained nurses in their hospitals, a clearly secular program, but they also evangelized there, an obviously religious activity. Hill responded that there was no explicit approval of federal aid for parochial schools in his bill, a true statement but one that also did not contradict the fact that it permitted such aid in states that already permitted it. Hill concluded by reassuring the pastor that "no one believes more strongly than I do in the complete separation of church and state and no one has tried to be more diligent than I in guarding against any breaching [*sic*] or weakening of the wall between church and state. We must keep the wall high and impregnable."[73]

At times, Hill became exasperated at the vehemence of some of the Baptist criticism of federal aid. When the executive secretary of the Baptist State Executive Board of Alabama wrote Hill opposing Hill's permissiveness on federal aid to parochial schools in states that permitted state aid, Hill replied that his bill upheld states' rights and the separation of church and state, two principles that both he and the minister held dear. Hill added that since the Supreme Court had allowed state aid to parochial schools in the form of textbooks and transportation, on the grounds of benefiting the child, not the church, changing his bill not to allow federal aid where state aid was allowed was an unwarranted intrusion of federal power into the affairs of states. On the copy of the Hill reply in the Hill papers, the phrase "not sent of course" was written at the top. A week later Hill sent a milder version of his earlier letter making similar points without making any explicit accusation of unconstitutionality about the minister's position.[74]

The amount of correspondence that Hill received on aid to parochial schools was enormous in this period. His responses were amazingly frequent, generally consistent, and usually solicitous of the views of his correspondents, but also rather firm in stating his own position. On this issue, Hill had a political response he thought was constitutionally as well as politically sound. He would countenance federal aid in states that condoned such aid, but not where it was prohibited. This allowed him to assure Alabamians that such aid would not be tolerated on constitutional grounds. At the same time he could point out to Alabama Catholics the provisions in other states as well as the aid given to Catholic and other private institutions in his hospital legislation. In spite of his confidence in his position on the church-state issue, Hill's federal aid to education legislation was defeated in 1950.

The development, consideration, and passage of the National Defense Education Act (NDEA) gave Hill a chance to reverse the negative outcome of his previous efforts on behalf of federal aid to education. One unusual aspect of the NDEA legislative process in 1958, however, was the relative absence of controversy, among Hill's constituents and nationally, over the issue of aid to Catholics and other private schools. Perhaps the major reason for this situation was that the Sputnik crisis alarmed the American public sufficiently to muffle any concerns that would be raised about the religious aspect of any federal aid to education program. Also, the multiple and complicated provisions of NDEA, and their consideration, meant that religious concerns were not allowed to overwhelm or displace the myriad of other issues important to consideration and passage. And NDEA did provide some benefits for nonpublic schools. For example, in Title III, which provided federal funds for public schools for laboratories and other equipment in the sciences and foreign languages, nonpublic schools received no grants, but were eligible for loans. Thus, religion did not impede NDEA to the extent that it had impeded earlier efforts for federal aid to education. Lister Hill was well aware of all of these considerations, and they clearly guided his actions in relation to NDEA.

The issue of race was substantially more important than religion in threatening the passage of the National Defense Education Act. Before considering the ways that race intersected with NDEA, a look at the rather complex interaction of Lister Hill with the race issue prior to NDEA is in order. Hill, in spite of his liberal reputation, was a white Democrat in a southern state that had experienced Reconstruction and whose white inhabitants largely subscribed to the racial attitudes and restrictions that characterized the Redeemer Democrats who ruled Alabama politics afterward. Born and raised in the state capital of Montgomery, Hill's father informed him of the atrocities committed against their ancestors by black politicians during Reconstruction. Luther Hill, however, had relatively enlightened racial attitudes for a man of his background. He treated both white and black patients in his medical practice. As a child, Lister had easy relations with the blacks who attended him and his family, though in no sense did equality characterize the situation.[75]

As a politician, Lister Hill seldom played the race card directly, though he was not averse to voicing white racism in veiled terms. For example, one week after election to the Senate in 1937, he took part in a southern Senate filibuster against an antilynching bill.[76] He also demurred from supporting Claude Pepper's proposal for the abolition of the poll tax because unless he could be guaranteed of its passage, how he voted for the measure would subject him to severe political distress. Hill also voted on more than one occasion against the federal Fair Employment Practices Commission (FEPC), which white southerners saw as an unwarranted federal intrusion into employment relations on the side of blacks and against whites.[77]

Yet Hill on occasion professed policies that sought to improve, not restrict, political opportunity. For example, he opposed passage of a measure in the Alabama legislature restricting the vote, agreeing with the National Association for the Advancement of Colored People (NAACP) and other liberal groups. Even here, however, his stated argument was that the measure harmed poor whites—true but also much more politically palatable to white Alabamians than pointing out that blacks were equally, if not more, disenfranchised by the measure.[78] It was mainly in comparison with other white politicians in Alabama and elsewhere in the South that Hill's racial views can be considered to be enlightened. Alabama racial conservatives, who learned quickly not to openly attack Franklin Roosevelt, felt much more comfortable attacking the racial tolerance and advocacy of Eleanor Roosevelt and trying to tie her to Lister Hill. In the 1944 Senate Democratic primary, for example, Hill's opponent tried to link advocacy of federal aid to education to racial integration of the schools. Yet Hill's careful avoidance of openly liberal federal measures such as FEPC, along with his considerable support from ordinary citizens in the state, and from its educators, inoculated him against these charges.[79]

On occasion, Hill had even heard from Alabamians, black and white, opposed to segregation. In 1948, for example, the president of the Tuskegee branch of the NAACP wrote Hill protesting a compact of southern governors that forced black medical students in the South to attend Meharry Medical College in Nashville rather than any white institution in the region. This was "segregation" pure and simple, said the black activist.[80] And a few years later, an Alabama Education Association official told Hill that the state group supported federal aid to education "for the benefit of 657,359 white and Negro children in our schools."[81] However, Hill's relatively enlightened views on race seldom embraced any controversial policies.

The 1954 *Brown* decision of the Supreme Court against racial segregation in education presented particular problems for Hill's advocacy of federal aid to education. The senator was not an immediate, visceral reactor to the decision, like many national and state legislators elsewhere in the South. In fact, in November of 1954, six months after the announcement of *Brown,* Hill had an exchange with an attorney from the northern part of the state about how the impact of the decision might prove to be positive. The attorney argued that now that segregation had been outlawed, Hill and other southern advocates of federal aid to education should push ahead with the campaign for the measure. The argument of southern opponents of federal aid that it threatened segregation in the schools was moot now, since the practice had been declared unconstitutional. Hill replied cordially to his constituent but questioned the conclusion the man had reached. Hill's response was that the court ruling presented a difficult political situation to both southerners and advocates of federal aid to education.[82]

In terms of federal educational legislation, the post-*Brown* period resulted in a formidable political challenge to southern advocates of federal aid like Lister Hill. In 1956, on the first occasion when a federal aid proposal came before Congress since *Brown,* Representative Adam Clayton Powell, an African American from the Harlem neighborhood of New York City, proposed an amendment to the House version of the bill that provided that states that operated racially segregated schools that violated the Supreme Court ruling could receive no federal funds.[83] Powell, who served on the House Committee that considered educational proposals with Carl Elliott of Alabama, vowed to attach his amendment to any proposal for federal aid to education. The debate over the Powell amendment occurred in the same year in which the Southern Manifesto, signed by Lister Hill and most other southern senators and members of the House of Representatives, was published. When Hill signed the Manifesto, he vowed to "do all in my power to maintain segregation."[84] Hill's political problem on this issue was made more acute during his campaign for reelection in 1956. In that campaign, Hill's opponent charged that Hill's advocacy of federal aid to education and his sponsorship of federal aid for hospital construction worked to break down segregation. Hill managed to defuse the situation, citing his signing of the Southern Manifesto as the true indicator of his intentions. Hill's biographer argued that Alabama blacks "sensed that Hill's words and actions on behalf of segregation were pro forma political expressions" and refused to take them as serious indicators of the senator's true beliefs.[85]

There is some evidence that Hill's liberal colleagues in the Senate from outside the South also were sympathetic to the political minefield that Hill faced on the race issue. Hubert Humphrey from Minnesota, for example, in 1956 informed Hill of a proposal that would prevent the negative consequences of Powell-like amendments to aid-to-education bills. Humphrey's proposal was a provision that "states and school districts are in compliance [with the desegregation ruling] until . . . the court finds that they are not." Humphrey elaborated that the "presumption is of compliance. The court would have to determine failure to comply."[86] Humphrey's proposal was not enacted and Hill continued to face pressure from diehard segregationists to maintain the southern way of life. In 1957, Hill responded to that pressure and joined with avowed southern conservative senators in an unsuccessful fight against a relatively mild civil rights bill.[87] Hill was increasingly being forced into a political corner by the segregationists.

Hill's personal views on race are difficult to discern completely. He was a private person and he guarded himself and his family carefully. The best evidence regarding Hill's position on race comes from an interview conducted with Hill's nephew by a biographer of Hugo Black, who left the Senate for the Supreme Court and was succeeded by Hill. Black became anathema to many Alabamians after the *Brown* decision, in which the vote to outlaw school segregation was unanimous. Hill, a close friend of Black, was forced for political reasons to distance himself from Black. This bothered Hill immensely. Hill's nephew reported his uncle's statement about the race issue. "I'm doing more good for people staying here [in the middle ground] than if I went out front on the race issue." Hill's nephew went on to add that Hill "didn't believe what he was saying about race, he had to say it. He knew it and it didn't bother him at all. He had made up his mind that was what he was going to do."[88] Thus, according to his nephew, Hill's position on the race issue, crafted to survive politically in Alabama, was not his personal position.

Fortunately for Hill, and for Carl Elliott, the opportunity presented by Sputnik for passage of landmark legislation in federal aid to education was not neutralized by the segregation issue. The federal administration that worked with Hill and Carl Elliott on NDEA was not inclined to support Powell amendments that prohibited racial discrimination, and Hill and Elliott were able to work successfully with the administration to neutralize the Powell amendment in the final version of NDEA that came from a conference committee of the House and Senate. What emerged was a bill that said nothing about racial discrimination but was interpreted to be antidiscriminatory in all its titles. Lister Hill and Carl Elliott were immensely pleased with this result. Thus, the NDEA that passed Congress in 1958 was a huge success for Hill, one he achieved without alienating the consistently anti-Catholic and increasingly vehement segregationist majorities of Alabama voters. Both Hill and Elliott would eventually fall to the white racist priorities of Alabama's voters, but not until several years after the passage of NDEA.

2
Carl Elliott, Liberal Politics, and the Gospel of Education

Like Lister Hill, Carl Elliott was known throughout Alabama, and nationally, as a political liberal. One prominent dimension of his liberalism that might seem unusual for a southern politician in his, or any, time was his support for organized labor, and its support for him. Labor's regard for Elliott was clearly illustrated by Barney Weeks, an Alabama labor leader who commented on Elliott's career in 1965, the year after his departure from Congress. Weeks responded to a request for an evaluation of Elliott's politics with a three-page account of Elliott's career, noting that on sixty-four

Representative Carl Elliott, coauthor of the National Defense Education Act. Courtesy of the W. S. Hoole Special Collections Library, The University of Alabama.

key legislative actions between 1947 when he went 'to Congress and 1964 when he left, the congressman had voted with labor on forty-seven of them. Weeks added that most of the seventeen differing votes were on civil rights legislation or education legislation with civil rights ramifications, or on measures involving Catholic school support. Civil rights and religion, as they were in the chapter on Lister Hill, were topics that were especially difficult politically for Elliott. We will discuss them both in a later section of this chapter.

Weeks's summary of Elliott's beliefs went on to detail numerous areas in which Elliott had supported organized labor, and Weeks concluded that "the average citizen or working man, be he union or non-union, had no better friend, no more effective champion, or more out-spoken leader working for him in Congress from any state in the nation comparable to Carl Elliott." Weeks added that because of Elliott's relatively poor, working-class background, he spent "his whole life—every waking moment—while in the Congress, trying to make it easier for others who followed after him. He understood the problems of the worker . . . and was sympathetic toward those problems."[1]

Weeks also discussed Elliott's laudable record in areas other than labor legislation. In this vein the labor leader praised the congressman's accomplishments in gaining approval for various public library measures that benefited at least "forty million people." Finally, Weeks mentioned Elliott's victory in achieving passage of the National Defense Education Act. The labor leader cited the U.S. Office of Education as his source for the conclusion that NDEA was "the most important piece of educational legislation in more than one hundred years—since the Land Grant College Act of 1862." Weeks added that NDEA had helped more than 60,000 students attain a college education, "more than 10,000 of these from Alabama." He went on to enumerate the number of technicians, graduate students, and guidance counselors that had benefited from NDEA and indicated the significant amount of aid it had provided to instructional programs in the schools. He concluded that, as of March 1965, when he was writing the letter evaluating Elliott, more than one billion dollars of federal aid had been invested in NDEA education projects.[2]

Barney Weeks knew well the accomplishments of the congressman from Alabama's Seventh Congressional District, made up of several relatively unpopulated counties in north and northwest Alabama. Elliott's constituents appreciated those accomplishments enough to keep him in Congress for almost two decades.

Early Life and Career

Carl Elliott was born and raised in the Seventh District, which encompassed much of northwest Alabama, and attended rural and town schools there, eventually graduating from high school in the small town of Vina in 1930. Elliott's background was one of relative, though not dire, poverty. He was raised among white tenant farmers who scrambled continuously to support themselves and their families. He recalled that many of these tenant farmers joined the Grange, an organization that helped them work against the local merchants and large businesses elsewhere in the state, the "big mules," all of whom were bent on economic exploitation of their inferiors.[3] This suspicion of the economically privileged was consistent throughout Elliott's congressional career. In a statement that likely undergirded both his economic and racial philosophy, Elliott noted in his autobiography that the common people of north Alabama "never were convinced, by and large, that the Civil War was a good idea."[4]

Carl Elliott was an avid reader from his early childhood, first under the tutelage of his grandmother and, after her death, of his father. Reading was a life-long habit, and it propelled him to excel educationally. Later in his life, in addition to his political achievements, Elliott became an accomplished amateur historian of northwest Alabama, publishing several volumes on the topic.[5] Elliott was valedictorian of his high school class and, after graduation, traveled to Tuscaloosa to The University of Alabama, where he worked his way through school at a variety of tasks, including that of houseboy to university president George Denney. He loved the university, and many of its faculty members, though not its social caste aspects. For example, he criticized the caps that freshmen were required to wear as demeaning, calling them "just another example of social stratification, like the fraternities." He further analyzed his social situation at the university, especially his nonmembership in any social fraternity, when he noted that "from the beginning I was ideologically as well as socially set apart from most of the other students at the university."[6]

Elliott graduated with honors in three years and immediately entered the law school. While a law student he ran successfully for the student body presidency, adopting a consciously anti-Greek emphasis in his campaign. He noted that his approach to the student presidency at the university was like the one he took in Congress. Elected by the less privileged in all cases, he worked assiduously in their interests throughout his political career. While the university was racially segregated, Elliott struck up a friendship with a black cook at the school who managed to put five of his children through colleges in the North. Elliott also mourned the suicide of a university professor who gained pariah status for his statement that the problem of race needed attention at the university and in the state.[7]

Elliott was deeply immersed in electoral politics outside of the university. He worked for Franklin Roosevelt in the 1932 presidential campaign, and testified in Congress on behalf of a Works Progress Administration (WPA) college scholarship proposal in 1936. As a young man, he had admired Alabama political orators and officeholders such as Hugo Black and Tom Heflin, and he was interested in a political career from an early age. He started a law office in the tiny town of Russellville in 1936 but quickly moved to the larger and more centrally located town of Jasper. A county seat and a coal town, it was in Jasper that Elliott first interacted with labor as it was represented in the United Mine Workers. In the 1938 Alabama senatorial election, Elliott was the Walker County (Jasper) campaign manager for Lister Hill. Elliott described Hill as at the "head of a wave of progressive southern Democrats whose careers blossomed with the New Deal." Although he and Hill differed widely in their social circumstances, Elliott admired the Montgomery patrician, noting that what "I liked about Lister was that although he came from a rich and powerful background, his heart still beat to the tune of the common man."[8]

Elliott ran unsuccessfully for a local judgeship in Jasper in 1940, continued to practice law after his defeat, married a local girl, and began a family. With his brother, Elliott entered military service in 1942. Injured in a training exercise, he was honorably discharged in 1944. Shortly after his return to Jasper, he was appointed to a city judgeship in 1945. He successfully ran for Congress in 1948, making education a large part of his campaign.[9] Carl Elliott summarized his political philosophy in his autobiography as follows: "I . . . never lost sight of the ends at which I aimed. They were the same things I cared about from the time I was a boy: seeing that folks got what they deserved, good or bad; seeing that the less fortunate weren't denied at least the same opportunity to get an education. To have a decent income, have a home and raise a family as people who happened to be in better circumstances." Elliott concluded this description by stating, "I never forgot where I came from."[10]

Elliott faithfully served his district and its interests throughout his career, yet he was not satisfied with this as his sole political task. He noted that the congressman's basic dilemma was "balancing your allegiance to your constituents with your allegiance to your conscience and your country," and added that "I always felt there was more to my job than simply making my constituents happy. . . . I wanted to be more, to be a national, an American Congressman."[11] Thus Elliott took his desire for the economic improvement of ordinary Alabamians and his suspicion of big business and allied economic interests that threatened that improvement to a national stage during his congressional career. This economic amelioration served as the core of Elliott's liberalism throughout his congressional career and cemented his ties to Barney Weeks and other labor leaders.

Yet Carl Elliott's priorities in pursuing political liberalism were not necessarily always those of organized labor. He discussed his main priority, educational opportunity, often during his political career. For example, in his description of his testimony on behalf of WPA scholarships in 1936, he noted: "I never forgot how hard it had been to get my education and how much it meant to me. If there was one issue that became a crusade in my life, the opportunity for education for the poor was it."[12] Elliott also stressed the importance of education in his initial successful campaign for Congress in 1948. Speaking of his campaign in that election, he remarked that "I focused real hard on education, telling those miners and farmers that there was no reason on earth their children shouldn't have schooling of the same quality as that of children who live in large cities."[13] Near the end of Elliott's political career, one year after his defeat for Congress in 1964, and shortly before his loss in the Alabama gubernatorial election to Lurleen Wallace, George Wallace's wife and surrogate in 1966, Elliott spoke to a Birmingham audience about the political future. The immediate context for Elliott's talk was the recent congressional passage of the Civil Rights Act that had been initiated by Lyndon Johnson. That passage meant for Elliott, as a former member of Congress, that "a man's color does not deny him the opportunity to any right enjoyed by anybody else in America." Much of the body of Elliott's speech was about his unsatisfactory record in Congress on civil rights.[14]

Elliott's conclusion that civil rights had been attained by the passing of an act in Congress proved to be an inordinately rosy view of the situation. It was Elliott's view at that time, however, and he was interested in what was to come after passing the legislation. The answer to the title question of the speech, "After Civil Rights—What's Next?" was that the burning issue that needed to be addressed was how to guarantee the opportunity of individuals to capitalize on their rights and advance. For Elliott, that opportunity was to be institutionalized through a door he had always wanted to open, "through education." After outlining the low percentage of Alabama high school graduates going on to college, and the even more dire high school dropout rate, Elliott restated his response to What's Next. "The answer is education. That must become very clear to all of us very soon. . . . Education is the key to a better tomorrow for all of us. Let's use it."[15]

This initial discussion has tried to detail in brief the liberal political philosophy of Carl Elliott and how it was related to his background and educational record. The importance of education in Elliott's political philosophy, which has just been outlined briefly, is the topic to be considered at length in the next section of this chapter.

Elliott and Educational Advocacy

Carl Elliott arrived in Washington after the 1948 election determined to attain his goal of an increase in educational opportunity. Since he had been loyal to the Democratic Party in that election nationally, refusing to support the Dixiecrat, racially based challenge to the Democrats, Elliott was immediately on good terms with President Harry Truman. Elliott recalled an initial meeting with Truman where the Alabamian told the president that in Congress his agenda was "to begin building a bill for education." Truman responded, according to Elliott, that you "don't want to fool with that . . . unrealistic objective." Truman added: "There's probably never going to be any federal aid to education in this country, at least not in your life time," and advised Elliott to concentrate on tangible, attainable goals for his district like roads and dams. In recounting this exchange in his autobiography, Elliott acknowledged the difficulty of attaining his educational objective but also stated that his resolve to pursue it never flagged. Elliott recounted how, "In every session of Congress from 1949 to 1958, I brought up some form of a student aid act, knowing that I'd get nowhere for awhile, knowing it might be years before my bill would get a hearing." Elliott added that the opposition to federal aid for student support, or any other kind of educational improvement, was motivated by a variety of factors including religion, economic privilege, communism, and race. More colloquially, he remarked that any federal educational law was blocked by "a politically paranoid version of the three R's: Race, Religion, and the Reds."[16]

Initially, Elliott pushed his scholarship proposal without a committee assignment related to the topic. Instead, he was assigned to the Veterans' Affairs Committee, and worked assiduously on behalf of the welfare of Alabama's veterans, a commitment he would maintain throughout his congressional career. In 1951, however, Elliott was made a member of the Education and Labor Committee of the House of Representatives, and took his place alongside of committee colleagues who would later rise to prominence, like John F. Kennedy and Adam Clayton Powell. He began a friendship with Kennedy because of their committee work, though he did not become close with Powell.[17] The chair of the committee was a southern conservative Democrat, Graham Barden of North Carolina, who bitterly opposed federal aid to education as well as any attempts to ameliorate the conditions of blacks, educationally or otherwise. Barden was characterized by a congressional staff member as "a tough, thick necked, immutable, immoveable, rock-ribbed chairman . . . [who] was in charge of education . . . [and] wasn't in favor of federal aid to school construction or teachers' salaries or anything like that."[18] Thus, Elliott's committee chair was a major obstacle to the Alabamian's aspirations for educational improvement.

In the first half of the 1950s, Elliott supported the same federal aid to education measures that had attracted Lister Hill's attention: aid for school construction as well as operating assistance for schools in federally impacted areas, and assigning federal oil revenues to education. In addition, Elliott continued to pursue his personal goal of federal scholarships for intellectually able students who lacked the economic resources to pay for college. He corresponded frequently and faithfully with his constituents and with Alabama educators, from his district and from elsewhere in the state, on behalf of the cause of federal aid to education. For example, he told one constituent in February of 1952, shortly after he joined the Education and Labor Committee, that no legislation was of greater interest than federal aid to education. He added that he saw the primary outcome of this legislation as that of "expanded opportunity" for the children of his district and his state.[19]

Later that month, he received a letter from the secretary-treasurer of the Alabama Education Association outlining the appropriations for local school construction from the Alabama legislature, and highlighting the insufficiency of those efforts. The only real improvement, said the state education leader, would have to come from federal aid in the form of a school construction bill. A few months later, Elliott informed a high school principal from his district of a federal aid measure for school construction in all school districts, not just in federally impacted districts, that Elliott was introducing in the Education and Labor Committee of the House.[20]

Any bill that Elliott introduced had to navigate waters controlled by Graham Barden, powerful chairman of the Education and Labor Committee. Elliott once discussed Barden's recalcitrance on federal aid, which was facilitated by the North Carolinian's mastery of the legislative process, beginning the account with a description of a 1949 federal aid to education measure. In that year, President Truman had acknowledged the need for federal aid and asked Congress to produce a satisfactory bill. Lister Hill maneuvered an acceptable bill skillfully through the Senate. In the House, the bill was developed in a subcommittee chaired by Barden, who had not yet become committee chair. While the amount to be appropriated in both bills was identical, Barden's bill made no provision for aid to Catholic or Negro schools, thus dooming the effort to failure in his own committee, then chaired by a Michigan congressman with ties to both the excluded groups.[21]

Barden became chair of the larger committee shortly after Elliott joined it in 1951, and Elliott carefully studied his adversary, knowing that any legislation he wished to see to a successful outcome would have to overcome the animosity of his committee chair. The election of Republican Dwight D. Eisenhower to the presidency in 1952 meant even more uncertainty for any kind of federal aid to education legislation. Elliott told the assistant superintendent of the Montgomery schools in February of 1953 that he and other members of the Education and Labor Committee were pushing federal school construction legislation, though they were not confident of support from the new administration on the issue.[22] Later that year, Elliott told the president of an Alabama classroom teachers group that he vigorously supported Lister Hill's bill for assigning federal oil revenues to educational purposes. He added that it was too bad the bill had been killed in a conference committee, indicating that the administration was not the only place where aid to education laws faced effective opposition.[23]

Like his Senate colleague Lister Hill, Elliott was a special friend of one federal measure that had been successful in many earlier sessions of Congress, aid to vocational education. The director of Vocational Education in Alabama, a position established by the vocational legislation passed earlier in the twentieth century, told Elliott that the national secretary of the American Vocational Association had been informed of Elliott's successful legislative efforts on behalf of stable vocational education benefits for states losing population in the 1950 census. The Alabama vocational education leader added that his state and other states in the same situation were in debt to Elliott and that Elliott should get together soon with the national vocational official to plan further efforts on behalf of federal aid to vocational education.[24]

In addition to his efforts on behalf of various types of federal aid to education, Elliott also made it his business to maintain direct contacts with the schools in his district. He frequently spoke at school commencements. Those speeches also served a distinct political purpose for the congressman. After giving a speech, he would gather a list of graduates from the school and then write to them, informing them that their name was now on the mailing list for Elliott's weekly newsletter. Thus Elliott tried simultaneously to participate in the educational affairs of his district and to make sure that he would garner the attention of large groups of prospective voters there.[25]

Although the cause of federal aid to education languished in 1954 and 1955 in the House of Representatives, Elliott learned to take the long-term view of the prospects for his education legislation. For example, in July of 1955, ever the political realist as well as the advocate of federal aid, Elliott told the superintendent of the Decatur, Alabama City School System that a bill for school construction would not get through the House Rules Committee in this session. He suggested working together to build up support for the next session. The superintendent responded positively, thanked Elliott for his work on behalf of school construction, and added that working with the National Education Association would be a great help in attaining sufficient support for passage.[26]

In 1956, the federal aid for school construction measure looked like it would, finally, pass in the House of Representatives. The bill failed, however, because of an amendment by Congressman Powell that any school construction funds pursuant to the legislation could be spent only in school districts that were not segregated by race. Approval of the amendment meant, practically, that school districts in Alabama and elsewhere in most of the South, which remained segregated despite the legal ruling against school segregation in *Brown* two years earlier, would get no federal aid. Elliott told the president of the Jasper teachers' association that approval of the Powell amendment made it "necessary for me, and all other southerners, to vote against the bill on the final vote." Elliott added that the situation was tragic and that he hoped that Powell's action "will so outrage public opinion that we can come back with a bill without his amendment before too long."[27] While there is evidence that Elliott was not as dead set against desegregation as he thought his constituents were, he obviously did not see this as one of the occasions on which it was politically safe to lead them in another direction.

Throughout 1955 and 1956, Elliott continued his long-lived public support for the cause of federal scholarship aid to college students. He corresponded in 1955 with a young Jasper resident who was a student at The University of Alabama on the topic. The student endorsed Elliott's advocacy of such aid, noting that it was an especially good idea for those who couldn't afford to attend college. Elliott responded that he was hopeful about the prospects for passage of a federal scholarship bill. He added that the political climate was such that it was not likely to happen before the next year, 1956.[28]

While the scholarship bill did not come to fruition in 1956, Elliott did manage to attain a position of substantial importance in relation to educational legislation in that year. In June of 1956, Elliott was appointed to chair a House subcommittee of the Education and Labor Committee to consider a proposal from President Eisenhower for funds to study problems in higher education. The proposal was for support to set up state groups to study higher education needs. Elliott immediately scheduled hearings on the proposal, noting that the need for additional facilities in the nation's colleges and universities had increased year by year, so rapidly that "the federal government must do something to help our states and localities solve this problem."[29]

The administration proposal for a study group to investigate having state studies of the educational situation in higher education followed the precedent set by the president's White House Conference on Education that had considered mainly elementary and secondary education needs, and the state conferences that were held as a follow up, earlier in the year. Educators were impatient with study groups, arguing that the time for study was past. Action was what was needed now, not study groups that would make recommendations that would be considered by new groups. Elliott's appointment as chair of the committee, however, gave hope to the educators that action was not far off.

That hope was intensified by an internal organizational change in the House Committee on Education and Labor that came with the advent of the new Congress that took office in January of 1957. The momentum for action that would loosen the iron grip of Chairman Graham Barden had begun in the previous Congress. In 1955, Edith Green of Oregon, Frank Thompson of New Jersey, and Stewart Udall of Arizona joined the committee. With two existing members, Elliott and Lee Metcalf of Montana, the three new members combined to form a liberal coalition that was ready to contest Barden's peremptoriness in conducting committee affairs as well as his substantive opposition to federal aid to education. In January of 1957, Ludwig Teller of New York and George McGovern of South Dakota joined the "liberal rebels" on the committee. The liberals gathered support from enough other committee members to persuade the chairman to establish five subcommittees that would conduct the initial stages of committee business, the holding of hearings, and the preparation of legislation for consideration by the larger group. Elliott had written to committee chairman Barden on behalf of subcommittees, suggesting that they did not have to be made permanent but that they did provide an opportunity for the younger committee members to attain visibility. He told Barden, the southerner from North Carolina, that he (Elliott) was for federal aid for school construction, but not for aid accompanied by a Powell amendment keeping funds from districts that were segregated. He reiterated his longtime support for a scholarship bill.[30]

Five subcommittees were established by Chairman Barden in January of 1957, on the topics of Labor Standards, Labor-Management Relations, Safety and Compensation, General Education, and Special Education. The chairmanship of these subcommittees would normally be given on the basis of seniority. Elliott was the sixth senior member of the Democratic majority, which meant that, if normal procedures were followed, he would not get one of the subcommittee leadership positions. The person immediately above him in seniority, however, was Adam Clayton Powell. Barden's racism, as well as Powell's diffidence about the committee's work and his willingness to routinely offer nonracial discrimination amendments on legislation where their presence was sure to obviate passage, made him unpopular, with the chair and with other members. Barden thus bypassed Powell in appointing subcommittee chairs. It was with great satisfaction that Carl Elliott greeted his appointment by Graham Barden to the position of chairman of the Special Education Subcommittee of the House Education and Labor Committee.[31]

The term "Special Education" subcommittee meant much more than it would mean later when it became the label for dealing with children with various mental and physical differences and disabilities. Rather, the Special Education Subcommittee of the larger committee was to hear and recommend legislation in areas of education other than general elementary-secondary education policies, such as school construction, that were the purview of the General Education Subcommittee. While intellectual disability and other disabilities were indeed part of the mandate of Elliott's subcommittee, they were only part. More importantly for the rest of the discussion in this chapter, Elliott's committee was responsible for higher education, including teacher education.[32]

Another area that was likely to come before Elliott's new subcommittee was vocational education. Although this topic also had links to agricultural and industrial development, if it were to be considered by an education committee, it would most likely be under the purview of Elliott's group, and not the General Education Subcommittee. Thus, a past president of the American Vocational Association congratulated Elliott after he was chosen to chair his subcommittee, noting that the congressman was now strategically placed to influence House consideration of the bill for area vocational programs introduced in the Senate by Lister Hill in the last session of Congress. The official advised Elliott to contact the executive secretary of the national vocational group to strategize on passage of the legislation.[33]

Within a few months of the establishment of the Special Education Subcommittee, Elliott scheduled hearings in communities in Wisconsin, South Dakota, Utah, and Oregon on his long-sought goal of federally funded scholarships for college students. In his weekly newsletter of August 12, 1957, Elliott announced to the voters in his district that his subcommittee would be holding the first ever hearings on a federal scholarship and loan program for college students. He justified the aid to students with the argument that it was essential to the success of the United States as a democratic society. He noted: "The base of any democracy is an educated society. Whatever happens in America's classrooms in the next fifty years will eventually happen to America." He concluded his announcement by noting, "I firmly believe that a Federal-state scholarship program is the long range answer to our shortage of expert personnel. It may also be the key to our survival on some future day when Russia provokes." Thus, two months before the launch of Sputnik shook the confidence of American society about its future and put the nation's educators under close scrutiny, Elliott was invoking the Cold War competition with the Soviets as a spur to pass his proposed scholarship program, putting international competition in the same priority position that the expansion of opportunity had in his advocacy of scholarships.[34]

Testimony in 1957 before Elliott's subcommittee on the scholarship proposal often combined two emphases—expanding opportunity and cultivating talent. This combination was clearly illustrated in the testimony of a University of Wisconsin administrator at the subcommittee hearings in Eau Claire, Wisconsin. This official gave several accounts of the results of studies of Wisconsin's high school students, showing that many of the leading high school students were prevented from advancing to higher education. He mentioned that almost 3,000 of the top 25 percent of high school students in the state were not planning on higher education and that one-fourth of these prospective nonattendees reported that their parents could "not afford to send them to college." He added that most parents did want their students to attend, if possible, and that half of the students had stated that they would borrow to finance higher education. The Wisconsin educator concluded that the "data . . . suggest to me that a program specifically directed at finding, encouraging, and assisting each year the 1,000 best qualified and most deserving high school graduates who without federal assistance could not attend college, would substantially reduce, if not remove, the financial barriers to educational opportunity for current top-ranking students in Wisconsin."[35]

Similarly, the director of the Western Interstate Compact for Higher Education told Elliott's subcommittee that half of the top 25 percent of high school graduates in the western region were not enrolled in higher education, and that half of the nonenrollments were due to financial factors. The other half did not enroll for motivational reasons, said the regional leader, but he added that motivation was hard to separate from finance in comprehensively explaining the reasons for nonenrollment. Most of the nonenrollees came from families with lower than average income, meaning that scholarships would both encourage talent and equalize opportunity. The answers given by both of these officials were prompted to a large extent by the questions developed by Elliott and his staff given to them to prepare their testimony. The questions prepared for Utah witnesses, for example, concentrated on the top 25 percent of Utah high school students, asking if scholarships for that group would mean too many students for Utah institutions to handle; whether aid should be in scholarships, loans, work study programs, or some combination; and seeking specific procedures that could be adopted to administer the aid. The scholarship hearings had been scheduled before the launch of Sputnik in October of 1957, but most of them occurred after that event. Thus, Cold War emphases on international competition and scientific education emerged in the testimony of witnesses, though in response to questions developed before the Sputnik launch. The combination of an emphasis on talent development and on expansion of opportunity was a constant in the testimony, as it was in the mind of Carl Elliott.[36] Neither the congressman nor those who testified noticed the possibility that the two options might not always coincide and, even when they did, that a choice might have to be made between them.

In choosing those who would testify before his subcommittee and providing them with questions to answer in their testimony, Elliott was participating in much more than garnering information to be used by his committee. As described by Lister Hill's chief clerk, Stewart McClure, committee and subcommittee chairs used questions astutely to shape what would be presented before their groups toward the political positions held by the chair and other influential committee members. As McClure noted, "hearings . . . can shape the form of anything. You get the right witnesses and ask the right questions and they give the right answers, and your opposition is slaughtered before they can open their trap."[37] Thus Elliott knew in advance largely what would be said before his subcommittee and planned the testimony carefully in each setting for the hearings so that it would culminate in a picture of widespread support for the scholarships that were his major legislative objective.

Elliott Anticipates the National Defense Education Act

The launch of the Soviet Sputnik satellite in early October 1957 intensified the Cold War–related push for technological advancement through educational reform. The Elliott papers contain a speech given in 1956 to the Alabama Association of College Administrators by M. H. Trytten, a noted scientist who held the position of director, Office of Scientific Personnel at the National Research Council. Trytten's speech outlined the contours of the mainstream view in higher education of the challenge, and opportunity, provided to American higher education by Russian achievement in science and technology a year before Sputnik began to orbit the earth. The speech, titled "Critical Days in Higher Education," ignored Elliott's long-cherished goals such as federal aid for classroom construction, for vocational education, and for college scholarships. Trytten, instead, gave full attention to needed improvements in the school and college curriculum, and to the related issue of how students chose to enter various fields of study. A special target for Trytten was the progressive ideology of school people, which supposedly hampered effective education in science and other subjects in the high schools.[38] Elliott was astute enough to save Trytten's speech and to use his ideas more than a year later when considering what to do after Sputnik.

By 1956, then, Carl Elliott was well aware of the Cold War rhetoric swirling around American education and the criticism of the progressive ideology and practices of the public schools that characterized that rhetoric. Certainly, Trytten's speech to Alabama's higher education officials represented a rather sophisticated version of the Cold War, science-oriented argument about higher education. College and university leaders, at least those outside of the field of education, were not likely to be as persuaded by progressive educational ideas as were elementary and secondary school leaders. The speech concluded with a reassurance to Alabama higher education leaders that it was "good to see that attention is now being given [to the crisis] by leadership organizations such as yours."[39]

Carl Elliott often gave similar reassurance to leaders of elementary and secondary education, in Alabama and elsewhere in the nation. Yet the speech to Alabama higher education officials must be read as a criticism of those groups. There was a tendency among school people, and their leaders, to maintain their commitment to progressive education, at least rhetorically, in the face of criticism from academically oriented higher education officials. As I will show in chapter 4, that tendency did not serve the educational profession consistently well.

Elliott understood the significance of Trytten's speech in shaping public opinion and so, before the launch of Sputnik, turned his attention to Cold War issues of international economic and political competition that could be addressed by needed changes in science and technology education. Elliott's frequently stated advocacy of scholarships as a way of widening educational opportunity was conspicuously absent in Trytten's speech to Alabama higher education leaders. If one attends only to this speech, despite its few references to the social studies and democracy, one might conclude that Alabama higher education leaders were less interested in educational aid to subjects outside of the sciences than were Elliott and Lister Hill, his fellow Alabamian and coauthor of the National Defense Education Act. Further, one sees in the speech how Elliott's commitment to scholarships as a device for expanding opportunity could easily fit with the argument that saw their main utility as a weapon in international competition.

Yet, these conclusions must be held in abeyance until we get a fuller look at Elliott's educational program and advocacy in the ensuing months and years of his congressional career. A conclusive characterization of Elliott's educational thought and action is the goal of this chapter. It will need to be sensitive to all of his educational pronouncements, the political contexts in which they were offered, and the ultimate priorities to which he subscribed, in developing and guiding NDEA, as well as in the subsequent years of his congressional career.

Just after Sputnik was launched, Elliott had an address prepared by the Legislative Reference Service of the Library of Congress that he would give on several occasions as he spoke throughout his state, and nationally, on behalf of education. The speech, titled "Education—Your Investment in Freedom," clearly had Cold War overtones and fear of Soviet advancement as a large part of its content. For example, it noted that "we know that the Russian artificial moons are a man-print in the sputnik sphere which represents a real threat to us. *It compels us to stop and think*!" It went on to report what it called the "astounding statistics that Russia has—right now—and is annually producing, a far greater number of teachers, engineers, scientists and technicians than the United States." It added that the scientists Russia was producing were not "hack scientists," but scientists who were "well equipped educationally." The Soviet scientific challenge was directed at the United States and its way of life, according to Elliott's speech. It was a challenge that needed to be met largely in the educational sector. The speech quoted from an Office of Education report on Soviet science published several months before Sputnik that noted: "Our survival depends upon maintaining the technical superiority of the free world over the Communists, and the maintenance of that superiority largely depends upon our having enough scientific, engineering, and other technical and professional personnel, with enough training of sufficient quality to outthink and outproduce them."[40]

Later in the speech, Elliott's hand becomes more visible in the content. He stated that there was "a real educational crisis in Alabama." Several statistics pointed to that crisis: first "Almost 1 out of every 4 of our citizens in Alabama, over age 25, has less than 5 years of schooling," which meant that Alabama "ranked forty-fourth among the forty eight states." Next, Elliott noted that "80% of our Alabama population does not have a simple high school education" and added that it was thus not surprising that "two years ago, 40% of our Selective Service registrants were disqualified because they failed to pass the Army's mental test." After commenting that Alabama's rejection rate was "40 times as high as Minnesota's or Iowa's," Elliott argued that in line with his own and Alabamians' love for their state, "there should be no place in America where it would be a disadvantage to be born." In the speech, Elliott next mentioned his four children by name, and added that it was they who caused him always to be interested in education. It was on behalf of them, and of all of Alabama's children, that education had become a necessity for survival. Elliott went on to note that "'survival' is a spine-chilling word" in the current climate of international competition with the Soviet Union.[41]

The speech then turned to a familiar theme that had been constant in Elliott's advocacy of federal aid to education, the expansion of educational opportunity through college scholarships. Elliott began this section of the speech by noting, "we in Alabama want adequate educational opportunity for all our children" and then added that he had "recently introduced into Congress a bill to provide for national scholarships for college and university undergraduate study." Elliott then quoted the language of the bill that established its purpose: "The Congress hereby finds and declares that the national interest and the national security of the United States requires the fullest development of the talent of its young men and women; and . . . to this end it is essential to reduce to a minimum the loss of such talent that results from the inability of many highly qualified young men and women, because of lack of means, to attend institutions of higher education. It is therefore the purpose of this Act to assist young men and women of limited means to further their education by establishing a program of national scholarships."[42]

Elliott's idea of "highly qualified" recipients of his proposed scholarships was less lofty than that of many other scholarship advocates whom we will meet in later chapters of this book. In contrast to the emphasis on high ability, talent, or giftedness, all qualities invoked by scientists and other academic advocates of federal scholarships, Elliott likened his proposed scholarships to the G.I. Bill and added that they would "ensure that many of our *mentally competent but financially needy* young folks get a chance for higher education." He then voiced the more traditional emphasis on the gifted as targets for scholarships, when he noted that each "year about 100,000 of our Nation's most talented high school graduates fail to enter college because of lack of funds."[43] Whether Elliott saw any contradiction between mentally competent and most talented is not clear. His long-standing advocacy of scholarships, begun well before the era of Sputnik and national concern over the scientific accomplishments of the Soviet Union, lead me to conclude that he was more on the side of generosity than exclusivity in his advocacy of scholarships. That is, he championed the larger group of "mentally competent" much more than the smaller group of the "most talented."

Additional evidence for the breadth of Elliott's vision for his scholarship program emerges from a consideration of the final paragraphs of the speech, where he discussed "exceptional children—those children who have some physical, emotional, or intellectual exceptionality." He went on to note that there were three million such children in the United States, and that they too also had a "birthright to education and to the personal and national freedom it engenders." He cautioned that these children were not to be "the forgotten ones," since, among them, "there may be another Albert Einstein, another Louis Pasteur, another George Washington Carver, another Carl Sandburg, or another Andrew Carnegie." These "exceptional children," Elliott remarked, "are more like average children than unlike them."[44]

This speech indicates that Carl Elliott's commitment to educational opportunity was broad, to say the least, encompassing talented children, mentally competent children, and exceptional children within its reach. This scope suggests that he was quite willing to use the advocacy of federal scholarship aid for the gifted or talented as a wedge in pursuit of his broader objective of equalizing educational opportunity. It also reveals that he was familiar with the national defense rationale that had made federal aid to education much more popular nationally, and in Alabama, than it had been before. Elliott ended his speech with an argument for educational aid that returned the attention of his listeners to the investment theme that was explicated in its title. He noted: "I'm not an expert at advising folks on how to invest their money on Wall Street, but I have no doubt that education, as an investment in freedom, will pay off with big dividends."[45]

Thus, in about ten pages, Elliott used a Cold War defense-oriented argument, a pro–G.I. Bill argument, a talent development rationale, a goal of serving the mentally competent, an emphasis on opportunity for special needs students, and an economic investment argument, all in pursuit of his objective of federal scholarships for college students. Elliott was versed in almost any conceivable argument to achieve his goal and probably believed to some degree in all of them. Concluding that his fundamental commitment was to expanding educational opportunity seems warranted, given that it pervaded his work in education long before the Sputnik era and that it was related to every one of the dazzling variety of arguments he proffered in support of the cause. With this judgment in mind, close scrutiny of Elliott's actions in the conceptualization and development of NDEA is the next concern.

Elliott and NDEA

When Sputnik was launched in October of 1957, when national reaction to the launch began to focus on presumed problems in the educational system, and when the Eisenhower administration began to consider a modest set of suggestions for its improvement, leadership in the House of Representatives in preparing and considering an education bill in response to Sputnik rested in the hands of Carl Elliott. Those hands were ready, even eager, to get on with the task. The introduction to this book gave a basic chronology of the congressional development of NDEA, beginning with the January meetings of Senator Hill and Representative Elliott on the general outlines of the bill. This section of chapter 2 will concentrate on Elliott's activities in pursuing passage of NDEA in the House of Representatives, illustrating both that the bill had a more difficult path to passage in the House than in the Senate, and that Carl Elliott proved up to the task of gaining its passage.

Not surprisingly, Elliott heard quickly from vocational educators fearful of being left out of the bill at the very beginning of his activities on its behalf. Early in January, like Lister Hill, he was importuned by the Alabama director of vocational education. Specifically, Elliott was asked to make sure to include boys and girls who want to prepare for employment in critical technical areas in his scholarship program. Three weeks later, the same official reminded Elliott that most students in Alabama did not go to college, but rather to technical schools, which should not be left out of the NDEA program. Elliott responded to the vocational educator with reassurances, noting that "I am for the Vocational Education Program first, last, and always" and adding that both his and Lister Hill's version of the legislation contained a title on vocational education in technical occupations necessary to national defense.[46] Elliott's attention to vocational education was sporadic in the entire process of consideration for the bill, however, overshadowed by other concerns.

Elliott's initial action after developing with Hill the two versions of educational reform to be offered in Congress was to set up more hearings of his Special Education Subcommittee on his scholarship bill. Meanwhile, the parent Education and Labor Committee was conducting hearings on Elliott's proposals for the larger NDEA bill. The specifics of the NDEA were less influential at this stage of the endeavor than the opinions that were offered before the committee and the purposes they served in shaping the bill that eventually was passed. Not surprisingly, some key insights gleaned from the NDEA hearings by the Elliott staff members responsible for digesting them paralleled to a large extent the national defense rationale for educational improvement that dominated in the months after Sputnik. The statement of Lee S. DuBridge, president of the prestigious California Institute of Technology and a prominent scientist and advocate of scientific excellence, spoke to three concerns related to Elliott's program. DuBridge stressed first the critical need for more and better science teachers, noting the particular need for teachers in the high schools and the relationship between more and better teachers and higher teacher salaries. He also remarked that far more important than increasing the number of college students in general was the task of enticing all of the best high school students: specifically he believed that the one-half of the top 10 percent of high school students who did not take advantage of higher education needed to be encouraged. Elliott's devotion to increasing the numbers of poorer students in college, as discussed in the previous section, had usually contained reference to those with high abilities, so he had no reason to see any direct conflict between DuBridge's views and his own. Unlike DuBridge, however, Elliott certainly envisioned a substantial numerical increase in the total college and university student population with passage of NDEA student aid measures.[47]

Finally, DuBridge advocated a rethinking of educational philosophy largely in keeping with criticism of the schools by academics from higher education. Especially needed, for DuBridge, was a stress on "intellectual attainments and achievements," an emphasis that clearly questioned the student-centeredness of much public education. DuBridge then noted the federal government's diffidence toward training in science education and advocated intensifying and improving that training with scholarships and loans based on merit, not need. This last stipulation, concentrating on merit and avoiding need in granting scholarships, was one that was much more limited in its conception of educational opportunity than Elliott's; however, the Alabamian chose not to stress his disagreement with DuBridge and was able later in the process of adoption of NDEA to address the issue to his own (Elliott's) satisfaction. DuBridge added that development of higher education in all areas of study was needed, the sciences, social sciences, and the humanities, a statement clearly in tune with Elliott's advocacy. Giving an emphasis that Elliott might have questioned, DuBridge noted that "our high school courses needed more subject content and *less vocational,* and that something must be done to make teaching attractive to college graduates."[48] Elliott's clear alliance with vocational educators did not incline him toward such criticism. All in all, however, Elliott had much reason to be pleased with the testimony of Lee DuBridge.

One potentially controversial area that was to be considered in relation to NDEA was the emphasis it might place on standardized tests. In preparation for the testimony of Henry Chauncey, president of the Educational Testing Service (ETS) that was developing standardized tests to measure student ability, one of Elliott's staff members prepared a list of questions to be addressed. The list included questions about the tests themselves, such as how reliable were aptitude and ability tests, their record in predicting college student success, how early students should be tested, the accuracy of the danger of the "big brother" charge against them, the adequacy of personality tests, and the relationship of tests to group guidance programs and their effectiveness. The other major area to which Chauncey was to respond was that of college scholarships: should they be granted on merit alone, or should need also be considered, and should they be available only in science and foreign language, fields of national need, or would such availability cause students to choose careers inappropriately. Finally, Chauncey was to be asked about how much interest high school students had exhibited in the sciences and the adequacy of the amount of interest indicated.[49]

The invitation to Chauncey to testify meant that the committee was certainly going to hear from someone with a point of view who was in favor of standardized testing. Chauncey, however, was an astute politician as well as a committed advocate of IQ and other standardized testing as important in indicating the ability and enhancing the opportunity of college students.[50] Thus, his testimony favored testing but did not go overboard in its advocacy.

But there was at least some effort in Elliott's committee to balance the consideration of this issue. The minority clerk assigned to the committee initiated that effort. He wrote to Elliott, attaching a list of possible names to testify before the committee that had been recommended by a minority member of the committee. Attached to the list was a copy of a letter from one of those listed as prepared to testify, Professor Pitrim A. Sorokin of Harvard University. Sorokin, a Russian by birth, was famous worldwide as a social scientist, but a maverick in relation to mainstream U.S. social scientists. Unlike most of his American colleagues, in his letter Sorokin expressed skepticism about standardized tests, especially but not exclusively personality tests. He added that his own views were characteristic of many European social scholars, even if they were not sentiments that were particularly popular in the United States. He mentioned that standardized tests were at best "supplementary tools" in making decisions about an individual's fitness for any career. He added that they were in no sense a substitute for "long-time continuous study of . . . vocal and written mental processes, and of . . . behavioral performances and achievements at home, in school, . . . and elsewhere."[51] Sorokin's letter was directed to Republican congressman Ralph Gwynn of New York. His opinions were not in opposition to any particular titles of NDEA, but more of a cautionary note about psychological testing, a cautionary note that was heard, though not necessarily followed, by Elliott and the others who developed NDEA.

A record of Elliott's views on testing is not extant. It is not likely that he was particularly persuaded by Sorokin's skepticism, however. More in tune with the provisions in the NDEA title of guidance and counseling that Elliott developed were the views offered to him about it by another official of the Educational Testing Service. That individual was happy about the testing and guidance provisions in Elliott's version of the bill. They helped achieve the objective of getting the best students into college. Scholarships also helped in achieving the objective of enrollment of the best. Refusing to join the chorus of advocates of science, the ETS spokesman added that what students studied was less important than that they were given the chance to study.[52]

In December of 1958, Mary Allen, Elliott's chief clerk, prepared a memorandum for him on aspects of Title V, the Guidance and Counseling title of the recently passed NDEA. The memorandum provided a rationale for the extensive testing that was at the core of the guidance and counseling provisions in the legislation. It made reference to talented high school students, this time specifying the talented as the upper 20 percent. One-half of them, according to the memorandum, were not taking the subjects they should be taking. Testing and a guidance program related to it would benefit this situation by treating it "scientifically." Test results, combined with a student's achievement record, yielded a prediction of a student's college success that was usually very accurate. Allen offered a caution about the testing program, however, in an extended discussion of the issue. The memorandum noted that tests measured academic talent, but said nothing about motivation. And, she added that no single test should be used to make a decision. Even more critically, she warned that the "test score is not to be worshipped." After these cautions, however, the report endorsed the substantial amount of testing embodied in Title V of NDEA. First, it indicated that testing and guidance programs were especially useful for students in acute need, such as the retarded and delinquent. Allen went on to add: "But there are students at the high end of the scale who present an equally great problem as far as their own self-fulfillment is concerned and an even greater problem as far as society is concerned. . . . We cannot escape the fact of individual differences, and we cannot escape the necessity for coping with them. Whether we like it or not, they are a central fact in any educational system—and in any society."[53] Thus Carl Elliott put himself in league with advocates of standardized testing who saw Title V of NDEA as the proper insertion of psychometrics into secondary schools, even though it seems clear that he had a view of expanding educational opportunity to attend college that was much more expansive than that of most of the testers.

Rather than engage in extended discussion of the virtues, and weaknesses, of standardized tests, much of Elliott's agenda in the spring in 1958 was devoted to finishing the hearings on NDEA and guiding a bill through the Education and Labor Committee and then through the House. This was not an easy task. While the bill passed the committee expeditiously, it next faced the House Rules Committee, a body that was infamous for blocking progressive legislation of many kinds. Two major objections threatened the bill. The first addressed cost. The federal budget was in a deficit and the extensive expenditures contemplated in the bill meant a significant increase in that deficit. Second, some members of the Rules Committee declared the scholarships in the bill to be undemocratic, discriminatory, and unnecessary. This second objection was based on the scholarships going only to the talented few high school students who would qualify for them, in spite of Elliott's contention that scholarships would go largely to able students who could not afford college any other way. Further, the scholarships were only partially awarded on merit according to the bill at hand. To answer these objections, Elliott persuaded the Education and Labor Committee to cut the number of scholarships in the bill substantially, and to provide that they be awarded only on a need and merit basis. Interestingly, though scholarships survived the Rules Committee, they did not ultimately survive the vote in the House of Representatives. The removal of scholarships was a bitter pill for Carl Elliott to swallow, though he would get a chance in the conference committee that had to reconcile the House and Senate bill to salvage the scholarships, which were in the Senate version. Here again, however, he was unsuccessful. Thus his cherished advocacy of scholarships that began with his election to Congress in 1948 was not to be realized. Especially galling to Elliott had to be the snidely moralistic arguments of some of those against scholarships, who were supported by the president at the last minute, that scholarships gave their recipients something for nothing.[54]

Ever the pragmatist, Elliott swallowed his pride and disappointment and accepted the appropriations for student loans in NDEA, which were boosted by the addition of much of the money that was supposed to go to scholarships. After passage of the bill, he was exceptionally interested in the student loan title, and, as will be shown in chapter 6, spent much time and attention on the numbers and amounts of the loans, the institutions that were dispensing them, and the recipients. During the final stages of the legislative process of NDEA approval, almost as if he anticipated the loss of scholarships, Elliott requested, and received, an analysis of the impact of the loan provision in the legislation from the Office of Education. That analysis predicted that over 200,000 students would be aided by loans in the four-year life of the proposed NDEA. It added that the prediction was realistic, based on the record of a previous loan program during World War II. The report added that loans would greatly expand the pool of students who would be helped by federal efforts, increasing enrollments and providing opportunity for good students who would not quite qualify for scholarships. Thus Elliott could take comfort in the projection that loans might be an effective vehicle for expanding educational opportunity, his long-sought goal.[55]

The issue of how Elliott defended the bill while it was being considered and passed, in relation to his earlier arguments for federal educational involvement, and his later analysis of what NDEA accomplished, deserves some attention. While NDEA was entering the final stages of consideration, a release for television from the Committee on Education and Labor, in which Elliott and his staff took a leading role in the preparation, stressed that the bill was addressing two weaknesses in the American educational effort: an "appalling waste of potential talent" and a substandard record in science, mathematics, and foreign language instruction.[56] The scholarship and loan provisions addressed the first issue and assistance to states for materials and equipment for the schools addressed the second.

These two emphases clearly represented the rationale for NDEA that Elliott, Hill, their congressional allies, and the Eisenhower administration all thought was needed to get the bill through Congress and to make it palatable to the American people. It also was the rationale that Carl Elliott used almost always in discussing the bill during the process of its consideration. In fact, as shown above, Elliott was not averse to using a national defense rationale that stressed the need for talent development and science education in his own speeches.[57] Yet this rationale lacked Elliott's emphasis on expanding educational opportunity, his interest in subjects not immediately related to educational defense such as the social sciences and humanities, and his concern for special education students. These interests were documented in discussions earlier in this chapter of his advocacy of federal aid before NDEA. They also were stressed in Elliott's autobiography, where he noted that the scholarships proposed in the bill would produce scientists, engineers, mathematicians, and linguists but that "the program we hoped to put in place was going to last much longer than any particular crisis." He almost immediately added the following: "Education has always been like a religion to me. I believed totally in its ability to empower every man to explore the limits of his potential. . . . An educational system available to everyone meets all those needs at once."[58] These are extremely generous statements about the liberating potential of education for the individual and about the broad scope that any educational program should have. It seems, however, that in the process of selling NDEA Elliott had to mute those sentiments and concentrate on the far more limited, and limiting, arguments about developing the talented few who would excel in science, mathematics, and related studies, to the end of pursuing the Cold War with the Soviet Union. It seems justified to conclude that the Carl Elliott of the period before and after NDEA, dare one say the real Carl Elliott, had much more liberal and liberating educational and social ideas than those he voiced during the debates over the bill's passage.

Race and Religion

The previous chapter showed how Lister Hill responded to the twin challenges of race and religion in his advocacy of federal aid to education. Carl Elliott faced similar, though not identical, challenges. On the religious issue and its relationship to aid to education, Elliott, in contrast to Hill, received minimal pressure in the 1950s. This was probably because of his relatively junior position in the Congress in terms of influencing legislation, particularly when compared to Hill's committee chairmanships in the educational field.

As Elliott ascended to a subcommittee chairmanship in 1957, however, he began to hear from partisans on both sides of the issue of aid to religious schools. In March of 1957, for example, Elliott received a copy of an Alabama Baptist newsletter that reiterated Baptist support for federal aid for public schools only. Anything else, the newsletter claimed, was a violation of the first amendment separation of church and state mandate. "Absolute religious freedom is impossible without complete separation of church and state." It added that if aid to nonpublic schools were to be allowed, they would have to rethink their position against having their own schools. On almost the same day, Elliott wrote to a Catholic priest, an official of a Catholic college in his congressional district. He told the priest that the House General Education Subcommittee, not the one that he chaired, was now considering a school construction bill sponsored by a Catholic congressman from the North that was supported by many Catholics. Neither of these letters reflected the heavy heat that often came with letters to Lister Hill on this issue in these years, and neither required Elliott to take a firm position.[59]

The religion issue was dealt with skillfully in both houses of Congress in the process of considering and passing NDEA. The final version of the measure contained some benefits to private schools: the loans for college students could be issued to students at private colleges, fellowship programs might be supported at private colleges, and private schools could obtain loans for equipment, as opposed to grants for the same purpose for public schools. Elliott worked assiduously for the bill and went along with compromises on the private school issue, as well as on other issues, in the interest of final passage of a measure that would pave the way for further, and perhaps different, aid programs in the future.

Shortly after passage of NDEA, however, Elliott became entangled with the religion and education issue in considering several higher education bills. In February of 1960, for example, he wrote a long letter on federal aid to religious educational institutions to the president of Howard College, a Baptist institution in Birmingham, Alabama. In this letter, Elliott stated that he had always opposed aid to private elementary and secondary schools, not mentioning the loan provision for laboratories or equipment for private schools in NDEA. However, Elliott added that he had recently been forced to change his position in regard to private colleges. In considering a higher education construction bill, Elliott told the Baptist college president that though it provided funds for construction on private campuses, Elliott had managed to insert a provision that the funds could only be used to construct facilities used for general education purposes, and not buildings used for religious purposes. Additionally, seminaries were specifically excluded from access to federal funds. Given these provisions, Elliott concluded, "I felt that I could not oppose the bill."[60]

In 1962, Elliott voted against a higher education facilities bill that included a more generous funding provision for private colleges than had the 1960 bill. An Alabama Catholic college official chastised Elliott for his vote but still made sure the congressman knew he was welcome on campus. Elliott replied that the bill had gone "too far and too fast" on aid to private colleges, but added that he loathed religious prejudice and respected the priest's views on the topic. In communicating about this same bill with a Baptist college administrator, Elliott informed the official that he had voted against this bill because of his allegiance to the principle of separation of church and state.[61]

In the judgment of Edith Green, one of Elliott's colleagues on the House Education and Labor Committee, intemperateness characterized the opinion of a Baptist college president with whom Elliott often corresponded. The president attached a copy of a letter he wrote to Green to a letter he wrote to Elliott that called the Oregon legislator either misinformed or "a liar" for claiming that Baptist colleges had received federal financial support. The president argued that since all the aid was in the form of loans or for construction of nonreligious buildings, or for summer student support, Green was incorrect. Green responded, with a copy to Elliott, that she had not misstated anything, and she listed specific Baptist colleges that had secured federal funds, including Denison College in Ohio, Linfield College in Oregon, Furman University in South Carolina, and Baylor University in Texas. She responded to the allegation that she had lied by stating: "May I say that I seldom have received as intemperate a letter as yours. I can only regret that it came from the President of a college."[62] There is no record of Elliott's position on this exchange, and he continued to correspond with the Baptist president, and to work closely with Edith Green, testifying perhaps to his tolerance as well as to his political realism.

Elliott had come upon a compromise on the finance for religious colleges issue that seemed to him both just and one that he could live with politically. Making a distinction between aid to construction for buildings without religious purpose, which he supported, and aid for constructing buildings that either trained ministers or otherwise served a religious purpose, allowed him to continue to correspond amicably with constituents on both sides of the aid to private religious colleges issue. Elliott's alliance with those opposed to aid for religious colleges was often cemented emotionally when he stressed that all of his four children had attended public schools. On the one hand, Lister Hill could not make the same claim, and he never did. On the other hand, Elliott's consideration of aid to religious colleges for nonreligious buildings, and other secular purposes, allowed him to discuss particular plans for buildings with Catholic college officials as well as possible approval for loans for private colleges, in place of grants.[63]

On occasion, a constituent would accuse Elliott of waffling on the issue of aid to private colleges, contrasting a statement in support of separation of church and state with a vote for an act that gave some aid to religious colleges. Elliott, however, was satisfied with his distinction between aid for religious buildings, which he opposed, and aid for secular buildings, which he favored. In a statement that greatly resembled Lister Hill's tolerance of federal aid to private schools in states that permitted such aid, Elliott told a constituent that since the facilities to colleges act would be administered by states, "we can rely upon the individual states to safeguard the doctrine of separation of church and state."[64] Very much like Hill, Elliott had reached a position he thought was both constitutionally justified and politically defensible, and it was this conviction that allowed him to correspond, rationally and amicably, with constituents who agreed with him, and those who did not.

Race, however, was not an issue that Elliott handled as productively, either politically or as a matter of principle. He had to confront the issue directly when Adam Clayton Powell offered an amendment to a federal school construction aid bill in 1956, denying aid to those districts that were racially segregated. Elliott told one constituent that the "Powell Amendment fans the flame of feeling . . . and, if adopted, will kill the legislation." When the amendment was approved and the legislation failed as a result, he told an Alabama teachers' association official that the passage of the Powell amendment made "it necessary for me, and all other southerners, to vote against the bill on the final vote."[65] Elliott added that the situation was tragic and that it hurt black people who needed new and improved school facilities more than whites.

A year later, he told George Meany that he agreed with the labor leader on the need for a federal aid for school construction bill, but added that he could not support one that came with a Powell Amendment. He elaborated on his position as follows: "I am sure that you have some conception of the situation we are now going through in the South. The changes in our basic way of live [*sic*] being brought about by court decisions, and by natural developments must not be hurried beyond the capacity of the people to absorb them. The Powell amendment violates that principle." In dealing with the northern labor leader, Elliott did not defend segregation on principle but rather asked for time to facilitate the changes mandated by the courts. He had expressed different sentiments to an Alabama high school student, who had asked him his opinion on segregation a few months earlier. He replied: "The South has had segregation of the races since the beginning. I am confident that legal means will be found to continue racial segregation. I favor continued segregation in the South." While these sentiments certainly were much milder than the views of those who advocated "massive resistance" to the Supreme Court, they reflected Elliott's judgment that he had to favor continued segregation in dealing with his constituents, advocating a legal defense rather than confrontation with the federal government. Of course, legal approval of segregation did not happen, and one might conclude that, as a lawyer, Elliott probably knew that what he was advocating was not possible, but that it was a position that allowed him some political breathing room.[66]

Later that spring, in a commencement speech in his district, Elliott told his audience in reference to the Powell Amendment, that "we have already had too much of the integration tail wagging the education dog."[67] Here he attempted to prioritize education over integration, putting himself on record as opposed to the court judgment that segregated education was a fundamental problem. In the fall of 1957, just after the launch of Sputnik, Elliott told an Alabama high school audience that the president's recent actions, sending federal troops into Little Rock, Arkansas, to enforce desegregation of Central High School, reflected more interest in race than in national defense. "I have been saddened as I realized how much valuable time we have wasted during the past year fighting among ourselves . . . when, with determined leadership, we might have raced ahead." Instead of pursuing the necessary international competition with the Soviet Union, Elliott told his audience that "our President was spending his time ordering the 101st Airborne Infantry Division into Little Rock, Arkansas, to force the integration of nine Negro high school students into the student body of a southern all-white high school. It is time that the President, and the Congress, realized that integration is [*sic*] southern schools cannot be accomplished, and will not be, as long as the vast majority of both races do not desire it." Elliott went on to maintain that race relations were best dealt with on the local level, "where the respect of both races for the feelings of the other can assert themselves" and that a solution would clearly "not be brought about by rabble-rousers from afar."[68] These sentiments seemed close to Elliott pandering to the racial fears of his white constituents, following them rather than attempting to lead them.

While Elliott undoubtedly believed his actions were necessary for his political survival, subsequent political events in Alabama showed that his tempered defense of segregation was not nearly enough to accomplish that outcome. George C. Wallace rode a wave of rabid, anti-federal-government resentment among Alabamians, laced with not so subtle racism, to the position of governor of Alabama. More importantly, as governor, Wallace became the arbiter of political succession in the state. Wallace skillfully manipulated a situation where the state was losing a member of the House of Representatives because of population change to oust Elliott from Congress in the fall of 1964, without Elliott ever losing an election in his own district. When Elliott ran against Wallace's wife in the 1966 gubernatorial election, offering a platform of reason and economic improvement against the hate that the Wallaces managed to inflame, Elliott lost badly.[69]

Elliott's position on the race issue changed somewhat, once he was released from the immediate demands of the Alabama electorate. After leaving Congress in early 1965, he quickly altered positions he had taken to defend segregation such as signing the Southern Manifesto against the *Brown* decision and criticizing the 1964 Civil Rights Act. In July of 1965, in a speech discussed earlier in this chapter to illustrate his commitment to the primary importance of education, Elliott applauded passage of the Civil Rights Act. Elliott added that his own vote was not part of the two to one majority in favor of passage of the bill, though he did not explicitly say that it was a wrong vote.[70]

When he ran for governor the next year, Elliott was positioned between Wallace and the Klan and other racist elements on one side, and a young attorney general who had made a reputation with younger blacks by criticizing Wallace's racial policies. Elliott thought he could win the black vote, given his record in Congress. "I assumed my actions—the color blind education and health bill I had pushed through Congress and the support I had given John Kennedy—spoke for themselves."[71] He ran his campaign as a man of the middle, "courting blacks and whites alike." He told a Selma audience: "I have not come to Selma tonight to stand on the Edmund Pettus Bridge and shout

'*Never!*' Nor have I come to stand in the Brown's Chapel AME church and sing 'We Shall Overcome.' There must be a middle ground for Alabamians." In 1966, the middle ground was small, and Elliott placed third in the primary election, behind Lurleen Wallace who won a majority of the votes cast and thus avoided a run-off, and behind Attorney General Richmond Flowers who commandeered the bulk of the black vote.[72]

In 1970, Elliott wrote to outgoing Alabama governor Albert Brewer, who had just lost the Democratic primary for governor to George Wallace, and commiserated with Brewer. Elliott described the political atrocities the Wallace gang had committed against him in the 1964 and 1966 elections. Elliott proudly told Brewer that in a recent conferral of an honorary doctorate, an eastern university had noted that Elliott "had steadfastly refused to make racism the platform" on which he stood. Elliott added that it is "morally wrong to stir up hate against 40% of our people."[73] Thus, Elliott continued to distance himself from actions on race that he felt he had to take while he was in Congress.

By the time he wrote his autobiography in the 1990s, Elliott had come full circle in his views of the race issue, to the point that he criticized his actions as a congressman, no matter that they had been taken for electoral purposes. Speaking of the 1950s and 1960s in that volume, he noted that a "course of reasoned moderation had become a tightrope almost impossible to walk. Lister Hill, who captained filibusters against civil rights even as he guided some of the most progressive social reform bills in the nation's history . . . wound up mired in the middle." Elliott agreed with a description of Hill's inability to navigate the political channels on the race issue, noting specifically that the reactionaries "didn't think Lister was enough of a racist" and the liberals "thought he was too much of one." Elliott was in the same boat politically as Hill was. One difference between the two was that Elliott stated that he had come to regret actions he had taken in pursuit of a middle position that proved to be untenable. Of the Southern Manifesto, which defended segregation, Elliott remarked: "Yes I signed it. I can say now that it was an evil thing, but I could not say it then. And I honestly did not feel it as strongly then as I do now." He further explained the reasons for his actions: "I knew there was no way I would survive, and I hadn't yet achieved what I came to Congress to do. It was that knowledge, along with my own personal concerns about the pace of the integration process, which guided me as I decided to add my signature to the others."[74]

Elliott went on to add that even the NDEA came to be used against him and Lister Hill in Alabama's dash to racist rage. "Both Lister Hill and I were heaped with praise in Alabama's newspapers after passage of our education act, but it would not be long before many of those same papers referred to that same act in language that damned both of us." Nevertheless, it was his educational accomplishment, and that accomplishment wrapped within a set of educational beliefs much more concerned with educational opportunity than with defense and scientific excellence, that Elliott offered at the end of his autobiography. He quoted from the speech he had given when he received a Profile in Courage Award at the Kennedy Library in the early 1990s. He noted that "early in my life I became aware that brains and ability knew no economic, racial, or other distinctions. When the good Lord distributed intellectual ability, I am sure he did so without regard to the color or station in life of the recipient." He then added: "I dedicated my public life to ensuring in every way possible that the sons and daughters of the working men and women of this nation would have the opportunity to achieve the highest levels of education commensurate with their ability, unfettered by economic, racial, or other artificial barriers, I am proud of the accomplishments that have been made to that end." He concluded, however, that his goals had not been reached completely. "As long as we have overcrowded classrooms, underpaid teachers, schools with inadequate libraries and young men and women who are denied an education because they do not have the resources, our work is not yet finished."[75]

This certainly represented Elliott's educational platform at its most generous: opportunity oriented and inclusive of all races and classes. While his words in support of NDEA during congressional consideration of the legislation did not always echo these sentiments, they seldom, if ever, directly contradicted them. Elliott was more often and more loudly a spokesman for extending educational opportunity than was Lister Hill, who focused on redressing the poverty of his state as a major goal. Yet their advocacy of NDEA was by no means contradictory and, further, was proffered in tandem with the goals of the Eisenhower administration. This meant that Elliott's goal of expansion of educational opportunity was to be achieved through reliance on educational testing that came to be used restrictively, as desired by most of its advocates. Also, Elliott's educational campaign flourished within a context of Cold War politics that look far less generous socially and politically than the educational opportunity he advocated or the regional educational redress that Hill sought for Alabama and its children. It is to the Eisenhower administration, and a consideration of its reasons for developing NDEA, that we turn in the next chapter.

3
Dwight D. Eisenhower, Elliot Richardson, and the National Defense Education Act

It should be clear by now that passage of the National Defense Education Act was a landmark accomplishment. Successful enactment of the legislation took an enormous, and courageous, effort on the part of both Lister Hill and Carl Elliott. These two congressmen were aided by several other members of Congress in sparking the effort to pass NDEA, and, further, passage was achieved through substantial negotiation and cooperation between Congress and the presidential administration of Dwight D. Eisenhower. That Hill and Elliott were Democrats, and Eisenhower was a Republican, is enormously significant for what it says about the promise and practice of bipartisanship during the late 1950s. Yet education was clearly an area of great promise for achieving bipartisanship in legislation, in 1958, as it was in 2001 when substantial majorities of congresspersons of both parties passed President George W. Bush's No Child Left Behind Act (NCLB). NDEA differed significantly from NCLB, however, in that NDEA represented a new and substantial infusion of federal funds into the American educational enterprise at a time when the prospect of such an infusion was clouded, at best.

Dwight D. Eisenhower, though elected to the presidency as a Republican, was not closely associated with party politics, Republican or Democrat, until he ran for that office in 1952. Eisenhower had made a name for himself in the military, rising to the position of leader of the forces that reclaimed Europe from the German army in World War II. Known popularly as Ike by his men and by the American public, both parties had eagerly sought Eisenhower as a candidate for high political office in the late 1940s. His choice of the Republicans in 1952 probably reflected his traditional beliefs as a midwesterner and as a war hero. However, he was never excessively partisan in his politics, and he was not predisposed against cooperation, and compromise, with members of the opposing party in Congress to achieve his goals.[1]

Eisenhower's postmilitary career as president of Columbia University, a leadership position in a nonmilitary context, had strengthened his reputation as one who was capable of leading the United States of America. It also meant that he was a familiar face to the leaders of American colleges and universities before he entered the White House. Eisenhower also had some experience with the leaders of American education at the elementary and secondary levels. For a few years in the late 1940s, he was a member of the prestigious Educational Policies Commission (EPC), a high-profile group chosen by the National Education Association (NEA) and the American Association of School Administrators (AASA) to discuss and develop the best professional wisdom that could be mustered to weigh and to recommend educational policies for the benefit of the American people. As a member of the EPC, Eisenhower interacted successfully with leaders of elementary and secondary education such as William G. Carr, executive secretary of NEA, and James B. Conant, then president of Harvard University and later to become perhaps the most famous analyst of the American high school.[2] In short, Eisenhower entered the White House with more familiarity with the American educational system and its leaders than most of his predecessors. While this certainly did not mean that he was, or would become, exceptionally responsive to the desires of the leaders of American education, it did mean that he was at least somewhat familiar with their problems and concerns and that they in turn had at least some sense that their programs and priorities would be intelligently considered, if not necessarily approved, by the president.

Of course, the fundamental problem for advocates of any educational program or policy at the federal level was that there was scant precedent for federal financial support for education. What precedents there were—the Morrill acts of 1862 and 1890, the Smith-Hughes and its successor vocational educational acts of the early twentieth century, and the various measures taken after World War II to increase access to higher education for veterans and to aid school districts burdened by the presence of the military—all contextualized the federal educational funds in terms of agricultural improvement, labor market needs, or the nation's defense. As discussed in the previous chapters, any attempt to win substantial funds for the nation's schools and colleges from the federal government in the 1950s faced strong and principled opposition from politicians in both political parties. They, along with many American citizens, claimed that the federal government had no business interfering in educational affairs, which were constitutionally the purview of state and local government. Further, advocates of federal aid to education were confronted with the thorny problems of religion and race. Catholic school interests, emboldened by several recent court decisions that provided public money for transportation and other nonsectarian services to parochial school students, sought to make sure that some of any approved amount of federal aid to education went to their schools. Blacks, after the *Brown* decision of 1954, sought to make sure that no money went to segregated schools. Schooling was thus an arena fraught with constitutional and political difficulties that needed to be overcome if any meaningful federal aid to education legislation were to be passed.

And President Eisenhower, in spite of his experience as an educational administrator and his service on a prestigious body of educational leaders like the EPC, was more inclined to the views of the critics of federal educational action than he was to those who advocated such action. Yet, as already noted, Eisenhower was not a rigid ideologue. His conservatism was cultural and instinctive rather than part of a view of the world that saw all concerns through the prism of political ideology. In campaigning for the presidency in 1952, he went so far as to indicate support for federal aid for school construction as part of the solution to the nation's needs for new elementary and secondary school classrooms.[3] As a president, however, he proved to be less easily influenced toward significant federal educational involvement than he was as a candidate.

Eisenhower was elected more as a representative of the moderate wing of his party than as a strict adherent to the beliefs of its more conservative elements. Yet Ike's personal conservatism appealed to all elements of the Republicans, and his openness and approachability had wide appeal for most Americans. The Eisenhower administrations, particularly his second administration after his reelection to a second term in 1956, often leaned toward the policy proposals of its centrist moderates, who were in turn willing to compromise with Democrats to achieve their objectives.

The passage of the National Defense Education Act owed much to the participation of moderate Republicans and to the willingness of Eisenhower and his administration to listen to their voice. Equally strong were the voices of Democrats like Lister Hill and Carl Elliott, who were devoted to the cause of federal aid to education, and those of Americans not especially identified with any political party who believed in improved education. In fact, there was a general realization on the part of many Americans in the 1950s, as reflected in Eisenhower's 1952 campaign advocacy of federal aid for classroom construction, that American education was in the midst of an enormous challenge from the sheer number of "baby boomers," the sons and daughters of the veterans of World War II who were entering the nation's elementary schools in large numbers beginning in the late 1940s. In the

1950s that onslaught was about to challenge the high schools, and eventually the colleges and universities. It was this demographic "time bomb" on the horizon that moved the Eisenhower administration to take some steps to address national educational issues near the end of Ike's first term.

In 1955, the president appointed a Committee for the White House Conference on Education. The recommendations of that group initiated the convening of an actual White House Conference on Education, as a culmination of numerous state conferences on education, to address the situation in the nation's elementary and secondary schools. While the conference was much more prone to discuss issues than to recommend action, and while it assiduously avoided any moves in the direction of increased federal government intervention in educational affairs, its existence at least drew public attention to the notion that all was not well with American education in the deceptively placid era of the 1950s. The many state conferences on education that accompanied the White House Conference reinforced the political primacy of the state as the locus for educational improvement and further intensified the sense of unease, if not of crisis, surrounding the nation's educational institutions, particularly its elementary and secondary schools. One tangible recommendation from the White House Conference, federal funds for school construction, was couched as an emergency measure only, provoking the head of the National Education Association to criticize the recommendation as too little too late. Such measures, according to the NEA official, did little to remedy the financial penalties put on several states through population shifts and uneven growth rates.[4]

Since the White House Conference had dealt only with the lower schools, the president appointed a group in 1957, after his reelection, to consider the situation in the nation's colleges and universities. The president's Committee on Education beyond the High School was chaired by Devereaux Josephs, an official of the New York Life Insurance Company and former head of the Carnegie Corporation who had relationships with many American college and university leaders. That committee, in its 1957 report, recommended to the president that a "modern revolution in education" was needed. The elements of that revolution, according to the committee, were more and better qualified high school and college teachers; greater financial aid for college students; more, and more diverse, opportunities for college attendance; an exceptionally needed increase in financial support for colleges; and improved relationships between colleges and universities and the federal government. Particular policies to be advocated in pursuit of these objectives, according to the committee, included higher teacher salaries, stronger guidance and counseling programs in high schools, more scholarships for students who were both able to succeed and in financial need, federal work study programs, tax deductions for parents of college students and for those who contributed financially to the nation's educational institutions, and the development of more community colleges to absorb some of the projected increase in higher education enrollment stemming from the development of the baby boom generation.

The issue of scholarships for students had a history that had long predated the Committee on Education beyond the High School, as indicated in the last chapter's discussion of Carl Elliott's advocacy of federal scholarships for college students from the beginning of his tenure in the House of Representatives in the late 1940s. In 1949, as Elliott pushed his scholarship proposal, the Division of Higher Education in the Office of Education prepared its own statement on scholarships, arguing that they were needed because financial difficulties were the main reason that so few "of the able continue their education." The statement advocated a system of federal scholarships for the best-qualified college students supplemented by a system of federal loan guarantees assuring low interest loans repayable "on long terms."[5] As early as November of 1954, President Eisenhower frankly stated that the federal government would probably be forced to inaugurate a system of scholarships for colleges and universities.[6] Eisenhower's opponent in the 1956 presidential election, Adlai Stevenson of Illinois, told the National Education Association at its convention in the summer of 1955 that a scholarship program was needed to "help supply the growing demand for more and better qualified school teachers."[7] By 1957, Congress was considering a number of bills for federally financed college scholarships, including the latest version of the scholarship bill sponsored by Carl Elliott.[8]

In addition to the White House Conference and the president's Committee on Education beyond the High School, alterations in the makeup of the Eisenhower administration after his reelection in 1956 gave some indication that increased federal activity, in education and in other arenas, might be on the horizon. In late 1956 and 1957 Eisenhower made a number of new appointments in various federal agencies, including the Department of Health, Education, and Welfare (HEW). Of particular interest for the nation's schools and colleges, Lawrence G. Derthick succeeded Samuel Brownell as U.S. Commissioner of Education, and head of the Office of Education (OE), in late 1956. Derthick quickly launched several new initiatives, including "a new cooperative program of research with colleges, universities, and state educational agencies."[9] By April of 1957, sixty-one agreements for cooperative research projects had been approved. Later in that year, an OE task force recommended a three-pronged program for federal aid to higher education: the expansion and improvement of graduate programs including fellowships for doctoral students to increase the number of available college teachers, an increase in the number of qualified undergraduate students through an improved guidance and counseling program designed to identify promising talent and scholarships and loans for students who needed them, and college-level programs below the bachelor's degree to train technicians and semiprofessional workers. While proposals like these were too radical to be endorsed by the Josephs Committee in its report, they indicated the direction in which professional opinion within the administration thought educational efforts should move.[10]

Elliot Richardson

At the same time that professionals in the Office of Education were moving in the direction of a markedly increased federal effort in American education, President Eisenhower made a political appointment in the Department of Health, Education, and Welfare, within which OE was housed, that would enhance prospects for the realization of that objective. Elliot L. Richardson, a young lawyer from the state of Massachusetts, and an active Republican, was appointed to the position of assistant secretary of Health, Education, and Welfare for legislation. Richardson's appointment, and several in other federal departments, represented a presidential investment in people with sound political instincts and connections whose main responsibility was to translate the programs and plans of the professionals in various federal agencies into legislation that addressed real problems. That translation, however, was to be accomplished without going so far in the direction of federal involvement in national affairs that the approach of the Eisenhower administration would be seen as more than moderate.

Massachusetts native Richardson was a prominent member of the moderate wing that dominated, and still dominates, the Republican Party in the Bay State. He had graduated from Harvard College and the Harvard University Law School, served in the military in the late 1940s, and been a member of a prestigious Boston law firm immediately prior to his appointment as assistant secretary for legislation of HEW in 1957. After serving in that capacity

Elliot Richardson, Assistant Secretary, congratulates a new employee of the Department of Health, Education and Welfare, August 19, 1958. Courtesy of the Eisenhower Library.

for two years, a period that included four months' service as acting secretary, he went on to a notable political career in Massachusetts and in national administrations, serving as attorney general and lieutenant governor of his state, and as the head of four cabinet departments in the federal government. Perhaps his most notable act while in the federal service was his resignation from the cabinet because of questionable actions of the Nixon administration in conjunction with the Watergate scandal.[11]

Born in 1920, Richardson was relatively young when he began his service to the federal government in the Department of Health, Education, and Welfare in 1957. One of his major successes in his role of assistant secretary for legislation of HEW was the passage of the National Defense Education Act. After leaving federal service in 1959, he went on to hold the numerous and significant elected and appointed positions mentioned earlier, in Massachusetts and in the federal government. It seems fair to say that Richardson's success with NDEA set the stage for the rest of his highly successful political career. That he never received the nomination of his party for the presidency was seen by Richardson's supporters as a loss for Republicans much more than any deficiency in Richardson's qualifications for the nation's highest office.[12]

The Challenge of Sputnik

The launching of the Sputnik satellite in October of 1957, for Elliot Richardson and the Eisenhower administration, as well as for Lister Hill and Carl Elliott, provided an opportunity to move on initiatives in federal educational responsibility that had been in place well before that time. Nevertheless, it is also the case for all actors in the NDEA drama that without Sputnik the federal educational legislation was unlikely to have overcome the constitutional objections of state and local government purists and the religious and racial controversies that plagued federal aid to education, constitutionally and, more importantly, politically.

For Dwight D. Eisenhower, Sputnik presented a challenge that was much more political than it was military or economic. Eisenhower was confident in the intelligence information that told him that, even though the Soviets had launched a satellite into orbit before the United States did, the overall picture was one of American superiority scientifically and technologically, rather than a situation that demanded crash programs to catch up. According to Robert A. Divine, noted historian of Eisenhower's response to Sputnik, "Dwight D. Eisenhower was . . . not impressed by the Soviet Fear. . . . He believed that American science and American education were much sounder than critics charged, and, above all, he was confident that the United States held a commanding lead over the Soviet Union in striking power." Divine added, however, that the president, "for all his prudence and restraint, failed to meet one of the crucial tests of presidential leadership: convincing the American people that all was well in the world." This was due, according to this analysis, to the fact that Eisenhower "simply could not comprehend why the nation refused to accept his reassurances: he finally was forced to go against his deeply ingrained fiscal conservatism and approve defense expenditures he did not believe were really needed."[13]

The president's political problem was how to reassure an American public that was being told by many politicians, by the media, and by some influential university leaders and scientists that the nation was in danger of lagging far behind its opponents in the Cold War waged with the USSR. While there is considerable evidence that Eisenhower was correct in his assessment of the larger strategic situation that faced the nation, that is, that American science and technology were superior to that of its rival, scholars also believe that the president was not sufficiently attuned to the political crisis that awaited his administration if it tried simply to convince the public that Sputnik did not mean what many politicians, journalists, scientists, and intellectuals said that it did mean, namely that the nation needed to take significant steps to deal with the Soviet technological threat or face a military defeat.

One prong of the plan that Eisenhower adopted to deal with the domestic perception of the Soviet threat sparked by Sputnik was to promote a short-term infusion of money and energy into the educational system of the nation to assure its citizenry that corrective steps were being taken. That infusion was advocated most prominently in the areas of science and mathematics education by a group of the president's scientific advisors, formed into a Science Advisory Committee that had been started by Harry Truman in 1951.[14] The scientists argued not that the United States was behind the Soviets scientifically, but that the Soviets emphasized science more than did Americans in their schools, and that this emphasis, unless countered, meant Soviet scientific superiority within a decade. These views had a profound effect on Eisenhower, according to the historian quoted above. According to this scholar, though the president "felt confident about America's satellite and missile programs, he had become aware of the danger of falling behind the Soviet Union in science and technology through complacency and . . . the fruits of material abundance. He was determined to do everything he could to . . . elevate the role of science in education, government, and American society at large" and thereby, to counter the "near hysteria" over Sputnik.[15] Clearly, the emphasis on science and mathematics and other technologically related subjects in the National Defense Education Act was a cornerstone of the administration's response to Sputnik.

Robert A. Divine concluded that the Eisenhower strategy of relying on science education to counter the Soviet threat represented a victory for Eisenhower's measured approach to temporary federal involvement in education over the more broadly based designs of Hill, Elliott, and other congressional advocates of more permanent, long-term, federal educational effort.[16] This chapter will argue later that this conclusion is debatable and that there is substantial reason to believe that Hill and Elliott achieved their objective in passing the NDEA as much as, or more than, did Eisenhower. Before that discussion, however, a look at the actual development of NDEA by the administration is in order.

Administration Activity Prior to Development of NDEA

The launch of Sputnik galvanized those in the Office of Education and elsewhere in the Department of Health, Education, and Welfare to try to put the ideas generated by the earlier mentioned OE task force into action. To accomplish this, both Congress and the administration had to be persuaded by the ideas of those in the Office of Education. Elliot Richardson, as assistant secretary of the department in which OE was housed, took the leading role, both in dealing with the rest of the administration and with the Congress. Richardson had begun this task in May of 1957, when he called for a discussion of the federal scholarship issue between the OE and the Office of the Secretary of HEW. The reason for this meeting was the "persistent rumors that the Subcommittee on Special Education of the House Committee on Education [the Elliott Subcommittee] may hold hearings on various Federal scholarship proposals shortly." Richardson's goal was "a carefully thought out Departmental position in advance of the [Subcommittee] hearings."[17]

Prior to a June 5 meeting of OE and HEW officials in Richardson's office, an Office of Education higher education official prepared a seventy-eight-page statement on financial aid to college students for the group to consider. This statement dealt with a full range of issues related to scholarships and other means of financial aid including factual determination of financial need, various methods to meet that need, a review of the situation in Congress and among private agencies sponsoring various kinds of student aid, and suggested responses to the situation.[18] This document provided the ideas to be used when various OE officials testified before the Elliott subcommittee. In the midst of the subcommittee hearings in early October of 1957, the first Sputnik was launched by the Soviet Union. To say the launch intensified the urgency surrounding the scholarships and other educational measures contemplated by Congress and the administration is to understate the significance of Sputnik. Whether by design, or by happenstance, probably by some of both, the turmoil caused by the launch of the Soviet satellite was channeled in large part into a critique of the nation's educational system for failings, particularly in the areas of science, mathematics, and technological preparation.

After Sputnik, OE and HEW, under Elliot Richardson's leadership, proceeded quickly to develop an administration proposal for educational reforms that addressed the issues raised by the satellite's launch. Richardson was briefed in full on the recommendations of the White House Conference on Education and the various state conferences.[19] The information he received stressed the ideas of concentrating on academic concerns in the schools, of providing both improved education for all and special attention for gifted students, and of addressing the need for capable teachers through various measures including some type of salary enhancement. He also learned, if he did not already know, of the need for maintaining a cooperative effort among federal, state, and local officials if anything was to be accomplished. On the political front, OE had just received a copy of a report on arguments for and against federal aid for college scholarships that had been prepared by the Legislative Reference Service, a congressional agency charged with providing assistance in developing legislative proposals.[20]

Immediately prior to both of these developments, Sherman Adams, the president's chief of staff, received a lengthy telegram from James B. Conant, former president of Harvard University who was becoming the most famous analyst of American education, about prospective changes in American schools to respond to Sputnik. Conant cautioned against any "crash program," noting that this approach caused damage "by confusing school boards and undermining [the] confidence of communities." He added that schools were easily damaged but that much more care was needed in turning them around than most change advocates realized. Conant reinforced the need for good school boards, superintendents, and principals if any genuinely positive change was to be accomplished. Using his own research to make the point, he noted that in "satisfactory schools" up to one-half of students with high academic ability "are being identified in the 7th and 8th grades and are urged to take mathematics and science adequate" for further secondary and higher education. In the same good schools, science and mathematics instruction was adequate; only "instruction in foreign languages was weak," stated Conant. He believed that what was needed was more of these good schools, an objective that could be accomplished by consolidation of smaller schools into larger institutions in which talent identification and rigorous academic education would be facilitated. There was, for Conant, a general "failure to recognize the national interest in early id [*sic*] of academic talent." Conant pointed to finances as a reason that many able students did not go on to college. He preferred solid education in all academic subjects to the existing situation where sports and other extracurricular activities dominated the attention of many students. If academics were stressed in high schools, Conant argued, the sciences and mathematics would not need extra development, and it seemed likely that "science and engineering would get their share of grads." Conant, a scientist but also a longtime university administrator, concluded this line of thought with a statement that stressed the need for improvement in the humanities as well as in the sciences: he argued that an age of intercontinental ballistic missiles required, more than scientists and engineers, "a people who will not panic and political leaders of wisdom courage and devotion with capacity for solving intricate human problems. Not more Einsteins but more Washingtons and Madisons."[21]

Conant's telegram was widely distributed among the Eisenhower administration, as was Adams's reply to Conant. In his reply to that telegram, the president's assistant noted that the president had stated that Conant's viewpoint "represents my thinking exactly."[22] Elliot Richardson quickly grasped the political boundaries implied in Eisenhower's approval of Conant's ideas. Any program that was to come from the administration needed to avoid crash or emergency approaches and to stress science and mathematics education, but without seeming to deemphasize or denigrate the social sciences and humanities. This was one tall order, but the HEW assistant secretary proved up to the task.

In mid-November 1957, Richardson noted possible sources of opposition to the educational ideas espoused by Conant or by other advocates of improvement through changes such as a federal scholarship program. He inserted a memorandum in his files discussing those who opposed educational plans, suggesting that much of the opposition could be neutralized by stressing national objective tests as a way to identify talent in schools. He had copied an article in the *Washington Post* that discussed the opposition of the state superintendent of New Jersey's schools to scholarships, because such a program meant federal control over education. Richardson argued that this was a misunderstanding of the issue, and he added that testing was not necessarily a national, or federal, program if states could be given alternative forms of tests to administer. Richardson further noted that reports that the executive officer of the Chief State School Officers (CSSO) association also opposed testing were exaggerated. Richardson stated that he knew the CSSO official and that neither he, nor the organization, was "inflexible" on the issue of testing.[23]

Richardson was not one to believe that the existing tests were a perfect way to achieve his goals. To a university president who thought that tests were needed to get at talent not identified by letter grades in high schools, Richardson responded that adjusting the tests to get at such information was an issue to be addressed through the testers, not the federal government. Thus Richardson, though a firm advocate of tests, at the same time understood that they certainly could be improved to achieve the desired goal of identifying talented students.[24] Whether or not he understood the kind of profound critiques of tests that were made decades after NDEA is not clear.

One potential internal obstacle to a productive response to the educational crisis by OE and HEW came from elsewhere within the Eisenhower administration. In November 1957, this obstacle was discussed in the midst of the flurry of activities geared to developing that response. The position of the National Science Foundation (NSF) on educational reform was a concern for OE-HEW. NSF was an independent federal agency that had been established by congressional action in 1950 to pursue the scientific welfare of the nation. More particularly, and in terms of interagency relations within the administration, NSF needed to be consulted, needed to know in advance of OE-HEW positions and proposals, and had to be viewed with a wary eye in terms of necessary budget adjustments made to respond to various proposals. In addition to budgetary concerns, NSF was a potential threat to OE for control of any science and mathematics pieces of federal legislation for education. The OE in late 1957 was poised to fight NSF, if it had to, for control over programs in science and mathematics education. There was no middle ground on this issue for the OE-HEW group.[25]

NSF and the scientific community it served were a formidable force for the OE to contend with. President Eisenhower had great confidence in the views of scientists, in some part because, like James B. Conant, they agreed largely with the president's views. Within days after the launch of Sputnik, Eisenhower met with several scientists, such as Detlev Bronk, I. I. Rabi, and Edward Land, to get their views on the situation. Two concrete results came directly from these meetings. Within a month of the first Sputnik satellite the position of scientific advisor to the president was established, and James R. Killian, president of the Massachusetts Institute of Technology, became the first individual to hold the post. In addition, a Scientific Advisory Committee that had existed in the Office of Defense Mobilization since its creation by President Truman in the early 1950s was upgraded to an executive level body, the President's Scientific Advisory Committee (PSAC). At the same time, new appointments were made to the PSAC with some fanfare. These formal actions followed Eisenhower's informal tendencies earlier in his presidency to turn to scientists for advice in strategic and defense matters. Now, a President's Scientific Advisory Committee aided the president in constructing a response to the political storm created by the Soviet satellite.[26]

The main job of the president's scientific advisor and the President's Scientific Advisory Committee was to help the president in strategic planning for national defense. The views of scientists on education, however, were also important, particularly as the president moved to generate an educational response to Sputnik. Thus officials in OE and HEW paid special attention to the science advisor and the President's Science Advisory Committee, as well as to the National Science Foundation, in developing their response to the situation.

In early December of 1957, Elliot Richardson addressed the relationship with NSF in a memo to his superior, HEW secretary Marion Folsom. Richardson reported on a recent meeting with NSF representatives in the office of Sherman Adams and stated that there was no dispute between the two agencies. NSF had been ordered to develop proposals for scholarship programs in the sciences and mathematics, as well as a loan guarantee program in those areas. While NSF would develop such a program, the preference of its representatives was for "an across the board scholarship program" that would be administered by OE. On the issue of equipment for science education, Richardson noted that NSF was "inclined to believe that a program taking in all kinds of institutions on an across-the-board basis should be administered by us [OE]." Richardson then characterized NSF in the educational arena as a "bystander willing to pick up any pieces thrown to them by the White House." Thus, he saw no need for any compromise with NSF. He did caution, however, that "there can be no assurance that NSF will give its strong support to any understanding we may arrive at with them. They will simply take the position that they are not competent in matters of political judgment and that the basic issues here involved are such matters."[27]

The fundamental problem for OE-HEW was not so much directly with NSF, but rather with a tendency throughout the administration, and in the public mind, to narrow the educational problem into one in the sciences and related fields and, thereby, to severely limit the role educational agencies could play. One HEW official voiced this concern to Richardson in a memo titled "Two of the Reasons for Broad Education as Against Excessive Emphasis on Education for Scientific and Engineering Pursuits." Rufus Miles, the director of administration of HEW, began the memo as follows: "I am greatly concerned about the tendencies being exhibited by the National Science Foundation, the Bureau of the Budget and even the White House to treat our crisis in education almost entirely in scientific and weapons terms." He added that according to this point of view the "only thing we need to do is to concentrate heavily on scientific and engineering education and research, and we will soon catch up and outdistance Russia." The problem, for Miles, was that seeking to outdistance Russia in those fields would yield a result in which "Russia will have run rings around us in other fields which we have neglected." The struggle with the Soviets, in this view, "will be won or lost as much or more in the political, economic, psychological, and cultural arenas as in the fields of weapons, technology, and military might." The Soviets, according to Miles, were "adept at economic and political penetration of middle and far-eastern nations," and were in the process of accomplishing this goal by purveying "technical help, trade relations, ideology, and perhaps music and art" with a clear understanding of how to adapt these to the target nations. To counter this move, he argued that "we need to think very carefully about the kinds of education which will permit us to compete successfully in these non-technological fields, and take all necessary steps to encourage such education . . . as rapidly as possible." Miles added that speakers of Arabic and other languages were needed as well as "those who understand the cultures of the nations of the Near East." Good grounding in economics, international law, and international relations were also essential for Miles, more essential than a scientific or technological program. He emphasized that it was "vital" to "give support to the non-scientific aspects of our proposed" educational program to avoid the conclusion by the larger public that the "non scientific aspects of the program are 'non-essentials,' or at least of lower priority than the scientific elements of the program."[28]

In addition to dealing with the influential science community within the federal government, as Richardson and OE officials developed their program for educational improvement they kept in close touch with leaders in both elementary-secondary and in higher education. Richardson and three OE leaders spoke late in November of 1957 to the American Association of School Administrators, filling in this group of school superintendents on the administration proposals, by then tentatively labeled the Educational Development Act of 1958. They outlined their plans on issues and asked superintendents for input on the matter of national testing, the ratio of scientific to nonscientific scholarships in any program developed, and the basis on which any money for school improvements might be apportioned to the states. One superintendent's response enthusiastically endorsed most of the administration's proposals, noting that improvement in science and mathematics education could help the schools compete with industry for the talent needed to teach these subjects. This superintendent worried, however, that too much attention would be paid to colleges and universities, at the expense of elementary and secondary schools. Further, he was concerned that aid for higher education would go to both public and private institutions, thereby threatening the wall of separation between church and state that supported the public schools.[29] These sentiments prefigured issues that would arise in the congressional course to passage of NDEA, and that have been discussed in the two earlier chapters of this book.

Elliot Richardson also vetted the particulars of his and OE's proposed legislation with university officials. For example, Richardson contacted McGeorge Bundy, dean of the Faculty of Arts and Sciences at Harvard, about OE plans for educational improvement. Bundy, a longtime Richardson associate, replied with a compliment for the amount of work that had gone into the proposals and added that he would respond only to the area in which he felt competent to comment, that of graduate fellowships. The OE fellowship plan, the stated goal of which was to increase the number of PhDs to address the increasing need for college teachers, proposed to achieve this objective by granting its graduate fellowships to students enrolled in "new or expanded programs." Bundy, who presided over many of Harvard's doctoral programs, opined that "there are a number of existing Ph.D. programs in which there is room for additional good students." While the OE language did not necessarily preclude adding students to existing programs, Bundy worried that adding students to existing programs might be interpreted as outside the stated objectives of the proposal. Furthermore, Bundy added that "the 'new' program is not always the good one, and in many major fields of advanced study, what we need is not more graduate schools but better work in the existing ones." Bundy's conclusion was that the "best way to achieve the objectives" of increasing the supply of PhDs would be simply "to state the purpose of expanding the production of qualified scholars and leave the precise method of" achieving that need to an appointed commission to award the fellowships that were also in the proposal. Richardson responded that the reason for new or expanded programs in the proposal was that the OE did not want simply to shift the cost of existing programs from institutions to the federal government. Rather, federal activity could be justified as an inducement to expand graduate education through the fellowships.[30]

Elliot Richardson was thus earnestly involved in November and December of 1957 in discussing the specifics of the proposed administration education legislation within his department with educators from elementary and secondary schools, as well as with college and university leaders. He also engaged in negotiations with the National Science Foundation and any other relevant federal actors as to who would be responsible for what aspects of the measure. By late January of 1958, the discussions were completed and the administration was ready to send its education program to Congress.

The Administration Educational Reform Proposal

On January 27, President Eisenhower sent the draft Educational Development Act of 1958 to the House of Representatives, along with a lengthy message. In that message he noted that the administration was "recommending certain emergency Federal actions to encourage and assist greater effort in specific areas of national concern." He added that his recommended program placed "principal emphasis on our national security requirements." He also noted that both NSF and OE-HEW were to be involved in the proposed program: NSF was due for a "fivefold increase in appropriations for the scientific activities" it was engaged in and HEW would receive funds for expansion in necessary educational programs, and especially for promotion of improved science education in elementary and secondary schools. Additionally, HEW would receive funding for scholarships, for a testing program helpful to choosing students for those scholarships, for guidance and counseling enhancement in the high schools, for improved foreign language teaching, for graduate fellowships for college teachers, and for facilitating improved data gathering by the states. These items—enhancement of science in schools; scholarships and graduate fellowships; testing, guidance, and counseling programs; better science, mathematics, and foreign language education in high schools; and better educational data gathering and analysis—were the essential parts of the administration's proposed legislation. The president concluded his message with the following admonition: "This emergency program stems from national need, and its fruits will bear directly on national security. The method of accomplishment is sound: the keystone is State, local, and private effort; the Federal role is to assist, not to control or supplant those efforts. The administration urges prompt enactment of these recommendations in the essential interest of national security."[31] Thus Eisenhower sought simultaneously to illustrate the acute need for his proposed changes and to indicate their temporary nature, thereby assuring the American people, and American educators, that he was not interested in radical alteration of the American educational enterprise.

Two days after the administration version of educational reform was put before Congress, Senator Lister Hill and Congressman Carl Elliott released their proposal for educational improvement. Their plan, as discussed in the previous two chapters, contained almost everything in the administration proposal. In addition, Hill and Elliott added a substantial student loan program and, a few weeks later, a vocational education title. Further, the Hill-

Elliott proposal was not presented as a temporary, highly targeted, measure, but rather as a long-range program for educational improvement that would meet the nation's current defense needs and lead it into the future. The Hill-Elliott proposal was also uniformly more generous in its financial provisions, calling for more scholarships than the administration did and advocating longer life and more funds for each of the titles in both bills than proposed in the administration's plan.[32]

Less than a week after Eisenhower's message to Congress accompanying the administration version of the Educational Improvement Act, administration officials began to testify on educational issues before congressional committees chaired by Carl Elliott and Lister Hill. OE staff prepared briefing materials and sample testimony for the chief administrators in OE, and in HEW, to use prior to testifying before a congressional committee. Sample testimony was developed in detail on several issues, including scholarships, loans, and mathematics and science instruction in public schools.[33]

On February 5, Elliot Richardson testified before Carl Elliott's House Subcommittee on Special Education. He began by recognizing that there indeed were deficiencies in the educational system, but adding that the "federal government cannot do the whole job" of repairing the situation. What the administration was proposing was the stimulation of work in hard academic subjects by able students, facilitated by the "testing, counseling and guidance programs" that offered incentives for rewarding hard work "through the award of scholarships on a competitive basis." Richardson added that the administration proposals sought to strengthen the teaching of mathematics and science in the schools, as well as the teaching of foreign languages. This targeting of efforts to specific programs was just the sort of thing the federal government should be doing, he argued. He stated his position on federal involvement explicitly as follows: "Should we, as the Federal Government, stand by and say we cannot do anything about this at all, or should we say we will undertake to do those things through stimulation of Federal programs that are appropriate for Federal action, realizing always that the primary responsibility is a state and local role?" In a spirit of respect for the congressional authors of alternative proposals, Richardson added that the administration plan was not necessarily the best proposal, that proposals like that of Carl Elliott were worthy of attention, and that the very best program should be identified through consideration of all proposals and testimony on their merits.[34]

In addition to testifying before the relevant congressional committees,

Elliot Richardson played a large role in specifying the others who would offer testimony. In communication with the minority clerk of the House Committee on Education and Labor, Richardson provided a lengthy list of those who could testify in favor of administration proposals and those who favored them, but with some reservations. Additionally, the list identified particular individuals who could speak to one or another of the subjects (titles) covered in the administration bill. He finally added a few names of those who were opposed to the bill and willing to testify, though he noted that this was not a large group of people.[35]

It took from February through August for the administration bill and the Hill-Elliott alternatives to coalesce into a single proposal and achieve passage. The process, though lengthy, was generally amicable, with all involved parties willing to compromise in the cause of seeking a productive outcome, a far from likely result given the history of federal aid to education legislation. One of the major issues of debate was the scholarship program, with the number of scholarships and the basis on which they were to be awarded the particular matters of concern. Generally, the administration on the one hand sought a smaller number of scholarships than did Congress, basing its limits on the idea that the program's fundamental goal was to raise educational quality and not to increase opportunity. The administration also advocated that merit be the only basis to qualify for award of a scholarship, and believed that any cash stipend go only to the meritorious students who had no financial need. Congress, on the other hand, pushed for scholarships to be awarded to all who qualified, regardless of need. A compromise was easily reached on this issue, with a minimum stipend attached to all scholarships, one that increased according to the amount of need that a student could justify. Other issues on which a compromise was reached relatively easily included administration acceptance of more scholarships as advocated by Congress and the addition of achievement in foreign language in high school as one of the criteria for awarding them. The administration also accepted the congressional desire for the addition of an area studies emphasis to the institutes for foreign language teachers that would be offered in the summers and a program of aid to improve audio-visual and other media related activities in schools.[36]

The administration successfully eliminated from consideration a work study program featured in the Hill-Elliott proposal, arguing that it was far afield from an emphasis on educational quality. The administration lost on a vocational education title it considered unrelated to the major purpose of raising educational quality. Hill, Elliott, and many other congressmen were staunch advocates of vocational education, and they pushed strongly, and successfully, with major assistance from a powerful vocational education lobby in Washington, for its inclusion in the final bill that was considered.[37]

Scholarships versus Loans

The student loan program advocated by Hill and Elliott was also an administration target, since it was judged to be not in conformity with a program to increase educational quality. In February of 1958, the administration considered a loan guarantee program proposed by Republican Senator Jacob Javits as a substitute for loans. Loan guarantees involved a federal commitment to back loans to students from banks and other private sector institutions, a commitment of far less federal money and much less federal intrusion into existing economic relationships than that which accompanied a full federal loan program. HEW secretary Marion Folsom told Senator Javits that the administration was not necessarily opposed to Javits's proposal, or to any loan program, but that any such program should not be considered a substitute for the scholarships that were a cornerstone of the administration bill. Loans in any form were, according to Folsom, "a means of general expansion of educational opportunity rather than of encouraging [the administration goal of increased] achievement." The secretary added that, unlike scholarships, loans were not likely to make the difference between attending college or not attending for students, and loans were more useful to business students than to teachers, that is, to those who could expect significant material wealth after college than to those who would receive modest wages and thereby be seriously burdened by debt repayment. Folsom concluded that he was not saying "that a loan program would not be a good thing. I believe, however, that any such proposal should be regarded as a supplement to, rather than a substitute for, a scholarship program limited in numbers and closely tied to a testing and counseling and guidance program; such as that proposed by the Administration."[38]

Loan guarantees were too far removed from a real loan program to be acceptable to Hill, Elliott, and other student loan advocates. The administration, as indicated by Folsom, would consider loan guarantees, and even loan programs themselves, if necessary. In March of 1958, Elliot Richardson wrote to a financial affairs official at Oberlin College on the topic of loans. Richardson noted that he was willing to discuss any specific proposal for loans, though he preferred those that fell far short of what was offered in the Hill-Elliott bill. Richardson added, however, that any specifics discussed did "not constitute an Administration recommendation as such—they represent, rather, the best judgment of this Department with respect to a federal student loan program, assuming that such a program is desirable (a point to which we are not completely convinced)." About a month later, an OE official told a Republican congressman that the administration had offered a loan proposal that they would be willing to amend to the congressman's wishes to have it be a loan guarantee proposal. The congressman was told, however, that Elliot Richardson could not guarantee support for any loan proposal but that he would support reasonable proposals in his discussions with the rest of the administration.[39]

The administration did indeed consider other alternative loan proposals. Richardson explained the fundamental difference between the administration and Congress over student loans in a letter to James Killian, the president's science advisor. The assistant secretary stated that loans were not an administration priority, since they "tend rather to enlarge enrollments than to create incentive for achievement." Yet the loans were popular with the public at large, according to Richardson, and so the administration had to negotiate with Congress on the issue. Those negotiations were ongoing and eventually resulted in a compromise, though rather late in the process of considering the legislation. The administration eventually favored a loan program that was funded at an 80 percent level by the federal government in conjunction with higher education institutions, which were required to produce 20 percent of the loan funds at their own institution. This arrangement, rather than State Loan Commissions, which were in the Hill version of legislation, was preferable to federal officials on the grounds of tighter fiscal control of federal funds.[40]

Loans

The Final Push to Passage of NDEA

By June of 1958, the situation regarding the educational legislation had matured to the point that final passage, or rejection, was on the horizon. An HEW official who monitored legislation described the situation to Elliot Richardson: "In its present form the [House of Representatives] Committee bill is so close to the administration's proposal, except for the inclusion of the loan title, that I don't see how the administration could make any serious objection to it. However, its chances of passage are, in my view, practically non-existent short of vigorous, all-out, whole-hearted support from the Administration."[41] Elliot Richardson proved to be the major agent in mounting that support within the administration. In late June, Richardson heard from one of his political staff in HEW on the prospects of the education bill in the House Rules Committee. That body, which had been an obstacle to federal aid to education for many years, was likely to approve this legislation, if given a nudge from the Democratic leadership of the House of Representatives.[42] In early July, OE-HEW staff huddled with Richardson and with Congressman Carl Elliott about who needed to be lobbied in Congress to gain passage of the education law and how that lobbying activity was to be conducted.[43]

Richardson, named the acting secretary of HEW in the summer of 1958 after Secretary Marion Folsom resigned for health reasons, participated forcefully in trying to orchestrate the support needed in the push for enacting the NDEA. He responded positively to a letter from Carl Elliott soliciting letters of support from leading scientists in the administration and noted military leaders to counter opponents of the legislation in the House who argued that the bill (now titled the National Defense Education Act) was not really oriented to the national defense. Letters from the president's science advisor and the head of NSF were quickly provided, the former concluding that "failure to enact this legislation would . . . seriously impede this country's progress in the development of its long-range defense effort."[44]

The major voice from the administration that needed to be heard, however, was that of the president himself. An exchange in July between a Republican member of the House Education and Labor Committee and the president was revealing in several particulars of the final position the chief executive took on NDEA. The congressman told the president that the house bill followed presidential desires in improving mathematics, science, and foreign language teaching; in expanding graduate education, in improving testing and counseling, and in providing scholarships. The congressman added that the loan provision "conforms to your philosophy of 'God helps those who help themselves.'" The president responded that the bill was a good one and that loans were a good device, though their inclusion should mean a need for fewer scholarships. Eisenhower, whose administration had consistently put loans in a secondary position to scholarships, was now giving evidence of his personal affinity for loans, which needed repayment, in opposition to scholarships, which threatened to give recipients "something for nothing." The president's preference in July was that "scholarship stipends will not only be restricted to those students who show outstanding ability, but will also be paid only to the extent that such students need financial help in order to get a college education." The president here was giving an early signal that his own devotion to scholarships might not survive a severe challenge to them on moral grounds as well as on grounds of insufficient availability of funds.[45]

The National Defense Education Act was approved, in different versions, by both houses of Congress in early August of 1958. The popular title of the bill, obviously geared to garner widespread political support rather than to logically characterize what it contained, came from Stuart McClure, chief clerk to Senator Lister Hill. McClure commented on his role: "I invented that God-awful title: the National Defense Education Act. If there were any words less compatible, really intellectually, in terms of what the purpose of education— it's not to defend the country; it's to defend the mind and develop the human spirit, not to build cannons and battleships. It was a horrible title, but it worked."[46]

After approval in each house of Congress, the bill had to be considered by a conference committee of members of both houses to come up with a final version. The conference process, as was often the case, produced a major surprise, at least for the bill's chief proponents. The scholarships that had been a mainstay of the administration's push for raising quality and the major plank in Carl Elliott's campaign to enlarge educational opportunity did not survive the Conference Committee. The published history of NDEA adoption credited this outcome to House conferees who believed that if scholarships were included, the Conference version of the bill would not be approved by the House of Representatives. Opponents of scholarships invoked budgetary concerns, as well as the idea of federal funds going to affluent students who did not need them, to justify their opposition. Just as importantly, the president failed to weigh in enthusiastically in favor of scholarships. In fact, in his memoir of the presidency, Dwight D. Eisenhower confessed that he never really did want scholarships to be included in the legislation.[47]

The loan program in the final version of NDEA followed more generous financial provisions of the House version of the bill instead of the administration proposal, with 90 percent of the amount of the loan fund coming from the federal government, and 10 percent from the institutions that granted the loans. Additionally, the bill provided that institutions could borrow their 10 percent contribution from the federal government if they could not raise their share of the money needed from other sources. The total amount of federal funds authorized for loans rose from $47.5 million in fiscal 1959 to $75 million, $82.5 million, and $90 million in the succeeding three years of the life of the bill.[48]

Carl Elliott, the longtime congressional champion of scholarships who was devoted to them as a device for expanded educational opportunity, saw the loan fund as an opportunity to achieve his goals. Elliot Richardson and his allies in the administration, however, had greater reason for disappointment, since the removal of scholarships struck at the core of their justification of the bill as one that raised the quality of the American educational enterprise. Richardson remarked that he and his allies "did not regard the loan program as a substitute for the scholarship program."[49] In fact, one prominent friend of the administration version of the NDEA, James B. Conant, espoused a conception of the importance of quality in relation to opportunity that differed substantially from that of other supporters. In an April article in the *Washington Post,* Conant was quoted as follows: "To my mind too many people are going to college, not too few."[50] It is doubtful that Richardson shared this belief. If he did, he knew better politically than to voice it. Richardson, like Carl Elliott, was a political pragmatist and he dutifully accepted the decision of the Conference Committee and touted the final version of NDEA as a victory for the administration and its educational agenda of educational improvement.

Prior to final passage, NDEA had to clear several high hurdles to obtain congressional approval, some reflecting opponents of long standing of federal aid to education and some relating to factors that had come into play more recently. The U.S. Chamber of Commerce, a longtime opponent of federal activity in American life outside of national defense, waged an eleventh hour campaign to stop NDEA, using a potpourri of arguments both old and new. The OE-HEW forces responded in a statement to a Republican congressman that included pointed rejections of the chamber's contentions. Beginning with an oft-repeated argument, the chamber charged that NDEA was a response to Sputnik, not a well-thought-out plan. The government countered that NDEA was rather the end of a chain of occurrences beginning with the White House Conference on Education of 1956, a logical culmination of a carefully planned campaign for educational improvement. To the chamber's contention that NDEA was not a defense bill, OE-HEW argued that the bill had recognizable defense benefits that had been acknowledged by the president as well as by the "considered judgment of leading scientists, engineers, and educators." To the chamber's argument that the federal aid in the bill did not attack any single great deficiency in education, the response was that it targeted the large purpose of preventing "the tragic loss of talent which occurs when our most able youngsters do not go on to college," and that other parts addressed problems in schools that hampered science, mathematics, and foreign language education. The administration advocates of the bill added that the "fact that the federal government does not seek in this bill to solve *all* the problems involved . . . is *not* a valid argument against attempting to solve those problems which can most effectively be dealt with by Federal action."

Finally, the government contested a new study from the state of Indiana that purported to show that new scholarships were not needed, since all existing scholarships were not being used.[51] While final passage of NDEA did not include the scholarships, the point-by-point rebuttal of the chamber's other arguments was used in Congress to help pass the bill, without scholarships.

Concerns about the racial issue plagued Carl Elliott as he assiduously worked for NDEA passage in the House of Representatives. In early August, as the final vote neared, he asked for reassurance from Elliot Richardson that NDEA did not mandate integration in schools that received its funds. Richardson responded that nondiscrimination language in the bill was "declaratory" and did not affect the distribution of funds through NDEA. For example, loan funds for "all eligible students" at any institution meant that segregated institutions could qualify for those funds, as long as the students met the eligibility criteria, which did not include race. Carl Elliott used these and other arguments to successfully defend NDEA against Powell-like amendments that prohibited federal funds from going to segregated schools and colleges.[52]

Dwight D. Eisenhower signed the National Defense Education Act on September 2, 1958, stressing the significance but also the temporary nature of the legislation. The bill in reality represented a long-term triumph for the U.S. Office of Education and the Department of Health, Education, and Welfare within which OE was housed. An indication of the magnitude of that triumph was given in a request from Elliot Richardson to raise the salary of the commissioner of OE, arguing that the increased responsibility given to the commissioner under NDEA justified the increase. Another missive from HEW to Congress indicated that the provisions for science and mathematics education, for counseling and guidance improvements, and for better data gathering and statistical analysis created a need for ten new positions of the highest grade in the federal service. The OE argued that it needed "the best people" to carry out the work of NDEA, and that existing salaries in the office would not achieve that result.[53]

As will be shown in the next chapter, OE was enhanced enormously in terms of personnel and budget by the tasks assigned to it by the NDEA. President Eisenhower's notion of a temporary bill for a limited purpose, seen as the outcome by both the president and a recent scholarly analysis of NDEA, was not the result.[54] Republican representative Keith Thomson from Wyoming spoke presciently against final passage of NDEA, cautioning those who thought the legislation was a "temporary" response to an emergency. He asked his colleagues whether or not they could name a single federal program of comparable substance to NDEA that was begun as an emergency response to a crisis, and then ended.[55] As renewals of NDEA occurred several times in the increasingly Democratically dominated, education-oriented next sessions of Congress, the provisions of renewal much more often contained additional appropriations and responsibilities for the federal educational efforts than curtailments.[56]

Nine of the ten substantive titles in NDEA gave responsibility to federal education officials for implementation. One that involved the NSF and its substance, the establishment of a science information service, posed no threat to the OE. Indeed OE used NDEA to become an equal, perhaps more than an equal, in relation to NSF in the universe of federal operating agencies. As members of Congress left for their homes after the end of their legislative session punctuated by the passage of NDEA, Commissioner of Education Lawrence Derthick and his staff set themselves to the task of administering the panoply of programs contained in the ten titles of the legislation.

The passage of NDEA, according to its supporters and to most analysts of the legislative process, was due in large part to bipartisan support for the legislation throughout the almost one year of its consideration and passage. Carl Elliott, Lister Hill, and Elliot Richardson were major actors in the legislative process. Their respect for one another, and for the different emphases each brought to the cause of educational improvement, permeated the process of committee hearings on the bill and congressional discussions of its merits. Richardson congratulated both Hill and Elliott when the bill finally cleared Congress, thanking the senator for "your many courtesies and kindnesses" and complimenting the senator's staff for its assistance; to Congressman Elliott, Richardson expressed his "deep personal appreciation for the thoughtful, fair-minded and unpartisan approach you brought to the struggle for the education bill." Hill and Elliott were equally complimentary of Richardson. Hill told the HEW official that it was "a pleasure to work with you," while Elliott was more effusive: he told Richardson that your work "was splendid; you moved with promptness, with discretion; and with determination." Carl Elliott concluded that "perhaps our most important accomplishment was that we gave our educational legislation a bi-partisan base. I think bi-partisanship is perhaps more important in the field of education than in any other."[57]

Ten years later, the personal situation of all three actors in the NDEA drama had changed drastically, but their positive opinions of one another had not been altered. When the Department of Health, Education, and Welfare of the Lyndon Johnson administration made plans for a tenth anniversary celebration of NDEA in 1968, they invited Lister Hill, Carl Elliott, and Elliot Richardson to participate. Hill was about to leave the Senate after a decades-long career, believing that he could not win reelection to another term in an Alabama that had leaned precipitously to the right politically, largely because of the race issue. Carl Elliott had not been in Congress for several years, the victim of that rightward turn in Alabama politics and its leader, George C. Wallace. Richardson, a Republican, was no longer in the administration, since the presidency had been held by a Democratic president since John Kennedy's election in 1960. Richardson was back in his home state of Massachusetts, serving as its attorney general.

Hill and Elliott were both present for the anniversary celebration, along with numerous current and former Office of Education and HEW officials and members of Congress. Attendees at the celebration heard Commissioner of Education Harold Howe's welcoming remarks that included discussion of the administrative progress in his office since NDEA. With NDEA's enactment, according to Howe, Congress "in a stroke changed the Office from the 97 pound weakling of the world of education into a robust organization whose importance to the country could not be overlooked and whose potential for leadership could not be ignored." Howe added that NDEA had increased OE employment "from 589 in 1958 to 900 the following year and finally to today's total of more than 3,000 men and women." Howe concluded that the "Office of Education and the entire educational enterprise had come a long way since NDEA passage." More pointedly, Howe noted, "starting with the National Defense Education Act 10 years ago, this country determined to reverse our educational decline and to commence building the schooling needed for the development of our people and the progress of our country."[58]

Additionally, the anniversary observance included remarks by HEW Secretary Wilbur Cohen, who reminisced about his reaction to the passage of the legislation. Ceremonies also recognized the recipient of the 2,500,000th student loan from NDEA and the recipient of the 25,000th graduate fellowship. Hill and Elliott concluded the ceremony with brief remarks. Both remembered their work with Elliot Richardson. Both, also, had to be heartened in this time of their own political decline by the tribute from Richardson that was read to the audience at the celebration. Richardson had written to HEW secretary Wilbur Cohen that he could not be at the celebration but that he wanted to participate through this letter. He noted that he had "served on the Task Force which developed the original bill, and worked so closely with Senator Hill and Congressman Elliott during all stages of the enacting process." He asked Cohen to please "give my warmest regards and best wishes to Senator Hill and Congressman Elliott and tell them for me that I shall always look back with tremendous satisfaction on having collaborated with them in bringing about this first major step in what you justly characterize as a decade of unprecedented legislative achievement in education."[59]

The lasting respect that Richardson had for Hill and Elliott was no doubt mutual. The efforts of these three were chiefly instrumental in the passage of a landmark federal aid to education measure, one that broke the back of the opposition to federal aid. In the first two chapters of this book, the liberalism of Hill and Elliott was discussed as a major cornerstone for their support of NDEA, and the differing emphases that each of these individuals stressed in their advocacy of the legislation were highlighted. What remains to be accomplished in the final section of this chapter is a discussion of Richardson's political philosophy and how it related to the liberalism of Hill and Elliott in the campaign for passing NDEA.

Moderate Republicanism

It seems clear that, on the administration side, NDEA was an accomplishment of the moderate Republicans, in the administration and the Congress. President Eisenhower's political position, as described earlier, was both moderate and conservative, depending on the issue. Marion Folsom, secretary of the Department of Health, Education, and Welfare during the time that NDEA was being developed, characterized the two sides of the Eisenhower ideology as follows: "When it comes to fiscal and monetary matters, be conservative: but when it comes to dealing with human beings, be liberal."[60] There is little doubt that NDEA represented the nonconservative side of Eisenhower's political position.

Elliot Richardson at the time of NDEA was a relatively young and upwardly mobile member of the administration. Given his relative youth and subsecretarial position in HEW at the time that NDEA was passed, and given his workload within HEW during, and after, its passage, it should not be surprising that Richardson had little to say publicly about his participation in the bill or the political ideas that guided him. Less than two years after NDEA's passage, however, in July of 1959, Richardson found a good reason to discuss the legislation and the political philosophy that guided him in working on it. The impetus for Richardson's discussion was a criticism of NDEA by Daniel Patrick Moynihan in *The Reporter* magazine, a periodical of some intellectual standing. Moynihan argued that the significance of NDEA was overblown, that it represented a "grab bag" achievement motivated by a political crisis fundamentally unrelated to education. Moynihan concluded that NDEA was basically unnecessary.[61]

Moynihan's criticism, and that of others, stung Richardson into action. In late July he published a pointed response to Moynihan.[62] He contested Moynihan's characterization of NDEA as a knee-jerk response to Sputnik, noting as he had during debate over the bill that it had roots in the 1955 White House Conference on Education, the report of the president's Committee on Education beyond the High School, and the June 1957 DHEW task force on education. He then argued that NDEA's significance could be inferred from the wide support it had received since its passage, noting that 65 percent of institutions of higher education participated in the student loan program, and that all funds available for graduate fellowships had been expended. Richardson characterized his commitment to NDEA, which according to Moynihan was a quick and dirty pragmatic response to a political situation, as, instead, a balanced response to a complex situation, a response that sought the middle ground between two extremes. The first extreme position was to do nothing about educational improvement and the other extreme position was that of many Democrats who thought NDEA fell far short of the permanent massive financial aid to education that was needed. The passage of NDEA, according to Richardson, had put the "no aid" group on the sidelines in discussions of federal aid to education, leaving the field now to the advocates of NDEA targeted aid on the one hand, and the massive, permanent aid camp on the other.[63]

While Richardson acknowledged Moynihan's claim that an acute need for school construction assistance was not addressed with NDEA, he argued that the Little Rock school desegregation crisis had made such aid impossible to achieve politically. Instead, NDEA achieved a different educational purpose that the public accepted. To the massive aid advocates' argument that the unequal distribution of wealth among states meant that the broad federal tax base represented the only answer to education's needs, Richardson countered that many states could come up with substantially more funds for schools than they were now raising. Richardson concluded where he had started, arguing that what was needed was not massive permanent federal assistance, but targeted, temporary aid that the public supported and that spurred states and local school districts into productive action. This was the NDEA and it, for Richardson, was a necessary and substantial achievement.[64]

In subsequent decades, Richardson published two books in which he elaborated on the middle political position in opposition to extremes that he had posited in 1959. In 1976, he pursued a "balance" metaphor of moderation in the political realm in a book titled *The Creative Balance.* He introduced that volume by discussing how the equilibrium he envisioned was one that addressed the gap between "innovation and conservatism." He described how the quest for such a balance animated many "of us who joined President Eisenhower's administration at the beginning of his second term [and came] to Washington in high hopes of helping to build a new political consensus." That consensus was to "rest on a strong belief in the individual tempered by the awareness that in a modern industrial society government must assume ultimate responsibility for protecting the individual against the harshest consequences of freely operating economic forces." This protection to which he and other activist Republicans in the administration committed, according to Richardson, was "an important joint venture whose goal was nothing less than the creation of an exciting new blend of conservatism and compassion."[65]

The brief description of NDEA in Richardson's 1976 book summarized it as a successful attempt to overcome the shortage of school and college teachers that plagued the nation in the 1950s. Richardson argued that by the early 1970s, that effort had been achieved, since the nation was then training more teachers than it could employ. Later in the volume, Richardson offered an explanation for Eisenhower's shift in position on NDEA that aborted its scholarship provision and seriously hampered its coherence. While Eisenhower, according to Richardson, entered his second term speaking positively of the moderate Republicanism that he wished to implement and proposed a budget that was far more generous than one normally expected from a Republican chief executive, he curbed his commitment to federal spending when his secretary of the treasury, George Humphrey, charged that a depression would be the result if federal spending were not reduced. Specifically, Richardson argued that the "Humphrey attack aroused misgivings in President Eisenhower which he never shook off. From 1957 on, the thrust of a confident new philosophy gave way to a halfhearted, halfway approach to domestic issues." Richardson added that in terms of his political activities in the administration, "instead of taking part in an exciting effort to build a new majority, I found myself spending large parts of the next three years doing battle on behalf of HEW programs against the chronic negativism of White House and Budget Bureau staff."[66]

Richardson did not mention NDEA in this discussion, but his analysis leads one to believe that he thought in 1976 that much had been lost when the scholarships were deleted, lost to the bogeys of budget deficits and moralizing about recipients receiving aid who did not need it. Whatever his reservations, Richardson still stood behind the NDEA, and the approach it represented to federal involvement in American life, seeing it as a balanced, moderate result that was appropriate both politically and as an approach to policy. Near the end of the book, he touted the virtues of moderation by quoting the noted jurist Learned Hand. In answer to the question of what is the spirit of moderation, Hand responded that it "is the temper which does not press a partisan advantage to its bitter end, which can understand and will respect the other side, which feels a unity between all citizens—real and not the factitious product of propaganda—which recognizes their common fate and their common aspirations."[67]

Richardson spoke eloquently about moderation and moderate Republicanism in 1976 because it was still a force in the American political arena. Richardson individually was also a popular political figure because of his resignation as attorney general of the United States in 1973, rather than fire Watergate special prosecutor Archibald Cox, as he had been ordered to do by President Nixon. The strengthening of moderate Republicanism under Gerald Ford seemed a distinct possibility as Richardson wrote, and as Ford campaigned for reelection.

In 1996, however, when Richardson wrote a second book, moderate Republicanism was on the verge of extinction, succumbing to the conservative revival initiated by Ronald Reagan and to the intensification of that revival initiated in the 1994 congressional elections by Republican representative Newt Gingrich of Georgia. In this volume, Richardson deplored the ideologically pure conservatism that Gingrich demanded of Republican congressmen and the sometimes vicious measures taken to enforce it. Richardson used the phrase "radical moderate" in the title of his book to indicate not that he was radical politically, but rather that there was a radical need for the moderation he had practiced for his entire career at a time when the political climate was plagued by the search for ideological purity and incivility. Much of this book contained a positive account of Richardson's work in the Eisenhower administration. He noted that he had been one of ten assistant secretaries that the president appointed in various agencies, charged with "across the board responsibility for legislation." He added that this work put him in touch with "gifted public servants . . . who held key positions in HEW." These individuals were products of the New Deal and World War II eras, individuals who spent the bulk of their careers in the federal service. Integrity was the watchword of these officials as well as of Richardson's superiors at HEW during the Eisenhower administration, Marion Folsom and Arthur Flemming.[68]

In Richardson's account of the campaign for NDEA in this volume, he noted that the chances for its enactment were enhanced by cooperation with many sympathetic national organizations, ranging "from the American Legion to the American Association of University Women." Notable also in passing NDEA was the resignation of Richardson's chief assistant from government service to lead a lay group devoted to its support. Richardson characterized the legislative climate in the 1950s as one of "comity" in which Congress, the administration, and organizations devoted to various causes such as NDEA cooperated to achieve legislative success.[69] The situation in Washington in the 1990s was markedly inferior to what it had been, for Richardson, with the federal service beginning with Ronald Reagan's administration full of political appointees zealously devoted to the cause of the president, and short on dedicated professional staff devoted to the nation, as well as to their departments.

The change in Congress was particularly troubling to Richardson. He contrasted interparty relations in Congress from the 1950s to the 1990s with the rabid partisanship that had been instigated by Gingrich and the House Republicans' Contract with America in the 1994 election.[70] Richardson believed that comity would have to return if there was to be any productive legislation coming out of Congress. His death in 1999 prevented him from seeing his belief repudiated, with the election of George W. Bush in 2000 and the achievement of Republican majorities in both houses of Congress, with few members of the majority party interested in the views of the Democrats.

Richardson's alternative to Republican conservatism was moderate Republicanism and its commitment to bipartisanship, since he believed that good Republicans and Democrats both adhered to the Lincoln view that the "legitimate object of government is to do for a community of people whatever they need to have done but cannot do at all or cannot do so well for themselves in their separate and individual capacities."[71] While moderate Republicans and most Democrats disagreed about where to draw the line between what the individual and what the government can do, both groups adhered to the dual need for individual and government effort.

There is an extreme chasm between Elliot Richardson and his belief in balance and moderation and most contemporary Republicans' affinity for ideological purity, whether it be economic, religious, or a combination of the two. In fact, moderate Republicans in our day are about as rare as southern liberals like Lister Hill and Carl Elliott. The obviously punitive No Child Left Behind Act as the center of current federal educational policy indicates how far we have moved away from NDEA and its subsequent attempts to construct a meaningful federal role in education such as the Elementary and Secondary Education Act of 1965. We will address this gap again in the conclusion of this book. Before that, however, a look at the political position on education in relation to NDEA taken by two professional groups, scientists and educators, is in order, as well as an evaluation of what each group gained and lost through passage.

4
Educators and NDEA

A Mixed Response, a Missed Opportunity, and an Expanded Agency

Clearly the category of "educators" is large, probably too large to be used precisely in any explanatory narrative. This account of educators and the NDEA confines the category to two groups, the National Education Association (NEA) and the teachers and administrators it claimed to represent, and the U.S. Office of Education (OE) and the individuals and groups, mainly in elementary and secondary schools, to which it was responsive. Limiting the educators to these two groups leaves out many significant educational actors—the teachers represented by the American Federation of Teachers (AFT), for example, as well as all the teachers and administrators involved in higher education. This latter group, as will be seen, became a more powerful constituency for OE in the aftermath of NDEA, replacing K-12 educators as the leading constituency group for OE. It is these two groups, NEA and OE, however, that are the focus of the chapter. They clearly can be said to have been the leading voices of the American educational profession in the 1950s.

The NEA was wide-ranging in its reach and it was clearly the largest organized group in the American educational profession when NDEA was passed, as it still is now. Before its transformation into a teachers' union in the early 1970s, NEA contained numerous subject matter "departments," as well as subgroups for teachers, administrators, counselors, and many others. Thus, the NEA could, and did, lay claim to being the one organization that represented all the working educators in the public schools. The strategic position of OE in relation to the implementation of NDEA, as discussed briefly at the end of the last chapter, marked it as a federal educational agency that was increasing greatly in prominence and influence on the American educational scene. Interestingly, that prominence was accomplished at the same time that the NEA began receding from its key position of significance on the national educational scene. The rise of OE as it planned and administered NDEA was accompanied by the beginning of the diminution of NEA influence. It is to the activities of each group that we turn initially, before addressing their differing trajectories after NDEA and trying to explain the reasons for these outcomes.

National Education Association and Federal Aid to Education

The National Education Association had been founded in 1857 mainly to pursue the recognition and expansion of formal education in a national climate that was, at best, mildly receptive to the effort.[1] For most of its first six decades, NEA functioned mainly as an annual forum for the voices of those who spoke for an educational profession that was in the process of establishing itself. The topics addressed by those voices varied substantially, but their devotion to the cause of education did not. The category "friend of education" fit almost all of those who were active in the early NEA, and they sought to use their influence to increase the amount of formal education offered to the people of the United States, as well as to raise the status of those involved in providing that service. Lines of demarcation between public and private education, though recognized as important at least since the time of Horace Mann and other common school crusaders in the first half of the nineteenth century, were not definitive. Similarly, lines between elementary, secondary, and higher education were also present, but were not as impermeable or restrictive as they became later.

Immediately after World War I, NEA underwent a significant alteration. It moved its headquarters to Washington, DC, and overhauled its internal organization and the way it conducted its annual meeting. One spur for this change was the increasing movement of teachers, particularly women teachers, to be heard, both on the larger educational scene and in NEA. The alteration of the association in the early 1920s into a formal national organization with state and local affiliates paved the way for a substantial increase in the influence of the NEA in that decade. Riding the wave of an antilabor political climate during the 1920s, NEA positioned itself as the "professional" educational organization in Washington, DC. Part of the NEA platform from the time of this remodeling of the association was the pursuit of federal aid to American education and the establishment of a cabinet-level Department of Education through which education would receive proper recognition and attention as a national priority.[2]

This pursuit of national recognition and federal financial assistance for education would consume a large part of the NEA's attention until 1979. The passage of NDEA in 1958 represented a significant, though complex and ultimately vexing, victory for the NEA advocacy of federal financial aid to education. The achievement of a Department of Education under President Carter in 1979 meant a successful result for the other part of the association's campaign for national visibility for the educational enterprise, with equally complex eventual results. The latter event is beyond the scope of this analysis, but NDEA, of course, is not. The irony of the successful accomplishment of NDEA in 1958 was that the NEA, longtime advocate of federal aid to American education, was largely on the sidelines while the bill was being considered and finally wended its way to passage. The reasons for this, and the less than enthusiastic support for NDEA by NEA after passage, tell us much about the politics of education in the mid-twentieth century and the subsequent trajectory of both American public schools and the National Education Association.

The NEA advocacy of federal aid to education, which began in the 1920s, was fervent, persistent, and punctuated by a series of setbacks. In the 1930s, in the midst of the Great Depression, NEA initiated a series of studies in educational finance that pointed clearly to the fundamental inequity of public schools funded largely by local property taxes and managed by local districts dependent for their life on state governments.[3] State and local control, seen by many Americans as the touchstone of the American educational system, were a distinct obstacle for the NEA and other advocates of educational equity between states and between school districts within states. The NEA worked assiduously on behalf of federal financial aid to education in the 1930s and, to a somewhat lesser extent in the 1940s, hampered in that latter decade by the fiscal constraints of the monumental World War II effort. A brief flirtation with federal aid by the noted conservative Republican senator Robert A. Taft of Ohio in the late 1940s gave a boost to NEA, but Taft and his allies in the effort such as Lister Hill of Alabama could not achieve enactment of the legislation they proposed.

NEA and the Eisenhower Administration

By the 1950s, the world war had been succeeded by an undeclared but real war in Korea, fought in the context of an ongoing Cold War with former ally the Soviet Union. The advent of a Republican administration, with a distinct preference for balancing the budget and avoiding large domestic expenditures, meant that the topic of federal aid to education was to become even more contentious than it had been in the previous decade, when Taft and a few other Republicans had modified their opposition to the policy. Although in the late 1940s President Dwight D. Eisenhower had been a member of the prestigious Educational Policies Commission, an organization cosponsored by NEA, this did not mean the educators had any special inroad to the administration on issues of educational finance.[4]

The social environment within which educational policy was developed in the 1950s was one in which anyone with any knowledge of the demographics of American society understood that the schools and colleges of the nation were about to face an overwhelming increase in enrollment. By and large, the educational institutions of the nation were unprepared for this onslaught, and NEA and the administration understood this though in very different ways. The association saw the demographic challenge as a spur to continue and intensify its campaign for federal aid to education. The administration saw the situation as critical but temporary, one to be met with a variety of responses that would last only as long as the social circumstances that prompted them.

The Eisenhower administration, on the one hand, was careful to make sure that any activity it undertook on behalf of the American educational enterprise had substantial political support nationally. This was the objective sought by the president in his 1954 State of the Union address when he proposed a White House Conference on Education to be held in 1955, as a culmination to a variety of state conferences to be held earlier in the year, or in conjunction with the national event. These conferences would establish a political base for any educational legislation, including federal aid, which the administration would propose to Congress. While Eisenhower was not inflexible on the federal aid issue, many members of his administration reflected more flat-footed opposition to the policy. Secretary of Health, Education, and Welfare Oveta Culp Hobby, for example, when asked in December of 1954 if the administration was prepared to recommend federal aid for school construction, replied simply "No, it will not." She added that the White House Conference and the state conferences associated with it were in the process of measuring a variety of educational needs and that the administration would not impose any policy prematurely.[5]

NEA, on the other hand, at least insofar as it was represented by its highest staff officer, was impatient with the administration, seeing the conferences as a vehicle to stall the needed movement for federal aid to education, rather than to facilitate it. For example, in his testimony to Congress on April 2, 1954, NEA executive secretary William G. Carr expressed frustration with the whole White House Conference plan. Carr remarked that the current population growth provided long-range problems for the schools, problems such as an increase in the number of students in schools of one million in the next five years. These problems, based on concrete enrollment trends, were well known to the educators and to political leaders in Washington. He concluded, "We do not need conferences to find out the facts" and added that "we have far more need for fact-facing than for fact-finding."[6]

Yet the NEA also realized it would be impolitic for the association not to cooperate with the White House Conferences. The last thing the association needed was to be seen as an obstacle to a grand national plan for discussing educational needs and indicating desirable policies to meet those needs. Thus, NEA turned to involving itself and its members in the various conferences in ways that could help meet organizational objectives. In this effort, NEA advocated teacher and administrator participation in the various conferences and wanted to make sure that state conferences were held in "close cooperation" with official state education agencies, bodies that were usually led by educators in close contact with the NEA hierarchy.[7]

The NEA pursued its campaign for federal aid to education at the same time the White House Conferences were being planned and taking place. In January of 1955, for example, NEA members were told of the names of the members of a prestigious advisory committee to the White House Conference Committee, one on which several NEA leaders served. At the same time, they learned that a special subcommittee of the House of Representatives, after hearing testimony from NEA interests, was recommending legislation for federal financial payments for school construction.[8]

NEA did not allow its perennial campaign for federal aid to lapse while waiting for the White House Conference findings. School construction and aid for teachers' salaries were major planks in that campaign, as was the stricture that aid be given to the states to use at their discretion, rather than in response to directions from the federal government. The last stipulation confirmed the third major plank in the NEA's campaign for federal aid, that the aid was to be general, apportioned to the states on some objective basis and spent by them according to their own priorities and needs rather than to those of the federal government. While teacher salaries and school construction were special, named categories of aid in some tension with the general aid provision, the need was so great in both cases, as well as congenial to the NEA and its interests, that the group chose not to see any inconsistency in its priorities.[9]

There was some convergence between the administration and the NEA on the issue of federal educational aid, even while the White House Conference movement was taking place. In April of 1955, for example, NEA leader William Carr testified before Congress on an administration bill for temporary aid to schools for construction. Carr welcomed the initiative from the administration but noted that the administration bill was inferior to another version favored by NEA. The NEA-preferred bill had more generous grants than the administration version, which also utilized loans as a substitute for grants; the NEA-backed measure was more of a permanent support for districts than was the administration version; the NEA bill determined the amount of funding to be offered on the basis of a formula applied in all states; and it provided the money to districts through state education agencies, a channel not utilized in the administration version.[10]

Congress approved funding for the White House Conference and state conferences in 1954 and they began to occur in the next year. In November of 1955, as the actual White House Conference was beginning, William Carr told NEA members it was an opportune time for American education. Noting that the Eisenhower administration had made school construction a legislative priority, Carr opined that the classroom shortage existed in tandem with a teacher shortage. He hoped the outcome would be more than recognition of these twin shortages, since they were well known, that it would be a statement of the need for federal aid to remedy them. Carr remarked: "The great national issue in education, at the moment, is the relation of the federal government to the support of the public schools. Unfortunately, this issue has been given little attention in the materials distributed to the state conferences." He concluded with a statement that mixed hope with caution. "If the White House Conference fails to come to grips with the central national issues, it will fall short of its highest potential value. If, on the other hand, conference members boldly confront these issues and refuse to be diverted by local and state problems, this conference may be a turning point in the history of American education."[11]

Two months later, Carr reported that NEA members should be buoyed by the outcome of the conference. He noted that with 1,800 in attendance, "The participants approved by a ratio of more than two to one the proposition that the federal government should increase its financial participation in public education. Of those favoring such increase, the overwhelming majority approved an increase in federal funds for school-building construction." This preference echoed the position of the administration and the NEA, both of which were supporting a school construction bill to be considered by Congress in 1956. Carr added that the White House Conference had yielded other positive results, including cooperation between educators and the noneducators who made up the bulk of the members. Also, the conference attendees exhibited a "well-balanced" understanding of American education, meaning that they were not hoodwinked by the antiprogressive education forces and their wish to undermine the student-oriented practices and priorities of American schoolteachers and their leaders. Carr concluded that the White House Conference would be of "continuing value" legislatively and in terms of other issues, and that it was sure to be recognized as "a landmark in the history of our country and its schools."[12]

Three months later, Carr continued to praise the White House Conference for identifying school construction as an area of critical need, but also noted its major deficiency. That deficiency was in its conception of the need for federal funds, for school construction or any other purpose, as a temporary response to a crisis situation. Carr stated that "the NEA is convinced that the need for federal assistance is neither temporary nor confined to school building construction." He added that dissenting statements to the recommendations of the White House Conference, statements that stressed the permanency of the need from two conference members, a classroom teacher from Oregon and a trade unionist, were on target. Also, he noted that the uneven growth in population and the great differences in wealth between states, factors that helped create the crisis, were "not going to be brought into balance and kept in balance by any temporary program." Carr then concluded with the warning that the White House Conference failed to consider the serious matter of school operating costs, such as teachers' salaries, as a critical and ongoing area of need.[13]

Carr's guarded optimism after the White House Conference meeting seemed in marked contrast to his testimony to the Senate committee discussed earlier. That Carr could interpret the conference's actions as in support of NEA's federal aid to school construction was clearly the reason for his change of heart. But Carr's hopes were to be dashed in the summer of 1956, when the House of Representatives rejected the Kelly Bill, the popular name for the federal aid bill for school construction. In reporting the reasons for this rejection, the NEA staff member responsible for federal legislation identified three major causes. First and most significant was the Powell amendment, which required desegregation compliance as a condition for federal aid. The success of the Powell amendment, named for the African American congressman from New York City who sponsored it, meant that almost all southern House members, even those who favored federal aid, voted against the bill. Less important but still significant as inimical to passage were the House Republican leadership, which failed to exert any meaningful influence on behalf of the bill, and the Chamber of Commerce and the National Association of Manufacturers, longtime opponents of federal aid who pursued their cause by lobbying vigorously. Parliamentary trickery by some Republicans had also hampered passage of the bill, but the largest reason for its failure was the Powell amendment. A large bloc of southern Democrats feared that federal school construction funds, with or without a Powell amendment, "would encourage integration of racially segregated school systems" and "adoption of the Powell amendment prevented southern members who favored the bill from voting for it." NEA, which had substantial numbers of members in its southern state affiliates, was sympathetic to the plight of southerners like Carl Elliott who were "forced" to vote against the bill for political reasons. Thus Elliott was listed as a strong supporter of school construction aid in the NEA magazine in spite of his vote against final passage of the Kelly Bill.[14]

The defeat of school construction in 1956 sent NEA back to the drawing board, but it rebounded as it had so often in the face of earlier defeats. The November election was on the horizon and NEA leaders apprised their members of the platform statements of both parties that favored various types of federal aid. Additionally, the association took heart from an increase in appropriations granted by Congress to the U.S. Office of Education, seeing this as a positive result of the impetus created by the White House Conference. OE was now publishing more information about American education, part of a general buildup in all of its existing services. The result was that one year after the White House Conference of November of 1955, national "interest in our schools still runs high, and an expanded informational program by the U.S. Office of Education will lend a welcome and sustaining vitality to this interest."[15]

As the next Congress took its seats after the 1956 election, NEA identified its major legislative priority—to "intensify efforts to obtain passage of a school-construction bill." This priority was offered with five particulars attached to it, including repudiation of any efforts in the legislation to enforce compliance with Supreme Court decisions on segregation since such a policy "contradicts the principle of federal aid without federal control." Such compliance for the NEA was properly a matter for the lower courts, and not for Congress. The association was heartened in its campaign for federal aid by a speech that President Eisenhower gave at the centennial celebration of NEA that was held at its Washington, DC, headquarters early in April of 1957. Basing his talk on the ideas of Abraham Lincoln, and alluding to education as important for defense of the nation as a democracy, Eisenhower turned his attention to issues of the school plant. He noted the problems caused by the Depression, World War II, and the Korean War in maintaining and improving school facilities, and advocated federal help to address them.

While Eisenhower was careful to note that the help he offered was temporary, a stimulus to correct an emergency situation, he reassured NEA officials with his statement of support that his administration would do something for the cause. Eisenhower ended his talk with praise for the recent White House Conference on Education as a vehicle for ideas to improve American education, ideas he hoped NEA would find useful in planning its own programs.[16]

At the midsummer 1957 meeting of the NEA's Representative Assembly, the association's annual convention, delegates voted to reaffirm, actually to reinforce, the NEA policy of support for federal aid for school construction. This action came along with support for maintaining federal aid to school districts impacted by federal military installations and other federal aid measures such as those in support of vocational education. Delegates also favored a more independent U.S. Office of Education, responsive to a national school board that NEA proposed to be established, and not to politicians. Finally, NEA supported tax deductions for teachers who used their own money for professional expenses. Thus NEA entered the 1957–58 school year by reiterating its long-held objective of federal aid for public schools and the major permutation of that objective that had captured its attention for nearly the entire previous decade, federal aid for school construction. This devotion to continuity in effort, in spite of the lack of success, was in many ways admirable. It would be tested, however, and found wanting in many ways, by the events that would ensue during the next school year.[17]

Sputnik and NEA

The successful Soviet satellite launch in October of 1957 caused a crisis for both the NEA and the Eisenhower administration. The crises were of a different order, however. As noted in the previous chapter, the administration responded slowly to the sense of national unease caused by the Soviet success in space, and made its response both careful and limited. In an early November address, Eisenhower concentrated on improving the schools, especially in science and mathematics, as the major initiative to be taken in response to Sputnik. The president was not convinced that Sputnik had identified any significant weakness in the U.S. defense effort. Thus his resort to education, and particularly science education, allowed him to respond to the Soviet challenge, but to channel his response into the arena of education rather than make it a direct defense issue.

The theme suggested by Eisenhower's speech, educational deficiency in relation to the Soviet Union, especially in the scientific realm, presented a significant problem for the NEA. As the leading organization in the American educational enterprise, it had to mount a response to any suggestion that the schools were somehow responsible for the situation. NEA's reaction was complicated by the debate that had raged over curriculum and pedagogy throughout the 1950s, sparked by analysts and others from outside of the educational profession rather than from within it. Specifically, progressive education, for the critics, was the cause of America's educational decline, and associating that decline with the emphasis on science achievement in Soviet schools linked it specifically to Sputnik. The NEA response was to locate any deficiencies in the schools in the lack of financial support they were receiving, particularly from the federal government, and to otherwise downplay the debate over curriculum and pedagogy.

Thus, NEA executive secretary William G. Carr responded to the president's November remarks by challenging him to follow through with meaningful financial support for science education and other areas. In January of 1958, as the administration was putting forth its own legislative proposal for education to Congress, Carr was more specific about its weaknesses, especially its stress on the area of science education in preference to general educational support. The real need in the schools was for first-class teachers, stated the NEA leader, and he added that we "will never get enough first class teachers until we pay salaries that compete for the best in business and industry." Rather than the administration program that advocated small expenditures for science education, "The NEA calls for strengthening American education right across the board." This strengthening included aid for school construction and for programs and services "in all areas, including science and mathematics." Carr noted that "a Federal decision to support any particular selected area of instruction carries with it some danger of federal direction of state educational policy. On the other hand," he added, "general federal support leaves the states free to decide how much stress to place on mathematics, or on science, or on other areas of instruction." Carr summarized his critique of the administration's proposal by stating that what was needed was not a "crash program" in science or any other area, but a "cash program" that served the real needs of the public schools.[18]

What Carr was doing here was trying to channel any impetus to educational change that came in responding to Sputnik, from the administration or from Congress, into the familiar NEA priorities of federal aid for school construction and teachers' salaries, and of general aid to be administered in conformity with state and locally determined priorities. Thus, insofar as William G. Carr spoke for the NEA and the American educational profession, neither the administration proposals introduced in January nor the program developed initially in that month by Lister Hill and Carl Elliott were worthy of complete support. This would be his judgment of the situation throughout the legislative process that yielded the NDEA in September of 1958. Fortunately for the sake of the NEA's credibility in Congress, it was not the only word from the association on the legislation.

Before looking more closely at the NEA responses to NDEA not orchestrated by William G. Carr, a close consideration of the ideological problem created by Sputnik for NEA is in order. The launch of the satellite was translated into a story of educational deficiency for the American public by the media, following a line of criticism developed by academic critics of progressive education and abetted by a presidential administration unconvinced that the defense situation was as dire as critics alleged it to be. Defenders of academic subject matter, mainly in disciplines represented in traditional arts and science faculties, had been critical of what they called the excesses of progressive education for some time. Arthur Bestor, professor of history at the University of Illinois, was perhaps the most prominent, and recognized, advocate of this position.[19] For Bestor, and others, education in the nation's public schools, particularly its high schools, had deteriorated greatly in the recent past, under the onslaught of life adjustment advocates and others convinced that most high school students had little interest in, and less need for, academic subjects.

Building on the arguments of Dewey and others that student interest was a preeminent need for an effective educational program, midcentury progressives advocated a variety of approaches that attempted to harness the disciplines to project or problem-oriented studies, or to abandon the disciplines in the pursuit of other goods such as social or cultural relevance.[20] With the furor over science education after Sputnik, the critique of progressivism intensified. National magazines such as *Life* featured articles critical of progressivism, and testimony before Congress by academics and others suggested a direct link between Sputnik and the academic deficiencies in American education.[21]

Other testimony critical of the schools was offered by military men such as Admiral Hyman Rickover, who would publish a book holding progressive education largely responsible for the intellectual, and physical, softness of American society. Rickover's shrill indictment of the schools, titled *Education and Freedom,* charged that the educational enterprise was rife with inanity and woefully lacking in rigorous intellectual inquiry, particularly in the disciplines immediately related to national defense, the sciences and mathematics.[22] The net result was that the public schools were placed clearly on the defensive and called on to answer the charges of their critics that they were a cause, if not the cause, of the Soviet primacy in science and technology evidenced by Sputnik.

NEA, as the leading organization in the American educational establishment, had to involve itself in the defense of the public schools. Fortunately, it had a body over which it had influence, if not control, that could, and did, respond. The Educational Policies Commission (EPC), mentioned briefly earlier in the chapter as a body on which Dwight Eisenhower had served in the late 1940s, held an emergency meeting in December of 1957 to consider a response to the crisis for the public schools caused in the aftermath of Sputnik. Seventeen of the nineteen members of the EPC attended the December meeting. The EPC membership represented more than public school officials: it consisted of three university presidents, one of whom was the elected chair of the group; a notable former university president; two professors of education and a professor of communications and journalism; and a state teachers' association leader from California. Public school administrators from city systems in Newark, New Jersey; Chicago, Illinois; Grand Junction, Colorado; and Westport, Connecticut were also members, as well as the president and executive secretary of both the NEA and of the American Association of School Administrators (AASA), all four of whom held ex officio membership. Perhaps the most prominent member of the EPC was James B. Conant, retired president of Harvard University, a noted chemist who had been involved in the scientific research that culminated in the launch of the atomic bomb on two Japanese cities, and who was in the process of developing a reputation as an educational expert through his own, Carnegie financed, study of American high schools.[23]

The full EPC met in December, a few weeks after a meeting of the Steering Committee of the group, called almost immediately after Sputnik's launch. The EPC's task was to prepare a document that needed to be published sooner rather than later, given the pressures under which the public schools had been placed by their critics. The record of discussion at the December meeting is 250 pages long, an indication that the group took its task seriously, and that the short document it was preparing needed to cover a wide variety of issues and to provide answers to many questions raised by critics. Generally, the group agreed that the response had to be a defense of the public schools, but that it could not exhibit an overly defensive tone. It needed to pay specific attention to science and mathematics education, in part to answer untrue charges such as that by former president Herbert Hoover that only 12 percent of American high school students were taking algebra and science. Also, a recent report on education in the Soviet Union, published by the U.S. Office of Education, had dealt at length with the place of science and mathematics in Soviet schools and was being used in the media to pillory American public schools. Finally, the injunction of President Eisenhower to the American people to "appraise" their schools carried with it a clear implication that he would not be surprised if they were found wanting.[24]

Conant, a four-time member of the EPC, advocated two strategies he thought essential to a sound defense of the public schools, particularly the high schools. First, he thought the real accomplishments of many public high schools in academic pursuits, particularly in the education of gifted students, should be stressed. The point was not that the schools were beyond criticism, but that in optimal circumstances, that is, in schools large enough to have a comprehensive curriculum and wealthy enough to support that curriculum with competent staff and carefully developed guidance and testing programs, the result was an educational situation that was exemplary and competitive internationally. Weaknesses indeed did exist in many schools, but they could usually be associated with small size and/or a lack of the financial support needed to achieve desirable results. Conant's second piece of advice was to avoid the tried and true NEA solution for educational problems, federal aid, in the document. He argued that invoking federal aid would cause critics to charge that the NEA was simply repeating its traditional theme and avoiding the real issues plaguing the nation's schools.[25]

The twenty-three-page document the EPC published early in 1958 heeded Conant's advice on both points. It stressed the progress made in educating gifted students and in identifying them through guidance and counseling and testing programs. It also discussed the financial difficulties endured in many school systems, but without invoking federal aid as *the* solution for what ailed the schools. On the issue of science and mathematics education, the report advocated offering those subjects in the context of a comprehensive high school curriculum that served all students, gifted as well as those who were not gifted. While Soviet schools could stress science and mathematics to the point that other studies were neglected, this could not take place in American schools, which were pledged to democracy as the context in which they operated and as the principle on which they developed their programs. The EPC report noted that the public was rightfully aware of the importance of science and technology for the future of the nation, and that science must be offered to those students who were capable of excellence in the area. It cautioned, however, that "scientific education is not the only need of America today. Fully important as progress in science are the promotion of American democracy and the preservation of peace." It concluded that peace called for "knowledge, insights, and abilities of many kinds" and mentioned specifically the contributions of "the philosopher, the historian, the social scientist, the student of language and literature" that all "shared with the scientist the promise of the future."[26]

The document went on to identify several specific areas that needed strengthening, as well as to indicate that much of that strengthening would come with better financial support for the schools. Major needs included "better opportunities for the academically able students; . . . better counselling [*sic*] and guidance; . . . improvement in the working conditions of teachers and in their social prestige and economic status; and . . . improvements in instruction in all subjects, including mathematics and science." To accomplish these objectives, the EPC argued, "there must be a breakthrough in educational finance; and programs which will contribute to the solution of all these problems must be developed at all levels of government."[27]

Later in the report, the EPC developed an important argument on the necessity of public support for the schools. No progress could be made without such support, and the group argued that "misinformation can cause serious damage to American education." Here it countered explicitly what it considered to be misinformation about the amount of science and mathematics offered in high schools, noting that the actual percentages of students taking mathematics and science far exceeded the figures that critics such as former President Hoover stated. It concluded this section of the report with the following admonition: "Citizens must recognize that careless criticism of education may actually result in a deterioration of quality rather than in improvement. An atmosphere of fear, distrust, or emotional antagonism is not conducive to those changes and tests of new ideas which are the basis of improvement." Finally, the report reiterated that the emphasis on freedom and democracy in American society and schools militated against the government-directed, overly rigorous selection and channeling of students into science and mathematics that prevailed in Soviet schools. American schools needed to honor the national ideals of freedom and democracy in their policies and procedures at the same time that they responded to the talents and needs of their students.[28]

The EPC report was an artful response to Sputnik and to President Eisenhower. It seemed designed, mainly, to buoy an educational profession that was being put under siege in the aftermath of Sputnik. In that regard, it can be judged to be a success. Readers of the NEA magazine were favored with a complete copy of the document; the only thing missing in the *NEA Journal* version was the appended statistical materials on American and Soviet education. Inserted in the middle of the article version of the report was the announcement that two television programs raising issues developed in the report were being distributed to educational and commercial stations.[29] Thus the thousands of teachers who belonged to the NEA, and those who didn't but had access to its published materials through their colleagues or school libraries, could be assured that their professional association was actively trying to project an image of intelligent responders to the Soviet satellite and the educational uproar its launch had instigated.

NEA and NDEA

While the publication of the EPC report assured the educational profession, at least insofar as it was represented by the National Education Association, it did little to allay the concerns of the public about American education, concerns that were aired frequently in the media and that were abetted by the Eisenhower administration and by members of Congress. Both the administration and Congress continued to push their versions of educational improvement and to work with each other to achieve a result. The NEA was aware of the administration proposal to Congress that came in January of 1958 and of the bills that Senator Hill and Representative Elliott were working on in response to Sputnik. It chose not to be negative about any of those efforts, but to point out the ways in which they fell short of NEA objectives. In February of 1958, for example, NEA leader William Carr testified before a congressional committee, though not one in which Lister Hill or Carl Elliott played a leadership role. Carr summarized the NEA position on the developing legislation when he remarked: "The NEA approves of the educational bills now before Congress, but we do not think the Administration's bill or any other is adequate to strengthen our entire public education program." Carr likened the various proposals of the administration and congressional leaders to "patches on the roof of a house when its foundation should be reinforced."[30]

Of course, that reinforcement would be accomplished, according to the NEA leader, by following the NEA program of massive general federal aid that would be used by the states for teachers' salaries and school construction. These recommendations were the heart of the NEA education program that was now also before Congress. That proposal advocated general federal aid to the states of one billion dollars for the 1958–59 school year and an annual increase that would eventually result in $4.5 billion in aid for 1961–62. The funds were to be turned over to the states under a formula that mandated initially $25 for every school-age child in a state, a figure that would annually increase until it reached $100. If, as NEA recommended, states would apportion 65 percent of their allotments to teachers' pay, this would boost salaries by $500 per year and by $2,000 at the end of four years. Similarly, if states spent 30 percent of their allotment over the next four years on construction, Carr noted that "a minimum of 83,000 new classrooms could be built." He argued that this number of classrooms "added to the present rate of construction would be sufficient to eliminate the existing backlog of urgently needed schools" and thereby "reduce the average class size to desirable levels." The NEA program for education described by Carr was introduced into both houses of Congress on February 17, 1958 by Senator James E. Murray of Montana and Representative Lee Metcalf of the same state.[31]

Carr also directly confronted those who saw American schools and teachers as implicated in a crisis of quality in science education and other areas related to national defense. He responded emotionally to the uproar, saying that "to the charge that public education is unconcerned about quality education, the teachers of the nation plead emphatically *not* guilty." He added that "with all its faults, the American public school system produces skilled scientists and technicians, and at the same time educates millions of free and thinking people."[32] Carr thus chose in his testimony to Congress, as well as in his involvement in NEA lobbying activity of Congress on education in 1958, to ignore Conant's strictures that repetition of traditional themes would further the image of NEA as a special pleader for money for teachers from the federal government rather than mark it as a serious player in the arena of drafting a successful federal educational response to the crisis situation, or at least to what seemed to be the crisis situation, created by Sputnik.

Carr and the NEA moved along their traditional path in the first half of 1958. In addition to pushing for Murray-Metcalf proposals, and thereby largely ignoring the administration bill and the Hill and Elliott alternatives, NEA also was active, and successful, in gaining Congress's attention on the issue of tax relief for teachers who spent their own money on materials for their classrooms. Several bills addressing this issue were introduced in Congress and, before any of them passed, in April of 1958, the U.S. Treasury announced that it had changed its mind on the issue and that expenditures by teachers for classroom materials were now deductible expenses on a federal income tax return. The NEA told its members that on average, teachers spent about $300 on educational materials and that, depending on their tax bracket, a portion of the amount they spent could be deducted. It also agreed to provide instructions to teachers interested in taking advantage of the deduction.[33]

As the NEA met at its annual convention in Cleveland, Ohio, in the summer of 1958, both houses of Congress were moving forward in considering the National Defense Education Act. In marked contrast, the NEA-backed Murray-Metcalf bill was mired in the committee process and unlikely to get any further, at least in the current session. The NEA response to this situation, like the NEA itself, was complex, diffuse, and difficult to characterize and evaluate. On the one hand, NEA executive secretary William Carr and the formal leaders of the group carried on as if the situation had not changed and as if the NDEA did not exist. Carr did not mention NDEA in his speech at the NEA convention in July and the Platform Committee developed a legislative plank that managed also to ignore it completely. The platform first sounded the familiar NEA priorities of massive federal funding, teachers' salaries, and school construction; it then called for more attention to higher education, urged a change in the selection procedure of the commissioner of the U.S. Office of Education to try and de-politicize that office, commended the Treasury Department for its recognition of teachers' deduction for classroom expenditures, called for retirement systems that were portable from state to state, urged greater recognition of international relations, and commended Congress for extending the special book postage rate to a wide variety of other educational materials. The absence of reference to NDEA in the platform was truly astounding, given that it was reaching a critical stage in the congressional consideration process and was likely soon to be either finally adopted or rejected.[34]

Fortunately for the NEA, it was a large and complex organization that had many ways of approaching an issue, in addition to the plans and policies of its leadership. Action taken by the delegates at the annual convention in support of NDEA provided one example of membership putting an issue on the agenda of the association that the NEA leadership did not necessarily want to consider. At the July 3 formal session of the Representative Assembly, the legislative body of the association, a former president of NEA, John Lester Buford, made an impassioned speech to the delegates, arguing that there had "been a let-down in the most important business that this convention has anything to do with and that is the program at the national level which will make it possible for us to do the . . . job that . . . we ought to do." Mentioning the importance that President Eisenhower had given to education in the past year, as well as a recent *New York Times* article by James Reston on the importance of education to national defense, Buford referred to the rocky road to be traversed on behalf of the Murray-Metcalf as a road worth taking, but made a significant addition to that priority.[35]

Buford told delegates that on July 2, the day before he was speaking, the House of Representatives Education and Labor Committee had approved Representative Carl Elliott's National Defense Education Act. That bill, according to Buford, encompassed scholarships and loans for students; grants to states to strengthen science, mathematics, and foreign language education; graduate education enhancement in the interest of creating more teachers for schools and for colleges; guidance, counseling, and testing provisions to identify gifted students; and research into more effective use of educational media in classrooms. He added that the NEA Legislative Commission now believed the Elliott bill "is in the most favorable position to be enacted into law of any proposed educational legislation now pending before Congress" and that the commission now "recommended that the NEA support HR 13247 [Elliott's NDEA bill]." He urged delegates to vigorously support the Legislative Commission in its advocacy of NDEA, and saw its passage as a stepping-stone to later passage of the NEA-backed Murray-Metcalf measure. The discussion of the NDEA bill from the floor was overwhelmingly in support of the following motion: "The NEA here assembled recommends that the National Education Association, the teachers of America, reaffirm their belief in and support of Federal funds for public education, and we further reaffirm our support of . . . the Murray-Metcalf Bill and . . . the Elliott Bill." The motion went on to recommend "that the *maximum* resources of the NEA . . . be employed in the promotion of this program. We here now, in this motion, mandate priority for the provision that will carry out this action for the teachers and children of America."[36]

The discussion that followed revealed overwhelming sentiment by delegations from many states in favor of NDEA as well as of Murray-Metcalf. Delegations that went on record either as seconding the motion, or otherwise favoring it, included those from Illinois, Idaho, California, Georgia, Michigan, North Carolina, Arizona, New York, Florida, Montana, Wisconsin, Indiana, Pennsylvania, Vermont, Alabama (twice), Washington, Tennessee, Ohio, Virginia, Colorado, Oregon, Missouri, Mississippi, Nevada, New

Hampshire, Alaska, Oklahoma, New Mexico, West Virginia, Maine, South Dakota, Kentucky, Minnesota, Wyoming, Arkansas, Utah, Delaware, Nebraska, Puerto Rico, Iowa, and Massachusetts. Louisiana reported a split in its delegation on the issue and Texas asked that the words "federal aid" not be used (actually *federal aid* did not appear in the motion). That the motion passed with a roaring voice vote was not surprising given the enthusiastic support exhibited by speaker after speaker who put his or her delegation on record either seconding or supporting the motion.[37]

The ringing endorsement of NDEA by NEA was noted in the next day's *New York Times* and undoubtedly heartened Carl Elliott and spurred on his efforts on behalf of his bill.[38] It would be an overstatement to say that the NEA rank and file overruled its leadership. The Legislative Commission, with a chief staff officer who was in close contact with other NEA leaders, provided the recommendation, understanding at the least that NDEA support might translate later into success for Murray-Metcalf. The emotion that swept the Representative Assembly, however, made sure that reports of their action would circulate in the media as well as undergird a significant rank-and-file campaign for NDEA in the ensuing month. How much of a role NEA had in the actual passage of NDEA is hard to estimate. The lukewarm support of its top staff officer, William G. Carr, and the pragmatic support from the Legislative Commission indicate that the outpouring of support of the delegates to the annual meeting was well beyond the sentiments of the leadership.

A report on the actions of the Congress on education, in the October, 1958, issue of the NEA magazine, reflected the recent NEA support of NDEA and the association's dissatisfaction with the final result. The article opened with praise for the 85th Congress as "a good, hard-working Congress regarding education." This praise was immediately balanced by mention that Congress had done nothing about school construction or the salary improvements contained in the Murray-Metcalf bill. The rest of the article was basically an account of the twists and turns that characterized the road to passage taken by NDEA, stressing the many parliamentary obstacles presented to passage from longtime opponents of federal aid legislation, particularly in the House of Representatives. The next discussion was of the contribution to passage of NDEA on the part of the NEA Legislative Commission and of state NEA leaders. The article concluded, "The National Defense Education Act of 1958 represents a major accomplishment." It then went on to contextualize that accomplishment as a step in the ongoing NEA campaign for meaningful improvement of the educational system.[39] Rather than a celebration of NDEA, the article was more of an analysis, one that saw the law's main strength in its precedential value for further legislation. Alas, that legislation, general federal aid with construction and salary provisions, did not ensue. NEA seemed insufficiently aware of the landmark status, in terms of federal dollars and cents for a variety of educational causes, that NDEA represented and certainly in this account did not show the same level of enthusiastic support for the bill that the delegates to the 1958 convention had generated.

Hesitancy over NDEA was even more prominent in an article in the same issue of the NEA magazine by Executive Secretary William G. Carr. This article began with a description of the mixed blessing for educators caused by the domestic reaction to Sputnik. While the satellite pushed education to the forefront of national concern, Carr argued that it did so in a way that threatened the schools through a movement to narrow the curriculum only to academics as much as it supported them. NDEA was similarly a mixed bag for teachers, according to Carr. While its passage "probably inaugurated a new era of shared federal responsibility for education," he opined, it did nothing for the crucial causes of "school construction and teachers' salaries." Carr characterized the final result of NDEA as a situation in which "educators are mixing gratitude and skepticism."[40] And the bulk of the article seemed to place Carr's dominant position in the skeptic camp, rather than that of the grateful.

Carr's refusal to declare a significant victory for NEA in the passage of NDEA is difficult to understand. While it surely did not meet all of his goals, it broke a dam that had been erected between the public schools and federal dollars. On that basis alone, it seems to have deserved a better evaluation from the leaders in the National Education Association than it garnered. William G. Carr, especially, seemed to exhibit a tunnel vision that served his constituency, and himself, poorly. He could have enthusiastically endorsed NDEA and used it as a springboard to seeking further support for bills like Murray-Metcalf that embodied his chief desires. Of course, as already noted, there was a logical inconsistency in those desires. Favoring general aid at the same time he favored school construction funding and teachers' salary support meant that Carr was not a consistent advocate of any federal aid policy. Whether or not that inconsistency had anything to do with the eventual negative outcome for Murray-Metcalf is hard to determine. What is not hard to determine is the gap between the purist William Carr and the enthusiastic delegates to the 1958 convention who endorsed NDEA and energized the campaign for its passage. In this case, it seems, the leader trailed far behind the members.

The U.S. Office of Education

The same fear of the federal government that animated much of the opposition to the NEA's pursuit of federal aid to education in the twentieth century had been present from the beginning of the federal educational agency in the middle of the nineteenth century. Established in 1867 as a Department of Education, though not with cabinet status, the federal educational agency quickly evolved into a Bureau of Education in the Department of the Interior and then an Office of Education in that same department. Opposition to institutionalizing a federal role in education was strong from the beginning, and based in large part on constitutional grounds, that is, that the U.S. Constitution did not mention education, which, pursuant to the Derived Powers clause of Article X, was a state function. Opposition was also based on protecting social and economic privilege by opposing any taxation scheme for public schools, especially though not exclusively at the federal level. The federal Office of Education continued into the twentieth century, leaving the Department of the Interior for the Federal Security Agency in a reorganization of the federal government in 1939. In 1953, as noted in chapter 3, another federal government reorganization resulted in OE moving to the newly created Department of Health, Education, and Welfare.[41]

Functionally, the original role of the OE, as developed by its influential founder Henry Barnard of Connecticut, was to gather and circulate statistical information relating to American education. Given Barnard's commitment to common school reform in his home state of Connecticut and elsewhere, gathering statistical information was accompanied by an earnest advocacy of educational improvement through enhancing existing schools and developing new institutions.[42] The second land grant college act of the 1890s increased the importance of the Office of Education, as did the vocational education legislation that began with the Smith-Hughes Act of 1917 and continued expanding in the 1930s and 1940s.[43] The vocational education acts provided grants for various vocational programs in schools, grants that were administered by OE. Similarly, legislation providing grant funds for school construction and operation in districts affected by federal installations (mostly military bases) was first passed in 1950, and expenditures increased significantly in the rest of that decade and later.

In spite of the statistical gathering function and the administration of vocational education and impacted areas grants, the OE was basically a backwater in the federal government through most of the first century of its existence. Congressional disdain for federal educational activity was a main source of OE's lack of influence, as was fear of federal control of education, a fear echoed by many citizens, organized interest groups, and several educators. The fear rose to the fore particularly whenever OE indicated that it might be interested in investigations of state or local schools, or of any other type.

The other main point to be made about OE prior to NDEA was its close relationship to NEA. The commissioners who headed OE usually came to that office from leadership positions in American educational institutions, mainly in elementary or secondary schools or in state departments of education, positions that were cemented with prominent committee work and/or elected office in NEA. In fact, in the early years of the NEA's Educational Policies Commission, the commissioner of education was an ex officio member of the group, a clear sign of the symbiosis between the federal educational agency and the nation's leading organization of educators. Even when that formal link was dissolved in an EPC reorganization in the late 1940s, the close relationship between the OE and NEA was not altered. NEA officials consulted informally with OE leaders on a myriad of matters, often seeking support for various causes, including federal aid to education, and pledging support for enhancement of OE. Part of NEA's campaign for federal involvement in American education in the 1950s, alluded to earlier in this chapter, was the establishment of a national board of education. The commissioner of education would serve that board in a capacity analogous to that held by state and local school superintendents in relation to their boards. This change was characterized as a removal of education from politics at the national level, a policy preference pursued by leading educational administrators at the state and local levels through much of the twentieth century.[44]

Just as significantly, NEA was concerned with the financial health of OE, a priority that was almost as important as the advocacy of federal aid for financial improvements for the nation's schools. NEA followed the federal budgeting process closely, especially the appropriations for the OE, and NEA sought to protect the OE role in disbursing federal funds for vocational education, impacted area schools, and any other purpose. Taking those funds out of OE represented an overt politicization of education that the NEA loathed, both in principle and because it meant a loss of their influence. NEA publications during the 1950s were full of reports on OE funding and program activities. The 1954 NEA platform indicated the rationale behind NEA interest in OE when it stated: "The NEA believes that as a component of the cabinet Department of Health, Education, and Welfare, the Office of Education should be strengthened with funds necessary for it to carry out its traditional functions unimpaired. The Association further recommends the adoption of such legislation as may be necessary to permit the Office to provide appropriate federal leadership in educational problems of nationwide concern." The NEA concluded its resolution by adding: "The Association pledges its active support to the Commissioner of Education and urges that he call on the Association for any support and assistance he may deem advisable."[45]

NEA-OE ties were particularly close in 1957 and 1958, the years when Sputnik was launched and NDEA was developed in response. That closeness was illustrated in the background of Lawrence G. Derthick, chosen by President Eisenhower to be commissioner of education in 1956. Prior to his selection, Derthick was superintendent of schools in Chattanooga, Tennessee, a prominent system in the safely Republican eastern part of the Volunteer State. Derthick had a strong NEA background as well. He had served as president of the American Association of School Administrators, the most powerful of the various subject matter "departments" and other subgroups of the educational profession affiliated with NEA. Derthick had also been a member of the NEA Legislative Commission immediately before assuming his position as commissioner, and had served on the Educational Policies Commission of NEA as well as in prominent positions in the Tennessee Education Association, the NEA affiliate in his home state.[46]

Derthick gave a speech to the delegates at the 1958 NEA convention, which endorsed schooling enthusiastically. While OE was working closely with Congress on the legislation, Derthick, perhaps in deference to William Carr's lukewarm attitude toward NDEA, did not mention it in his speech. One major topic in that talk did, however, relate directly to NDEA. Derthick recounted that he was part of a delegation that had recently returned from a month of study of schools in the Soviet Union. In discussing that visit, he highlighted the devotion of the Soviet system to schools as the most significant institution in determining the future success of their nation. This devotion, to Derthick, was a direct challenge to the American people to invigorate their educational enterprise to compete with their Soviet rivals. There was no doubt, for Derthick, that education was now the leading front in the Cold War between the two societies. Derthick did not mention science or mathematics in his speech, nor did he mention them in an editorial he published in the NEA magazine a few months later. In both venues, however, he did stress the challenge to American teachers to invigorate their educational system by reinforcing its democratic principles in order to compete with a nation devoted to education that did not base that enterprise on democratic principles. Whereas the Soviets had a definitive blueprint for their educational effort, Americans had a principle, freedom, on which to base their response. Derthick called for "a great awakening and an old-time revival of the American spirit" in its application to educational improvement as the desired alternative to the Soviet social engineering approach to the problem. Derthick's refusal to stress science and mathematics in his remarks echoed the NEA line that education needed to be improved across the board. Further, he refused to join the chorus of critics of American educational achievement in science, mathematics, foreign language, and other academic subjects, another position in which his remarks paralleled the position of the NEA.[47]

Derthick's call for a revival of democratic spirit, among educators and in the American public, was not a priority for OE staff who dealt with Congress on NDEA. Congress, particularly its leaders Lister Hill and Carl Elliott, knew that educational help was needed in areas besides science and mathematics, but they were willing to foreground those subjects in their plans as a way to justify helping in other subjects. Congress also refused to approve the NEA priorities of general aid, school construction, and teacher salaries embodied in the Murray-Metcalf bill. What is important to remember here is that OE in this arena played both sides of the fence. Derthick echoed the NEA line without specifically endorsing NEA priorities in his speech and article for the association. His staff, and staff from the Department of Health, Education, and Welfare, played a different game in their negotiations with Congress, trying to compromise Eisenhower administration priorities in science and mathematics with congressional desires for improvements in other subjects and in other arenas such as student aid. One might say that OE and NEA were on the same page with their hearts, at least as evidenced by Lawrence Derthick, but also that OE policies could not afford to be those of NEA. The federal agency had to follow the desires of the administration of which it was a part and work with the Congress that was responsible for its funding. Following its head instead of its heart eventuated in an enormous increase in funding, power, and influence for OE, the topic of the next section of this chapter.

NDEA and the Office of Education

Implementing the ten titles of the National Defense Education Act enumerated in the introduction to this volume changed OE dramatically, beginning almost immediately after the enactment of the legislation. NDEA broke the dike on federal aid to education and the amount of money spent by the federal government on education. As of 1961, three years after passage of NDEA, total federal expenditures on education exceeded $32 billion, "an increase of over 300 per cent since 1945." That amount of money did not all go through OE, but a significant portion of it did. Those expenditures meant an enormous increase in staff at OE, an increase that began in earnest almost immediately after passage of NDEA. Shortly after NDEA was implemented, OE was reorganized into a relatively complicated bureaucratic agency that sought to carry out its historic functions of data gathering and research and analysis, alongside administering the grants for vocational education and for schools in federally impacted areas, and developing and administering the grants for scholarships, fellowships, school improvement, and state educational agency enhancement, all called for in NDEA.[48]

Speaking specifically of NDEA, in its first five years, 1958–1963, over $170 million was distributed to the states, three-fourths of which went for science, mathematics, and foreign language education. The graduate fellowship program of NDEA also increased expenditures and oversight enormously in OE. By 1964, $41.5 million in stipends was going to graduate fellows and another $38.5 million was devoted to supporting grants to institutions where these fellows were enrolled.[49] The fellowship programs, as well as the student loan title of NDEA, put OE in a position of direct involvement with American colleges and universities. The relationship between OE and higher education had been present and real prior to NDEA, but also relatively informal. Now the two groups were in direct and formal contact with each other, a contact that would change them both. This relationship with higher education meant that a significant segment of OE was now dealing with a part of the American educational enterprise that had, at best, enjoyed a distant relationship with NEA in the past. While NEA had a higher education group, it was more of a study group and not one that enrolled institutional leaders in the way that the NEA-affiliated American Association of School Administrators enrolled school principals and superintendents.[50]

The enormous increase in complexity and funding of OE meant, inevitably, that it would undergo a change in relationship with NEA. This change was not anticipated by anyone in NEA headquarters, nor was it on the forefront of the agenda of OE. Both groups went on with their priorities after passage of NDEA, with NEA continuing to work for passage of Murray-Metcalf and OE beginning in earnest to administer the funds and the activities thrust upon it by NDEA. NEA did pay some attention to what was going on in NDEA, particularly as it impacted public schools. In January of 1959, for example, readers of the NEA magazine read a summary of the implementation activities for Title V of NDEA, the title devoted to testing, counseling, and guidance. The programs under the title were described briefly and the expenditures allotted for each program discussed. Since implementation was at the beginning stages, the article was not exact in indicating the specifics of institutions and individuals involved in the various institutes being set up.[51]

The same issue of the NEA publication carried two articles on the legislative future for education, both of which stressed the prospects for passing Murray-Metcalf. One, by the staff chief of the NEA Legislative Commission, talked of the political climate in the Congress and compared and contrasted it to that in the previous Congress that had passed NDEA. The second tried to answer opponents of Murray-Metcalf who argued that it meant federal control of education by claiming it meant no such thing. While the legislation did provide funds designated for construction and salaries, the article pointed out that each state was free to determine the amounts that went to each area. In February, the NEA published a two-page article on the particulars of Murray-Metcalf, and in May, subscribers to the NEA magazine learned of the long list of congressional sponsors of Murray-Metcalf. The May discussion also referenced NDEA and sought to attain passage of Murray-Metcalf on the broad back of the NDEA legislation.[52] Thus did NEA try to use NDEA to attain its program as embodied in Murray-Metcalf. The causes of the eventual negative outcome of that effort are complex and difficult to delineate. What seems clear, however, is that rather than trumpet the achievement of NDEA, the NEA hitched its star to a future outcome that did not occur. The consequences of that failure surely harmed the association's image, particularly in the minds of its members. Yet NEA had failed before. What is odd in the case of NDEA is its refusal to participate enthusiastically and at length in celebrating a victory that it had ample reason, organizationally and politically, to celebrate.

Returning to the topic of NEA-OE relations, things seemed to go on as usual in the first few years after passage of NDEA. A change in presidential administration after the 1960 election meant a change in the office of commissioner of OE, however, that provoked a firestorm of anger on the part of NEA executive secretary William G. Carr. This change brought to the surface the fault line in OE-NEA relations that was laid with the expanded responsibilities given to the federal educational agency by NDEA. According to Carr, discussing the situation with members of the Educational Policies Commission, the first OE commissioner chosen by President John F. Kennedy was handpicked for that role by the Ford Foundation. Carr recounted that, as usual, NEA and other educational groups presented their preferred list of names to Abraham Ribicoff, secretary of Health, Education, and Welfare. The individual chosen for the position by the administration was Sterling McMurrin, a professor of philosophy from a university in Utah. Carr was flabbergasted, noting that "this name wasn't on anybody's list" and adding that he and the other education groups "didn't have the foggiest idea" about the background of the new commissioner.[53]

What Carr either did not know, or chose to ignore, was that McMurrin was also a stranger to Kennedy; in fact, according to Hugh Davis Graham, when McMurrin resigned from the position of commissioner of education, Kennedy did not know who he was.[54] For Carr, however, the choice of McMurrin as President Kennedy's first commissioner of education, facilitated by the Ford Foundation, furthered the cause of private school advocates, particularly but not exclusively Catholic school interests, and diminished the influence of public schools and their constituencies. Carr stated his belief explicitly and explored its negative consequences for public schools briefly: "I perceive the Ford Foundation as moving into a position in this country—in fact it is already there—where, without being responsible to anybody, to no body of citizens, to no group of the profession, it can take and enforce decisions of very wide-spread importance."[55] Additionally, though Carr did not note this, McMurrin's experience was in higher education and not in public education, both of which augured poorly for the nation's public elementary and secondary schools represented by NEA.

Carr's experience with McMurrin during his brief tenure as commissioner of education did nothing to allay his suspicions. On October 22, 1962, shortly after his resignation as commissioner of education was announced, McMurrin was interviewed in *The New York Times* about his tenure as the nation's chief school officer and his relationship to the NEA.[56] McMurrin was quoted on several items in this interview that infuriated William Carr. Carr wrote to McMurrin on October 24, 1962, and asked if the interview reported accurately the commissioner's statements that the NEA "is in danger of moving toward national control of education," that the NEA "is not responsive to its membership," that the NEA's chief executive officer "has too much authority," that "members of the NEA 'rubber-stamp prepared resolutions,'" that the NEA "dominates state associations," and that the NEA "is not interested in higher education, is cool to the private schools and is pathologically opposed to the parochial schools." When Carr did not receive an immediate reply to his letter, he again wrote McMurrin and almost demanded a reply, telling the former commissioner that "statements attributed to you in the *New York Times,* concerning which I wrote you last week, are now being quoted and requoted to the considerable detriment of the National Education Association." McMurrin's eventual reply stated first that he might simply say he had been misquoted, but that this would be misleading. McMurrin explained further that while he might qualify the quotations somewhat, they all expressed sentiments he held, even if they did not do it precisely. McMurrin concluded that, in spite of his criticisms, and in spite of personal differences over policy, he had great regard for Carr and for the NEA, a body "that I have no desire to injure."[57]

Carr refused to be mollified by McMurrin's reply. The NEA leader disputed each of McMurrin's charges, whether in their original language or with a qualification McMurrin had added in his letter to Carr. Challenging McMurrin's contention in his letter to Carr that he had "no desire to injure the NEA," Carr responded that whatever "the desire, your continued, vague, uninformed, and unsupported generalizations are not apt to help." The NEA leader then added: "No Commissioner of Education ever assumed his office with less knowledge of the NEA than you revealed and cheerfully admitted during our first interview, and no Commissioner ever left the office with so much misinformation." Carr concluded that he did not wish to separate himself from his association, and added that since "I am its executive officer, your attacks, both in public statements and on many other occasions, display a lack of confidence which makes your professions of personal esteem difficult to comprehend."[58]

McMurrin was, indeed, chosen as commissioner of education without consideration of the desires of the NEA and other powerful educational organizations. The new commissioner came from a higher education institution, and a humanities department within this institution, both extremely unusual qualifications for the position of head of the federal educational agency. McMurrin's lack of public school experience, as well as his unwillingness to acknowledge that lack as a weakness, marked the new commissioner of education as someone who needed to be monitored closely by NEA. Carr's interactions with the commissioner, as mentioned in their correspondence, failed to repair the chasm in experience and in orientation that existed between the two men. While Carr's comment that he refused to separate himself from his association was offered in defense of that association, it seemed also to reflect a reality that the teacher leader indeed felt that he personally, as well as through his position, was a leader of the educational profession, of the public schools, and of the interests of all those Americans who sent their children to public schools. Unfortunately for Carr, the world was becoming more complex politically, and the interests he claimed to represent, and very probably did, at least in some sense, represent, were being challenged by newer political forces and coalitions. John F. Kennedy, a Catholic who had tried to distance himself from his church in his presidential campaign, nevertheless unleashed, or at the least abetted, the rise to influence of urban politicians and concerns, including the Roman Catholic interests that influenced many of the urban political machines of mid-twentieth-century America. The working-class political liberalism that Kennedy reflected was not uniformly pro–public school. Just as importantly, beginning with Kennedy and continuing in succeeding administrations, colleges and universities received as much attention, and support, or more of both, from the federal government as elementary and secondary schools. Finding an educational administrator conversant and comfortable with both sectors of the educational enterprise would prove to be a difficult task in the future.

McMurrin's successor as commissioner of education, Francis Keppel, was welcomed with open arms by Carr and the NEA. Both the leader and the group were insufficiently sensitive to how Keppel's qualifications failed to mesh with the NEA agenda, however. Keppel had been chosen as dean of the School of Education at Harvard University by then President James B. Conant in 1948, plucked from elsewhere in the Harvard administration to lead the education school. Keppel had no experience as a teacher or administrator in public schools, or even in private elementary or secondary schools, for that matter. When he chose Keppel as dean of Harvard's education schools, James B. Conant rationalized the choice by arguing that "education was too important to be left solely to educators." Conant introduced Keppel to superintendents and other prominent educational administrators, and Keppel proved able to bridge the gap between his, and their, experience.[59]

Like McMurrin, Keppel came from higher education, with no background in public education. This should have put the NEA on guard that it was in grave danger of losing the influence in the federal educational agency it had exercised for several decades. William Carr chose, however, to rely on his friendly relations with Conant as a guide for his contacts with Keppel. That choice, in retrospect, seems not to have served the NEA, or public education, very well.

One indication of the long-standing relationship between OE and NEA that ended with the choice of McMurrin was the assumption of an executive position at NEA by retiring Commissioner of Education Lawrence Derthick, when he left OE in 1961. Derthick, however, proved to be the last commissioner with a real affinity for NEA and the public schools. McMurrin and Keppel both came from higher education, a sector that NEA had sought to ally itself with, and to influence, with relative success until the 1960s. After NDEA boosted the role of higher education in the federal educational agency, through administering loans and fellowships for students and grants for institutions, colleges and universities assumed a position of significance for the federal government at least equal to that of elementary and secondary education, if not superior to it. Politically, Keppel, from New England and prestigious Harvard University, represented a new breed of federal educational leader, one much more in tune with private schools and the private foundations such as the Ford Foundation, headquartered in the Northeast, than with the state school officers, school board association officials, schoolteachers, and others allied with, if not represented by, the NEA.

The final conclusion to be drawn about educators and the NDEA, then, must attend to the shift in political power signified by the legislation and its aftermath. While the OE, on the one hand, prospered through administering NDEA, its leadership drifted away from the close affiliation it had enjoyed with the NEA. The educators' group, on the other hand, failed to capitalize on the victory its participation, however late, in passing the NDEA represented. Rather, NEA continued to seek approval of its federal educational policy program, one that was becoming increasingly distant from the tidal forces enveloping American education. When urban poverty and race came to the forefront of educational policy, and politics in the mid-1960s, the NEA, a group with a membership concentrated outside of the nation's biggest cities, was poorly equipped to participate in the dialog over these issues and to influence the federal legislation that addressed them.[60]

5
Scientists and NDEA
Maintaining the Momentum

Science was transformed and scientists were empowered socially and politically by World War II and its Cold War aftermath. Beginning with work on weapons systems and allied military matters during the war, conducted under the aegis of the federal government, scientists, particularly physical scientists, found themselves in a very favored position because of their research and its successful outcome in pursuing the war.

On June 14, 1940, a little more than a year before the Pearl Harbor attack that officially drew the United States of America into World War II, a National Defense Research Council (NDRC) of several leading scientists and scientific administrators was formed. Vannevar Bush, head of the Carnegie Institution of Washington, DC, a leading philanthropic supporter of American science, and James B. Conant, president of Harvard University, were two of the most eminent scientists in the founding group. Bush, who had been educated at Harvard and the Massachusetts Institute of Technology (MIT), and served the latter institution as a faculty member and administrator prior to his coming to Carnegie, moved quickly to obtain support for NDRC activities from the Roosevelt administration, using his personal relationship with FDR aide Harry Hopkins as his major conduit to the president.[1]

While Bush was the leader in establishing NDRC, Conant took the lead in recruiting to its ranks eminent scientists, many if not most of whom came from his campus in Cambridge. Conant initially had believed that radar was to be the scientific frontier in the war effort but quickly realized that atomic energy was where the weapons race was headed. In fact, Conant had taken action on his campus in anticipation of the war prior to the founding of NDRC, facilitating the establishment of a New Committee on Nuclear Physics at Harvard in February of 1940. In addition to several physicists who served on that group, George Kistiakowsky, a chemist who had immigrated to the United States from Russia earlier in the twentieth century, was a member. Conant had hired Kistiakowsky for the Harvard chemistry faculty, luring the Russian away from Princeton University. Conant, Kistiakowsky, and many others were soon embarked on the Manhattan Project, the outcome of which was the explosion of atomic bombs at Hiroshima and Nagasaki some five years later.[2]

Conant, in spite of earlier nonalignment views on foreign policy that questioned American participation in the war, had become a full supporter of the war effort in 1941. He described the situation as he saw it in December of 1941, two weeks after Pearl Harbor: "This war is in many ways a race of scientific developments and devices."[3] While that characterization of the situation gave short shrift to the many human lives that would be lost on the various battlefields of the war, Conant was correct in his assessment and acted with conviction on it through the war, and afterward.

The awesome destructiveness of the atomic bombs brought a swift end to the war and, as the work of scientists in developing this arsenal became known, they rose stratospherically in the esteem of the American public to the point that they received near irrational approval. One historian of the late 1940s noted the "veneration of atomic scientists" as a key feature of the era.[4] President Harry S. Truman expanded the importance of scientists in the Cold War–Korean War context, both publicly and within the administration, with the creation of a Science Advisory Committee (SAC) within the Office of Defense Mobilization (ODM) in 1951. Arthur S. Flemming became head of the ODM under Truman's successor Dwight D. Eisenhower; as shown in chapter 3, Flemming was appointed secretary of Health, Education, and Welfare just after the passage of NDEA in 1958. Important figures in the early SAC included James R. Killian, president of the Massachusetts Institute of Technology, neighboring institution to Harvard University in Cambridge, Massachusetts and home of a number of prestigious scientists who had cooperated with their Harvard colleagues in the Manhattan Project and other World War II endeavors. That cooperation between Harvard and MIT scientists continued in the SAC as it consulted on the development of new weapons and other aspects of defense research in the 1950s.[5]

The establishment of the National Science Foundation (NSF) in 1950 was perhaps even more important in terms of the long-term success of science in the federal government and in the nation at large, and particularly in the departments of the nation's most prestigious universities. This body was led, like the SAC, largely by physicists. The relationship of physicists to the development of the atomic bomb was well known to the administration, members of Congress, and the public at large. NSF and SAC were founded to facilitate the productive participation of scientists, particularly physicists and other physical scientists, in the national defense arena and, more particularly, in weapons research. The munificence of the federal funds being spent, mainly on weapons related science, stood in stark contrast to the meager amount of federal money spent in other academic fields. Even paltrier were the dollars that found their way into the budgets of elementary and secondary schools. The ability of the scientists to assuage academics in the social sciences and the humanities, at the same time that money poured into science, is one major theme of this chapter. The second, and more important for purposes of this book on NDEA, is the scientists' steady, though subtle, attack on the schools and the people who worked in them.

National Science Foundation

Vannevar Bush was the architect of the National Science Foundation, as he was a prime mover in founding NDRC and in many other scientific developments in this era. In 1945, Bush submitted a report to President Truman titled *Science: The Endless Frontier.* The report was written in response to a request from President Franklin Roosevelt that Bush prepare answers to four questions relating to the place of science in the coming postwar era. Two questions dealt with biomedical research and the place of public and private support for scientific research, two thorny issues that were more likely to cause controversy among scientists than the other two questions Roosevelt asked. These dealt with the timing of the release of scientific insights gained through World War II research and the prospects for effective education in science in the near future.[6] Bush, using a classic bureaucratic technique shared by many academic administrators, including those in science, established four panels to help answer each of the president's questions. Bush managed to broker the interests of each panel to the extent that they all agreed to the recommendations he would publish in his report, with the answers of each panel to the four specific questions appended to it.

Bush's report was carefully designed to make the case for a new federal agency, a National Research Foundation, the purposes of which were to "supplement the basic research resources of colleges, universities, and research institutes," to support defense research for the armed services, to "administer a national program of science scholarships and fellowships," and to "develop and promote a national policy for scientific research and scientific education."[7] Bush did more than outline purposes in his report. He proposed that the new federal agency be controlled tightly by scientists and not by the normal administrative procedures in the federal government. More specifically, members of the proposed foundation were to be free to be employed privately, in addition to their research work with public support; the grants made by the foundation bypassed the normal bidding procedures of the federal government; and grant recipients were not to be subject to the onerous auditing requirements imposed on other federal agencies and programs. The fundamental value protected in the Bush proposal was the autonomy of scientists in the nation's universities and research agencies to be the proponents and judges of their work, its promulgation, and its evaluation. Bush's proposal was faithful to this priority and, as such, it won wide support from scientists. In addition to submitting his report, Bush had prepared rough budget estimates for the proposed agency's activities and had arranged for legislation to be introduced in Congress shortly after its publication that would implement its major provisions.[8]

An alternative proposal to Bush's for a federal scientific research agency was circulating in the halls of Congress. The differences between the two proposals were over issues such as the appointment powers of the director in relation to that of a board that appointed the foundation director, patent policy, and the place of the social sciences in the new agency—all controversies that were real enough to drag out the legislative process to the point where the disputes took on a significance far greater than seemed necessary. Eventually, political tensions between advocates of two major versions of the proposal escalated to the point that the future of the measure was in doubt. When scientists began to bicker with one another over the particulars of the new agency, the politicians felt little pressure to impose on themselves a unanimity that had escaped the proposed beneficiaries of the legislation. Subsequently the American Association for the Advancement of Science (AAAS) tried to bring the scientific interests into agreement on the bill and proved to be moderately successful in that effort. In the next congressional consideration of the proposal, however, the measure foundered on a dispute between interests that wanted to broaden support for research to a wide geographical range of institutions of higher education and those that sought to confine the bill's research grants largely to institutions where high-quality scientific effort was already concentrated. When Congress eventually approved a version of the bill that emphasized quality over quantity in institutional support (fewer rather than more institutions and scholars supported), scientific interests coalesced in support of the measure. President Truman ultimately vetoed the bill, however, not because of the nature of its provisions for scientific support, but, instead, because of a dilution of presidential authority over the appointment process that caused the Bureau of the Budget to oppose the measure.[9]

Lacking a Sputnik to galvanize scientists and politicians into action as it would a decade later in the case of NDEA, the proposed foundation, now known as the National Science Foundation (NSF), languished in Congress, eventually becoming enmeshed in a partisan dispute between the Democratic president and the Republican-controlled Congress. If there was an underlying intellectual issue embedded in the political fight over NSF, it was the tension between the Bush proposal's commitment to basic research as the fundamental task of NSF, and Bush's opponents, mostly in Congress, who wished to see a body that would help "to solve recognized national problems."[10] For Bush, basic research, that is, research that followed the intellectual interests of the scientists who proposed it, was essential to ultimate scientific progress of any meaningful kind. To many congressmen, basic research was scientists at play and not at work on pressing national needs. The bill creating the NSF that was finally signed into law in 1950 generally followed Bush's prescriptions, though it did not completely close the door to the practical concerns of his opponents.

The new National Science Foundation was overseen by the members of the National Science Board, the body that was also responsible for setting foundation policy. The NSF pursued Bush's agenda to the near exclusion of more practical concerns, choosing at its first meeting in 1951 to specify the foundation's responsibility in the areas of basic research and training in science. Congress responded negatively to this priority by recommending paltry sums for NSF research in its initial appropriations for the measure. While NSF officials expected to receive the full $15 million that had been authorized for fiscal year 1952, for example, Congress initially approved only a $300,000 appropriation. Vigorous lobbying by the new NSF director, Alan Waterman, and other scientists, persuaded Congress to relent a bit and to adjust the appropriation upward to $3.5 million, still a long way from the authorized amount.[11]

Waterman was a physicist with a PhD from Yale University who had worked in the federal operating agency that employed scientists during World War II, the Office of Scientific Research and Development (OSRD). In spite of his successful experience as a scientist directly employed by the federal government to help conduct the war effort, Waterman subscribed fully to Bush's emphasis on basic research as the mission of NSF. To conduct that mission, Waterman and others believed, scientists had to be free from oversight from Congress or an administration with a particular set of priorities or issues to be addressed.

Responsiveness to national needs was not the only pressure that NSF sought to deflect. The McCarthyite political climate of the 1950s meant the new agency was often criticized in Congress over the political orientations of the scientists it supported, with little attention paid to the topics for which they were being supported. In fact, in the creation of NSF there had been a conflict over loyalty requirements to be imposed on NSF personnel and beneficiaries that ended in a compromise that reduced more exacting requirements in favor of a simple loyalty oath. As in the case of NDEA, university faculty had objected strongly to the excessively burdensome requirements that were being considered by Congress, an effort that was successful enough to get them reduced to only one oath. The fact that the oath was between the scientist receiving support and the NSF meant universities did not have any role in its administration.[12]

Congress's subsequent treatment of Manhattan Project scientist J. Robert Oppenheimer as a security risk, because of his left-oriented political affiliations in earlier decades that were well known while he worked on the atomic bomb, only reinforced the fears of scientists concerned about unnecessary and restrictive political oversight. In 1955, Alan Waterman published an article in a scientific periodical that worried about the possible rejection of science by a politically aroused electorate and politicians. He feared that science and scientific work would be subject to control from politicians consumed by, or at the least responsive to, the anti-intellectualism of Senator McCarthy and his allies.[13]

During President Dwight Eisenhower's first term, from 1953 to 1957, the public image of scientists gradually freed itself from the McCarthy web of insinuation. Public relations work by scientists through organizations such as the American Association for the Advancement of Science was partially responsible for this development, but perhaps even more responsible was the gradual decline in domestic political tension that followed the end of the Korean War. Beginning in the middle 1950s, scientists with NSF support also became actively involved in curriculum reform movements, in the high schools but also in colleges and universities, one outcome of which was more acknowledgment of the important work done by scientists and more respect for the scientists as the authors of that work.[14]

Involvement in curriculum reform, particularly in the high schools, allowed scientists to contrast their accomplishments with the grossly insufficient efforts at science education, if not downright antipathy to science itself, of educators. Jerrold Zacharias of MIT and other physicists organized into a Physical Science Study Committee (PSSC) and began to develop an academically rigorous high school physics curriculum. Zacharias and his colleagues, on the one hand, had little faith in the scientific abilities, or even commitments, of teachers of physics in the high schools, and took steps to make sure their new course of study would be impervious to intellectual dilution or other adulteration by teachers. Denigrating educators served the scientists well, as it allowed them to bolster their public image by contrasting it with that of a group, schoolteachers, which had far less public prestige to begin with. PSSC offered the work of scientists as an antidote to the inferior efforts of the school people.[15]

NSF, on the other hand, could remain above the intellectual and political fray caused by the work of their grantees at PSSC. NSF director Waterman, in this as in other cases, proved to be a consummate administrator equipped with needed political skills, guiding his agency skillfully through the national political waters and maintaining, largely unchanged, the initial orientation toward basic research proposed by Vannevar Bush and enacted into law. Waterman, Zacharias, and other physicists associated with NSF celebrated quality in scientific work as the ideology of NSF. Quality, of course, was to be judged by the eminent members of scientific fields who made up the leadership cadre, and the most eminent beneficiaries, of NSF.

Historical evaluations of NSF and its commitment to quality have been infrequent, though usually favorable. The official historian of NSF, J. Merton England, a well-published American intellectual historian, indicated his approval of the agency and the program adopted under Waterman in the title of his published history, *A Patron for Pure Science*.[16] The purity of NSF's commitment to basic research impressed England, though he certainly was aware of challenges to this orientation from outside the agency. Another historian, Daniel Kevles, whose field of specialization was the history of science, offered a significantly different view of the early NSF, though not necessarily in direct opposition to that of England. Kevles characterized the establishment of NSF under the leadership of Waterman and other physical scientists as a "victory for elitism."[17] The use of the term *elitism* by Kevles did not necessarily indicate wholehearted disapproval of the attitudes and orientations of physicists. At the least, however, it suggested that physicists were not inclined to consider seriously the views of others whom they considered to be their inferiors, including academics in other fields, physicists in higher education but not at prestigious research institutions, and high school physics teachers and other educators.

The prestigious scientists from MIT and other distinguished universities that manned the PSSC and held most NSF grants certainly had no qualms in considering themselves to be greater authorities on physics than mere schoolteachers. They also considered themselves the intellectual superiors of the many physicists who held positions at universities inferior to MIT and the other high-status institutions, mainly the public universities that proliferated in the Midwest and the South. These universities, and their scientists, however, did not consider themselves inferior to the private colleges and universities in their own states and regions with whom they competed for enrollments and for funds, or to the MIT-led group that influenced NSF. Rather, the public university scientists saw their service mission, epitomized in the land-grant philosophy that formally animated many of their institutions, as a necessary and legitimate alternative to the pure research mission espoused by NSF. The attitude of the NSF constituency, however, differed sharply. It was expressed, rather starkly, by James B. Conant in the first annual NSF report: "In the advance of science and its application to many practical matters, there is no substitute for first-class men. Ten second-rate scientists cannot do the work of one who is in the first rank."[18] That statement leaves no doubt that in the minds of the NSF leadership the issue of quality versus quantity was decided, in favor of the former. Kevles's term *elitism* thus seems clearly appropriate to use to characterize the hierarchical view that NSF and its scientists had of those scientists who occupied positions in institutions not normally associated with the leaders in the field.[19]

Scientists, the Soviet Union, and the Schools

While science and especially the academic leaders of science involved with NSF were prospering in the 1950s, they became increasingly concerned about the challenge to the dominance of their scientific accomplishments from scientific developments in the Soviet Union. This challenge was refracted through the lens of a larger Cold War political climate that amplified any Soviet achievement that might in any way be related to weapons or armaments to the point that it was seen as a direct challenge, not only to American science but also to American power in the world. While Sputnik in October of 1957 was the greatest single instance of Soviet accomplishment and of American fears of that accomplishment, scientists had begun to take notice of Soviet science well before the launch of the Soviet space satellite.

For example, in April of 1957, James R. Killian, whom we will discuss at length later in the chapter, gave a judicious estimate of scientific accomplishment in the Soviet Union. Killian noted that Soviet science had advanced substantially, especially after the death of Stalin released scientists from the ideological blinders that governed what they could say in public. Soviet science was advancing because of financial support from the government, especially in industrial applications, including those related to defense. Killian also noted the successful strengthening of science instruction in the Soviet school system. He concluded that Soviet scientific accomplishment was worthy of respect and concern for the impact it might have on "the balance of military and industrial power." Killian admonished, "We in the United States cannot lag or flag one minute in our scientific, technological, or educational effort if we are to avoid dropping back into a position of disadvantage."[20]

In discussing the Soviet challenge, most scientists sought a response not in the conduct of their research, under the auspices of NSF and other agencies, but rather in an alteration of science education in American schools and colleges. It was clearly in the interest of research scientists not to locate the difficulty directly in their own efforts, and it must be said that it made some sense to do so. It might also be said that scientists were likely to mount an attack on science education in the high schools to deflect any negative response to their efforts, even if there were no real problems there.

Many speeches and articles written by scientists indicated the nature of the concern of the American scientific establishment over Soviet science and American science education. For example, consider a speech given to an audience of Alabama higher education administrators in May of 1956, well over a year before Sputnik. The speech, titled "Critical Days in Higher Education," was by M. H. Trytten, one of the many physical scientists in government service, who had been the director of the Office of Scientific Personnel of the National Research Council, a government body that preceded NSF and that was responsible for direct government funding of research in defense and other related areas.[21] In early 1958, nearly two years after he gave the Alabama speech, Trytten would be one of the prestigious scientists called to testify on the proposed NDEA before the Senate committee chaired by Lister Hill.

In his speech in 1956, Trytten gave a lengthy description of Soviet education, basing it on recently published reports on the topic, including one by the U.S. Office of Education. Trytten's description of the Soviet educational effort marked it as a clear challenge to the U.S. system. He compared the two systems to each other in their outputs, a comparison that largely favored the Soviets. Trytten noted that the proportion of Soviet higher education graduates in engineering was about four times greater than those in the United

States (30.6 percent to 7.8 percent); the Soviet graduate percentage in health and medicine was almost twice as high (13.9 percent to 7.5 percent); the Soviet percentage of agriculture graduates was nearly three times that of the United States (10.4 percent to 3.4 percent); while the percentage of graduates in all other fields ran in the other direction, with the U.S. graduates making up 81.4 percent of all those graduates while the Soviet percentage was 45.1. Clearly, to this scientist, and to his colleagues, the burden of any American underachievement in science was to be laid on the shoulders of American educators, not American scientists.[22]

Trytten went on to say what had only been implied in giving the numbers of graduates in respective fields. To him, the Soviet accomplishment in education was considerable, as judged by the output mentioned above, and, more importantly, as illustrated in his discussion of mass education and of teacher education in the Soviet Union and the USA. Trytten argued that Soviet education at all levels was more scientifically oriented than it was in American schools, and that the USSR trained its teachers, particularly its secondary teachers, more rigorously in science and in other subject matter fields than their American counterparts. The situation was particularly disturbing for Trytten, given the recent statements of Soviet leaders that "we shall see who has more engineers, the United States or the Soviet Union." Trytten characterized this statement as an example of the new "cold war of the classrooms," and he added a warning about the danger of "the vast technocratic Sparta that is burgeoning in the U.S.S.R." The American scientist concluded that he was convinced that "Russia's classrooms and libraries, her laboratories and teaching methods, may threaten us more than her hydrogen bombs or guided missiles."[23]

Trytten believed there was a dangerous international dimension to the educational issue. He noted that the long-range Soviet plan was to school, both technically and ideologically, thousands of engineers and other technicians who would then help develop the economies and societies in third world countries. As a specific example of this impulse, he discussed the Soviets' promise to build and staff a technical institute in Rangoon, the capital of Burma, a developing country in Southeast Asia. He went on to name several other proposed beneficiaries of Soviet educational aid, including India, Egypt, Afghanistan, and several countries in Latin America. While the Soviets were intent on educational achievement in technology, and export of the achievement, Trytten remarked that they also were intent on exporting their political ideology to these undeveloped nations as the appropriate point of view for economic advancement. He warned that the educational system in the United States needed to realize that it was involved in international competition for educational and economic influence with the Soviet Union. Trytten described U.S. education as an individually, and not nationally, oriented endeavor and criticized U.S. schools further as anticompetitive, diminished in their attention to talent, and focused on the average and the laggard at the expense of the talented. In this regard, Trytten added, "While I hope we can continue to have a decent concern for all students, it is time we worried about our ablest."[24]

Trytten identified high school size and teacher training as major obstacles to be overcome if U.S. high schools were to be reformed. U.S. secondary education was handicapped, he believed, by the numerical dominance of small high schools, which in turn meant small faculty size that precluded specialization in the teaching force. This resulted in high school students in science and mathematics frequently having teachers not trained in those subjects. The situation needed to be addressed in two ways: consolidation of high schools to the point that their size permitted rigorous classes in the sciences and a faculty size that could encompass science specialists, and teacher training that assured that teachers in science, and in all subjects, had substantial preparation in the content of those subjects. Trytten added that his views were not his alone, but rather were represented strongly on recent committees appointed by the president on science and technology and on education beyond the high school.[25] He also could have added that these views were becoming more and more prominent among critics of public schools, particularly public high schools, and that these critics included many university professors, not just those in science, as well as journalists and politicians who were influenced by the academic criticism of the schools from scientists.

The content of Trytten's speech was prophetic of much that would be said about American education by scientists in the discussion of NDEA that would ensue after Sputnik. It anticipated many points made by Admiral Hyman Rickover, who would testify before Congress on the possible content of NDEA in 1958 and who in 1959 published a stinging criticism of high school education, particularly in the sciences. Trytten was not as shrill or accusatory as Rickover, but the two analyses closely paralleled each other. Trytten's ideas also dovetailed nicely with the recommendations that James Bryant Conant would make for the reorganization of American high schools in his Carnegie-supported report to the nation on that topic in 1959.[26] Trytten, then, in 1956 was making what was becoming a prominent, if not dominant, critique of U.S. education that excoriated (without mentioning it by name) the emphasis on progressive education in the public schools. It was progressive educators who believed in education for the promotion of democracy and of individual student interests rather than for the dissemination of subject matter and the propagation of talent for the cause of international competition. For scientists and other critics of the schools, progressives had come to epitomize most of what was wrong in those institutions.

Trytten made his case against neglect of subject matter, however, not against the democracy and democratic education that educational progressives frequently invoked in their defense. In his speech Trytten made sure to placate, as much as he could, those Americans, citizens or educators, who believed it was essential that a commitment to democracy be maintained, notwithstanding needed changes. He added specifically that a defense of educational democracy was a priority. He linked this commitment, however, more with nonscientific subjects in higher education institutions than to elementary and secondary curricula. He noted specifically that study "of the social behavior of human beings in our society, whether it be in an economic context or a political one . . . is essential to the well-being of our democratic society." When it came to discussing higher education institutions specifically, he refused to concentrate solely on the sciences, and thereby ignore subjects other than the sciences, mathematics, engineering, and related technical fields. He added that "much of our legitimate concern over our educational problems is based, not on the demands of science or technology, but on a need for new knowledge and new leadership in areas of experience not generally related to technology in the public mind. . . . I refer to the fact that we in our country live in a society where, to a large extent, we operate by consent rather than compulsion." Trytten went on to state his belief that the "atmosphere of democracy is precious to us. But it does not propagate itself without effort. In fact the processes of democratic living in our society must be continually re-evaluated as our kaleidoscopic civilization shifts and turns and changes like the current in an undying stream."[27]

Trytten added to his approval of a democracy addressed in political and economic studies in higher education settings a statement of approbation for the humanities, noting particularly the importance of classical studies, of philosophy, and of literature as all contributing to a "system of value judgments which guide us a hundred times a day." He concluded this discussion by stating that he thought the need for truly qualified teachers in these fields, in higher education and in the high schools, was perhaps even more in danger of not being met than the need for scientific and technical teachers. In the same vein, near the end of the speech, after a long discussion of the scientific challenge of Soviet education, Trytten noted that "we must not forget the areas of the curriculum devoted to our studies of human institutions and human relations, and to the heritage of the past. We cannot afford to be merely technical specialists. . . . These [Soviet] challenges will require that we reexamine many of our practices and our philosophies."[28]

The favorable discussions of democracy in education and of the value of nonscientific subjects represented about one-tenth of the total length of Trytten's speech. Further, they focused on higher education and left the schools to languish as the true targets of his indictment. Thus Trytten presented himself to his audience of college administrators as an advocate of rigorous education in all fields, and of democratic education in all fields, particularly in the social sciences and especially in higher education, where it was an appropriate focus. It seems, however, that considering the speech as a whole, Trytten was much more concerned with the deficiencies in the high schools in the training of teachers and the existing curricula in scientific and technological subjects, and in the use to which these fields needed to be put in a time of international competition with the Soviet Union, than he was with democratic processes, commitments, or understanding, or with nonscience subjects.

Trytten's speech to Alabama's higher education officials in 1956 represented a sophisticated version of the Cold War, science-oriented argument that scientists were making, and would continue to make, before, during, and after Sputnik. College and university leaders, especially those outside of the field of education, were likely to be soothed by Trytten's defense of democracy centered in the social sciences and of the humanities as evaluative studies. Higher education officials also were not likely to be disturbed by Trytten's critique of the progressive educational ideas that dominated, at least rhetorically, the discourse of elementary and secondary school leaders. Trytten ended his speech with a reassurance to the higher education leaders that it was "good to see that attention is now being given [to the crisis] by leadership organizations such as yours."[29]

Other members of the scientific community were more explicit about the crisis in science education than Trytten was in his speech. In November of 1956, the director of the federally sponsored Scientific Manpower Commission published a critique of science education in the *Bulletin of the Atomic Scientists.* In this article, Howard Meyerhoff began with a discussion of the critical situation in the nation's leading universities. In spite of their excellence in research, they provided "only mediocre and uninspired instruction at the undergraduate levels." He added that nearly half of the vacancies in science and mathematics teaching in the high schools were being filled by persons not competent in the subject matter they were asked to teach. Another disturbing development he noted was that only a fourth of the nation's high school students took two years of algebra and "fewer than 10 percent acquire a mathematical foundation for college study of science and engineering." For Meyerhoff, these unfortunate developments were due largely to "scientists' indifference" toward quality teaching and the teaching profession. One consequence of this indifference was that there was little regard for or understanding of science in the population at large. The remedy for these situations began with scientists' need to become aware of their duty to communicate their enterprise, its needs, and their concerns to the public. Lack of such concern for communication was causally related to the shortage of qualified science teachers and the dearth of science students. The remedy, for Meyerhoff, was to be found in scientists choosing to address themselves to the crisis of science in the schools. They needed to do this by concentrating more directly on the quality of their own teaching, as well as the quality of teaching in the schools. Meyerhoff concluded as follows: "Good teaching must be employed to inspire more students to enter the teaching profession, particularly at the secondary level. Self-preservation requires the restoration of learning, the resurrection of scholarship, the reentry of science into education."[30]

Still another 1956 article pointed more directly at the deficiencies of American high schools in science education, compared to the schools in the Soviet Union. The article was focused on the shortage of engineers in the United States. The author, Elliot Tozer, noted that graduates from Soviet secondary schools had ten years of mathematics, one year of astronomy, four years of chemistry, five years of biology, and five years of physics. He also pointed out that close to half of the high schools in the United States did not offer any instruction in chemistry, physics, or advanced mathematics. Tozer argued that drastic upgrades in the offering of science courses in American high schools were in order, as well as a substantial increase in the production of teachers for those new courses. Only with these necessary improvements would the United States be able to compete successfully with the Soviets in the production of engineers and other science-based professionals.[31]

The sentiments in these articles were echoed in many other similar publications by prestigious scientists, as well as by academics in other fields and by leaders in business and industry. The opinions of scientists, however, garnered special attention from President Eisenhower and others in his administration. The relationship between the president and scientists is the next topic to be considered here.

Eisenhower and the Scientists

As discussed above, President Harry S. Truman had created a Science Advisory Committee before he left office. After Sputnik, the Eisenhower administration undertook three additional initiatives related to science and scientists. One was the development of NDEA, building on existing work by the administration and responding to the proposals from Congress. The second was the elevation in prestige of the SAC when it became the President's Science Advisory Committee (PSAC), housed within the president's Executive Office, and thereby attained a more influential role in government that was symbolized by the frequent meetings of the group with the chief executive. The third was the appointment of a special assistant for science and technology, or scientific advisor, to the president.

President Eisenhower sought the counsel of scientists for many reasons. Consultation was a good move politically, particularly at a time when the nation was alarmed about Soviet scientific accomplishment. Obtaining advice from scientists like those who had pioneered the development of the atomic bomb told the public that the president was going outside of his regular channels to a group of successful, ostensibly nonpolitical, people for advice. Another reason was the desire of the president to garner information on military issues and other science-related matters from academic scientists who were not compromised by allegiance to specific programs or weapons. Eisenhower was a military man who knew intimately the tendency of military and civilian defense officials to pad their budgets with unneeded projects and materials. He trusted scientists to be less privy to the disease of institution building that plagued defense bureaucrats and military officials. The scientists who were chosen for the PSAC were almost all academics whose allegiances were to their fields and their institutions rather than to building any department or program in the federal government.

Eisenhower had developed a working relationship with academics in science and in other fields when he was president of Columbia University shortly after the end of World War II. In that capacity he became well acquainted with I. I. Rabi, a longtime faculty member of the Columbia Physics Department. Rabi won a Nobel Prize in 1944 for his work on hydrogen. This work was theoretical but it also was clearly linked to the development of the hydrogen bomb that would succeed and surpass in destructiveness the atomic bomb used at Hiroshima and Nagasaki. Rabi and Eisenhower met frequently during Eisenhower's Columbia presidency, and the trust between the two was a significant factor in Rabi being selected as chair of the PSAC.

Eisenhower with his 1961 President's Science Advisory Committee. Standing left to right: George W. Beadle, Donald Hornig, Jerome Wiesner, Walter Zinn, Harvey Brooks, Glenn Seaborg, Alvin Weinberg (in front of Seaborg), David Beckler, Emanuel Piore, John Tukey, Wolfgang Panofsky, John Bardeen, Detlev Bronk, Robert Loeb. Seated left to right: James Fisk, George Kistiakowsky, Dwight Eisenhower, James Killian Jr., Isidor Rabi. Courtesy of the Eisenhower Library.

According to James R. Killian, who was Eisenhower's first science advisor, "the President had a high regard for him [Rabi], and this brought about a new relationship between the old style Science Advisory Committee and the President."[32] Killian also noted that Eisenhower was animated and involved when he met with his Science Advisory Committee. The president's interactions with the PSAC were "lively, spontaneous meetings in which there was free-for-all discussion, with the President at ease" in the give and take of the discussion.[33]

Rabi and other members of the PSAC discussed the appointment of the new science advisor to the president at a meeting with Eisenhower just before Sputnik was launched in October of 1957. Almost immediately after the launch, Eisenhower, with consultation from Rabi, chose Killian as his first science advisor. Killian's memory of the situation was that it was a time of "deep concern and fear that perhaps we were being surpassed by their [Soviet] military technology." The appointment of Killian, president of the Massachusetts Institute of Technology, put a representative of the scientific community in direct contact with the president, and, in conjunction with his duties as science advisor, Killian took over the directorship of the PSAC. He became an essential conduit between the group and the president, with direct and relatively unencumbered access to Eisenhower, and he exercised his influence both forcefully and judiciously. Additionally, the president was also in direct contact with all the members of the PSAC, meeting frequently with them and often discussing many issues related to science as well as specific agenda items. Relations between the president and his group of scientific advisers were good, according to Killian. Eisenhower looked forward to meeting with the group, and its members, in turn, felt honored to be consulted by the nation's chief executive and confident that the advice they gave him would be seriously considered in policy development.[34]

Killian's successor as science adviser, George Kistiakowsky, had the same favorable sentiments about Eisenhower that his predecessor and other members of the PSAC held. Kistiakowsky spoke of the friendship he developed with Eisenhower during his time as science adviser and noted that he had "great admiration for Dwight Eisenhower." In comparing Eisenhower to John Kennedy, the other president that Kistiakowsky served, the science adviser allowed that while Kennedy might have been better intellectually, Eisenhower developed a much closer working relationship with scientists. Kennedy's lack of such a relationship, among other factors, resulted in a decline in the influence of the science adviser and the Science Advisory Committee during his time in office.[35]

Killian echoed Kistiakowsky's preference for Eisenhower over the other chief executives under whom he served. He noted that he and the other scientists involved in the PSAC were much more at ease with Eisenhower than they were with Kennedy, Truman, or Lyndon Johnson, even though most of the scientists were Democrats. According to the science adviser neither the president nor the scientists took partisan stances as they discussed various problems and issues. Killian had only one reservation in his discussion of Eisenhower and scientists: he remarked that one thing about Eisenhower he found troubling was the president's "almost exaggerated confidence in the judgment of the scientists that he had called upon to help him." For Eisenhower, the scientists possessed a quality of "objectivity" that he trusted; for Killian, the president overrated the "objectivity" of the scientists and had "excessive confidence" in their judgment.[36] Killian, however, criticized the influence of his colleagues over the president long after the relationship was developed and did not make such statements while he served Eisenhower. Nor did Killian make any move to temper the influence of his colleagues and the fields of science they represented over the president.

James R. Killian

James Rhyne Killian received his bachelor's degree in business and engineering administration from the Massachusetts Institute of Technology. He went on to serve as a journal editor at MIT for more than a decade, and then became executive assistant to the president of the institute in 1939. During the war, he took on demanding duties related to MIT's role in the defense effort and was rapidly promoted for his successful performance, becoming executive vice president of MIT in 1943, a member and vice president of the MIT governing corporation in 1945, and president-designate in 1948. He was inaugurated as president in April of 1949. Killian was not a scientist, but an administrator of science, and he did not make his reputation as a teacher or as an academic researcher, but rather as a facilitator and public advocate of the research of others. Killian was an exceptional organizer and administrator of scientific effort during wartime, when his talents were sure not to go unnoticed.[37]

Killian's presidency at MIT was also a great success. He increased the budget of the institute carefully through the use of a long-range planning mechanism that meant the funds were acquired consciously and used judiciously. As president, Killian added a Humanities School, an Industrial Management School, and a Center for International Studies to the institute. His description of what he was trying to accomplish was the establishment of a "university polarized around science, engineering, and the arts." Killian also distinguished himself through service to the federal government, holding a position on the inaugural Science Advisory Committee established by President Truman and continuing in that service when he was appointed special assistant for science and technology (science advisor) to President Eisenhower. Additionally, he had served President Truman as a member of the Communications Policy Board and the Advisory Committee on Management, and he was chairman of the Army Scientific Advisory Panel under both Truman and Eisenhower, serving in that position from 1951 to 1956. For Eisenhower, Killian also served as a member of the Committee for the White House Conference on Education, which was discussed in chapter 3 as

James R. Killian Jr. is sworn in as President Eisenhower's science advisor in November 1957. Courtesy of the Eisenhower Library.

a body that laid the groundwork for the administration's version of NDEA, and on several other national committees and commissions. From 1953 to 1955, he was on the Board of Visitors of the United States Naval Academy. Killian continued to serve the federal government after Eisenhower's terms in office. The MIT administrator retired as chairman of the president's Foreign Intelligence Advisory Board in 1963; he had begun his service on this board under Eisenhower.[38]

Killian's position about the consequences of the Sputnik launch for the United States mirrored that of the larger scientific community. He remarked that he "was not immune to some of the sense of concern with what it [Sputnik] might demonstrate by way of a great and unexpected advance in the technological capabilities of the Soviet Union." He added, however, that "*it was silly to conclude* from Russia's launch of Sputnik that all of our own scientific programs both within and without government had been brought into serious question, or that *it meant any really significant weakness on the part of our own science.*" Killian, in a speech shortly after Sputnik was sent into orbit, "sought to express reassurance that Sputnik was a tremendous achievement but it in no sense justified conclusions that American technology had fallen far behind." He added that he was confident in "regard to our industrial, our military, and our scientific capacity."[39]

Like his scientific colleagues discussed earlier in this chapter, Killian believed the Russian advances over the United States were mainly in the educational realm rather than in scientific accomplishments. He acknowledged that well before Sputnik "it was perfectly clear to some of us that the Russians had been making great advances in education and particularly in the education of scientists and engineers." He also qualified any sense of immediate alarm that he or other scientist felt about the situation, noting that "the Soviets were not making as spectacular advances in education as the general public discussion might indicate." He added that there "was lots of use of loose numbers in appraising the Soviet effort." To Killian, it became increasingly clear "that the Soviets were doing a kind of crash educational program in which they were training people to do very specific kinds of jobs, the kind of educational program that we [in the USA] undertook in time of war, particularly World War II."[40]

Thus the president's science advisor echoed the concerns about the schools that his scientific colleagues had been voicing well before Sputnik, though he did not see them as some sort of profound dilemma. Of course, voicing these concerns and acting on them in developing the National Defense Education Act put the schools under the public microscope and simultaneously removed from scrutiny the efforts of American science and technology that related most directly to what the Soviets were doing. In a way, the situation was almost too good to be true from the point of view of the nation's leading scientists. Sputnik proved to be a vehicle to facilitate their involvement in reforming secondary schools, thereby leaving their enterprise almost completely unexamined in the process.[41]

Killian, like James B. Conant and other prominent scientists, believed that true progress in the sciences could not be attained by neglecting other fields. This emphasis was often in the foreground of Killian's efforts on behalf of NDEA and other of the administration's education proposals. For example, in late December of 1957, as the Eisenhower administration was preparing its post-Sputnik education proposals to go to Congress, Killian spoke to the American Association for the Advancement of Science meeting in Washington. He described the proposed education act as both "designed to aid education generally" and containing "important provisions specifically directed at strengthening science education." The speech contained only slight reference to proposed legislation, however. More importantly, it laid out a general philosophy of the interrelationship between science and other fields. Killian noted that "the quality of our science and our science education cannot be separated out from the quality of our intellectual life generally." He went on to argue that the "current emphasis on science, if it is not to cause reactions adverse to science, also requires of the scientific community humility and a sense of proportion." These orientations pointed to the necessary recognition that "science is a partner, sharing and shouldering equally the responsibilities which vest in the great array of professions which provide the intellectual and cultural strength of society."[42]

As the presidential science advisor, Killian followed Waterman's tactic at the National Science Foundation and developed a system of panels within the PSAC for conducting the business of the group. One of those panels was devoted to the topic of education. In May of 1958, Killian wrote a memorandum for that panel as it prepared a report on science education. The theme of their work, he told the group, could be "the overriding need for higher quality and performance." This need required a productive interaction between science and the nonsciences. Specifically, Killian stressed that the chances of producing great science required "an educated community that understands science and values it as well as the Humanities, that views them both as essential parts of our common culture and the wholeness of learning." The education panel of the PSAC and Killian were definitely in agreement that science not be stressed to the omission of other fields. In December of 1957, the chair of the panel, Lee S. DuBridge, president of the California Institute of Technology and another prestigious scientist who served on many influential advisory groups and testified before Congress as it considered NDEA, remarked to Killian that schools needed "more and better teachers" at all levels and in all subjects. DuBridge added that the "primary goal" of educational improvement was necessarily general, that is in all fields, without regard to any specific subject-matter field.[43]

Scientists and Educators: A Distinctly Unequal Relationship

In chapter 4, I argued that the educators in the U.S. Office of Education (OE) benefited greatly from the passage of NDEA. I also argued, however, that this benefit accrued more directly to the federal educational agency than to the educational profession at large. In fact, the passage of NDEA coincided with the beginning of a long decline in the public image and influence of professional educators from elementary and secondary schools, and from teacher education programs in higher education. In contrast with the situation of educators, scientists maintained their position of prominence throughout the passage of NDEA, even enhancing it somewhat at the expense of educators. Also, there is no doubt that NSF suffered little, if at all, from the institutional success of OE with NDEA. Thus scientists and NSF emerged from the period of passage of the NDEA with an enhanced sense of their own worth that was matched by the political influence, and the public image, of the group and the agency.

Arguing that scientists flourished at least somewhat at the expense of educators during and after the passage of NDEA necessitates explaining how that was the case, given that NDEA increased educational expenditures significantly, as shown in chapter 4. The explanation is complex, involving both personal and institutional factors. Institutionally, increases in expenditures, in the number of employees and in the influence of OE were accompanied by similar developments in NSF. For example, following an end-of-the-year meeting in 1957 between Science Advisor James Killian and President Eisenhower, just before the Eisenhower administration version of what was to become NDEA was introduced to Congress, there was a dramatic increase in appropriations for NSF, the total amount of money for the agency almost tripling through an additional $40 million item for the NSF budget. This expenditure, according to Killian, was as much as scientists and NSF could use efficiently. Killian intimated that there might have been more coming from the administration, but that this amount was what he told the president was needed to implement a "full employment" policy among first-rate scientists. Killian also mentioned that Sputnik marked the beginning of a time of high expenditures for NSF. The budget after Sputnik, according to the science advisor, "went up tenfold." He added that this increase was "completely coherent with the understanding we had of science and its need."[44]

Killian acknowledged that, as science advisor, he had taken on a wider role, that of an informal "education advisor in the White House," after Sputnik. Part of that activity was playing a large part in the administration lobbying for NDEA, though Killian added that this effort was undertaken in close cooperation with HEW secretary Marion Folsom and assistant secretary Elliot Richardson. Killian added that Folsom was ill for most of the period during which NDEA was under consideration by Congress and that this led to an increased role for him as science advisor in promoting NDEA, especially the scholarship program that was so important to scientists. Killian also noted that he was influential in bringing Eisenhower around to the support of a loan title within NDEA. The president's initial opposition was based mainly, according to Killian, on a loan program at the Columbia University medical school while Eisenhower was president that went largely unused. Killian remarked that he was able to counter that experience by explaining to Eisenhower that the Columbia loan program was a financial operation initiated by bankers with interest and term policies that were more in tune with financial industry standards than with aiding students. The former MIT president added that during his own presidency, his institution had set up a student loan fund with a low interest rate that was "used right up to the hilt by students." In fact, more students applied for the loans available at MIT than anyone in the faculty or administration had anticipated.[45]

When asked specifically if he was representing all of education during the consideration and passage of NDEA, Killian did not answer the question directly. He responded, however, that he "gave great support to the overall philosophy and effort to bring the bill about, and to get support for it within the administration as well as Congress." This response revealed some of the conflict within the administration over the bill, resolution of which in favor of the bill was an acknowledged Killian accomplishment, and of the larger role a scientific advisor who spoke directly to the president exerted on behalf of a bill that contained much more in it than support for science.[46]

Eisenhower acknowledged the significance of Killian's activities in the administration, both in the service of science and in the larger educational arena. After Killian had announced his resignation as science advisor in May of 1959, to return to his MIT administrative position, Eisenhower wrote a personal letter to his first official advisor from academic science. Beginning the letter with "Dear Jim," Eisenhower acknowledged the vital service Killian had performed for his nation, contributing to its security and "to the strength of a large and fundamental section of our whole system of Education." Killian responded to the president, noting that the educational programs developed under Eisenhower "will stand as a milestone in the progress of American science and its effective use by Government."[47]

Recollection of these events from the education side of the Eisenhower administration was not at great variance with Killlan's account. HEW secretary Folsom remembered Killian entering the picture regarding the particulars of NDEA after the latter's appointment as science advisor. Because of the involvement of budget-oriented people in the administration who wanted to be careful about spending, Folsom added, he and Killian went over the administration version of the measure carefully in an effort to trim costs, partially by cutting the number of scholarships proposed in the bill. At a December 1957 cabinet meeting that discussed the administration's proposals for education, Folsom used Killian's views as support for his own advocacy of the education measure. He began by stating that "Dr. Killian believed this is a very good program" and added that Killian believed the proposed program needed "close coordination" with existing NSF programs.[48] Folsom later noted that HEW assistant secretary Elliot Richardson had worked with several university loan officers to make sure that a loan program, if it became part of the bill, would be seen favorably by university leaders. This recollection bore no mention of Killian's influence on President Eisenhower's position on the issue of loans, but, given that Killian had a more direct and regular line to the president than did members of the cabinet, it is not surprising that Folsom did not mention it. All in all, Folsom and Killian recorded parallel versions of administration activities on behalf of NDEA.[49]

Relations between NSF and OE were a topic of conversation in many corners of the Eisenhower administration, not just in the two agencies. In November of 1957, for example, presidential advisor Arthur E. Burns argued that any science education program proposal that would come forth should stress NSF involvement at the expense of OE participation. Burns argued that NSF was much better placed than OE to produce the scientists the president had called for in a recent speech on the topic. At the moment, both agencies had proposals for creating more scientists. NSF, for Burns, had the better proposal for several reasons. First, it already was authorized to do such work, and did not need a congressional authorization in support of the work like OE needed, but only an appropriation. Burns added that NSF would do the necessary work sooner than OE, because it already was operating with universities, the American Association for the Advancement of Science, and other scientific societies in supporting various science training programs. Finally, and perhaps most revealingly for the purposes of my argument about the greater influence of NSF, Burns argued that "HEW, and its Office of Education, does not have the prestige that NSF enjoys. Nor do the state offices of education with whom HEW would work. HEW simply would not get the support from scientists that NSF now has." Emphatically, Burns remarked, "These are some hard facts of educational life." He went on to note that the existing NSF science support programs involved stipends going directly to individuals, research grants to institutions, and scholarships to students, all of which avoided the OE debility of having to set up "another grant-in-aid program in the state offices of education." Such a cumbersome procedure that amounted to "establishing state organizations under subsidy from the Federal government with federal standards" would be "less effective [than NSF sponsorship] and would involve the Administration in the political difficulties that go with a grant program to 'control' education in the states." For Burns, the national objective was "to develop more scientists." He added that such development was "the job of scientists working with the National Science Foundation." Burns summarized his argument by noting that the NSF program was more effective in reaching the President's goals, that it was legislatively easier to accomplish than the HEW program, and that it avoided the political difficulties inherent in creating another large scale grant-in-aid program.[50]

As shown in chapter 3, the eventual proposal that came from the administration involved institutionalizing a program that put responsibility for federal support for science improvement in the high schools in OE. This support was not just for science education, however; it involved aiding foreign language instruction and counseling and guidance in the high schools, along with the sciences, and provided for a fellowship program in universities that supported many fields besides the sciences. The sciences, in addition to receiving a good deal of the money expended by NDEA, also benefited greatly from enhanced appropriations to support the existing research grants and allied programs in NSF. Science, and NSF, emerged stronger than ever with the passage of NDEA.

An internal administration memo acknowledged this reality. On August 26, 1958, less than two weeks before President Eisenhower signed NDEA into law, an NSF official remarked that his agency "had no objection to approval of H.R. 13247." According to the NSF official, the legislation addressed the need for progress in science, as well as the need for "the ever increasing attention [to] be given to the education of the young people in the United States." For NSF, the memo noted, NDEA met the spirit of the president's education program as he had outlined it in January 1958, and it acknowledged that both OE and NSF had proper responsibilities in the education arena. The memo ended with the reassurance that "we believe that the two agencies can work cooperatively."[51]

The belief in interagency cooperation of this NSF official was shared by the OE staff. The two agencies were able to work together without visible conflict for the next several years, as OE implemented the various titles of NDEA and NSF greatly expanded its research and higher education programs in various science fields. NSF made sure its effective advocacy of science was not undertaken in any obvious denigration of other academic fields, particularly the social sciences and the humanities. Since faculty members in all of these fields were likely to be housed in some version of a College of Arts and Sciences, the scientists knew instinctively that they should not alienate their colleagues in other disciplines at the same time that they were receiving financial support in the form of grants and fellowships from NSF that far outstripped anything that went, or would go, to the other fields.

The Education Panel of the President's Science Advisory Committee

The scientists discussed above were generally of one mind regarding the propagation and development of their group of subjects in the 1950s and 1960s. While scientists engaged in the same scholarly battles within their fields that characterized most scholarly endeavor in other fields, scientists, regardless of their special field, usually agreed with one another on what was necessary for the institutional health of their work. Presidential science advisor James Killian, who also served as chair of the PSAC, conducted the business of that group through an assortment of panels. One of those panels was an Education Panel. Its task was to consider and recommend policies relating to the education of scientists. This was a major task that had much to do with the preservation and improvement of the scientific enterprise.

The late spring and early summer of 1958 were a landmark time both for the Education Panel of the PSAC and for the National Defense Education Act. The importance was very different in each case, however. NDEA was wending its way toward passage, a process in which scientists had an important stake. As shown in earlier chapters, science education was not the most important priority for any of the sponsors of NDEA, nor was NDEA the most important priority for scientists. The development of a statement on science education by the Education Panel of the PSAC had begun well before the 1958 development of NDEA. During that year, the two tasks proceeded in parallel fashion, but also discretely.

In addition to developing its report on education, however, the panel kept a careful eye on NDEA. Just as it was to be signed into law by President Eisenhower, the chair of the PSAC panel on education invited the new secretary of the Department of Health, Education, and Welfare, Arthur Flemming, to meet with his group. The invitation was accompanied by a message of congratulations on Flemming's recent appointment, and a statement of widespread concern in the panel that within the Office of Education there was "a tendency to have the program directed by the 'professional educationists,' as contrasted to the scholars, scientists, and other teachers in subject-matter fields." Education Panel chairman Lee S. DuBridge did not indicate that this concern bothered him personally, but he suggested to Secretary Flemming that it could be countered by "the appointment of an advisory committee of scientists and scholars to avoid the danger of this fear." There is no record of Flemming's response to this invitation or suggestion from the PSAC. It seems clear that he had enough to do in his huge department without involving himself personally, or the department, in establishing a committee of scientists that necessarily involved intramural relationships within the administration over which he had no formal control. The hubris of the scientists in suggesting a group of scientific advisors for the HEW secretary was obvious, and it stood in clear contrast to their consideration of issues in science education without any help from professional educators or school administrators.[52]

But, as suggested earlier, the major work of the Education Panel was development of its report on science education. A structure for the report was suggested in January of 1958, when the panel chair wrote to three influential members of his group, two of whom were Jerrold Zacharias and Alan Waterman. The chair suggested that the report address the task of solving educational problems and that it be broken down into four sections: elementary education, secondary education, undergraduate education, and graduate education.[53]

The report of the Panel on Education was published in the spring of 1959. Its structure did not follow the suggestion of Chairman DuBridge as made in January of 1958. The report, *Education for the Age of Science,* did not say a word about elementary education. The extant panel records do not indicate a reason for this absence. It seems logical to conclude, however, that it was related to the fact that the scientists knew nothing and cared little about science in the elementary school, a topic that differed drastically from the research enterprise in which they were engaged. They had much to say, however, about science education in high schools, as well as in undergraduate and graduate education.[54]

Most of the education panel report echoed sentiments already discussed in this chapter. In other words, there was a broad consensus on issues related to the education of scientists among the scientists, mostly the physical scientists, who were prominent in research and government service related to that research. The first and politically the most important item in that consensus was in the first sentence of a brief statement from President Eisenhower that prefaced the report. According to the president, "This report makes clear that the strengthening of science and engineering education requires the strengthening of all education."[55] The first chapter of the report echoed the point made by the president when it discussed the educational enterprise in general, stressing the social importance of education and its intimate relationship with the goal of meeting the individual educational needs of each American child. After identifying the goal of a full educational opportunity for each child, and indicating that this did not mean the same program for all children, the report mentioned brilliant children, slow children, and artisans (as distinguished from intellectuals) as areas within which different program emphases might be expected. Next, the report cautioned against allowing the tendency to reward practical achievement to become an anti-intellectual stance that devalued intellectual excellence. Finally, in the introductory material, the report identified two desirable goals: the first was achieving excellence in development of various specialized talents and the second was the desirability of a general education program for all in our democratic society that allowed the latter group to understand and appreciate the accomplishments of the former.[56]

The report then moved to a brief consideration of the importance of science and technology in society and an identification of the major educational tasks to be addressed. The first task was to attend to the development of intellectual excellence.

The next major task addressed in the report was the improvement of the teaching force in both the high school and in higher education. After a few paragraphs on the numbers of teachers that would soon be needed in all subjects, numbers that could not be produced without a significant alteration of the existing system, science teachers were mentioned specifically as a group that was woefully short on subject matter knowledge. This shortage was due in large part to the "competing requirements of 'teacher-training' subjects." Given the rapidly expanding boundaries of science, the high school science teacher, "sometimes inadequately prepared in the first place, . . . tends to fall further and further behind with each passing year."[57] The report posed several solutions to the situation, including freeing teachers from nonteaching tasks, increasing salaries, providing the opportunity for teachers to increase their understanding of their subjects, and renovating teacher training to stress substance in subject matter as a requirement for initial licensure and for salary increments or other promotions.[58]

After another lengthy discussion of talent, and the necessity of a large, comprehensive high school in order to develop that talent properly, the report discussed a few other aspects of education for science. In another nod to general education and those who were responsible for its development, the panel argued that the future scientist in high school needed "adequate preparation in English, history, and languages," and recommended minimum years of study in these and other fields. The recommended minimums were four years for English, three of mathematics, two of science, three in one modern language, and two in social science, including history. After the panel added that exposure to subjects such as art and music was also desirable, it concluded that the recommended program "obviously leaves little room for nonintellectual subjects in the curriculum," subjects it termed as being offered in "less vital courses." In case the meaning of the recommendations for more occupationally oriented fields was not crystal clear, the panel concluded that subjects "like shorthand, accounting, or home management ought to be reserved primarily for those for whom academic work is not appropriate."[59] Interdisciplinary, or problem-related courses, those that combined various subject matters in a push for relevance and problem solving were not even discussed in the report. Obviously, the panel had little use for such studies, which were often the favorite devices of school administrators, professors of education, and other educational leaders to liven up the high school curriculum and make it attractive to students. The panel saw these types of studies, and their advocates, as rivals of the subject matter competency that was its primary goal.

After discoursing briefly on needed improvements in undergraduate science education, science education for adults, and graduate education in the sciences, the panel returned to the high school science teacher as a major focus for its conclusions. Its recommendation was that high school teachers should collaborate with scientists and engineers so that high school students could be brought into more productive relations with practicing scientists. Additionally, it advocated cooperative work on curriculum reform by scientists and science teachers to develop curriculum, "especially in the sciences and mathematics, with the aims of reducing the alleged conflict between subject matter and methodology." A drastic improvement in teacher training was an immediate goal for the education panel. Just as importantly, reform was to "bring about a better understanding between scholars, scientists, teachers, educators, and the public in regard to the philosophy, goals, and methods of the educational system."[60]

There is little doubt the high school was the major target for the reforms advocated by the education panel of the PSAC. There is also little doubt the educational leadership cadres that shaped the high school curriculum, especially educational administrators and professors of educational methods in the various subjects, were the group the panel believed needed to have its influence on the high school curriculum severely reduced, if not altogether eliminated. In many ways, the education panel simply encouraged and attempted to build on the work being done on the new high school science curriculum by physicists and mathematicians, seeking its extension into the other scientific subjects. This should not be a surprise, given that Jerrold Zacharias, MIT physics professor and leader of the Physical Science Studies Commission (PSSC) that was developing a new physics syllabus for high schools, was a prominent member of the education panel.

Thus the enmity between scientists and educators proved to be a major force in the activities of the Panel on Education of the PSAC. While the group was careful to cultivate other academic specialists in the humanities and social sciences in order to enlist them in the campaign to alter the high school curriculum, and while it preferred not to criticize the educationists directly, the major target of the PSAC education panel's criticisms of the high schools was clearly the leaders of the nation's schools, particularly its high schools, and the schools of education that claimed far too much responsibility for training high school teachers.

The Gifted and Talented

The identification and encouragement of gifted and talented students was a major concern for scientists, including those on the panel on education of the PSAC. As scientists engaged the issues of school improvement, through NDEA or through the other organizations discussed above, they expressed special concern for the able students in high schools and elsewhere. Talent was of such importance to the scientists that I have chosen to discuss it separately. The goal of this discussion is to gain perspective on how the scientists saw their pursuit of talent and excellence in relation to an educational system ostensibly devoted to democracy.

It would be tedious to indicate the many invocations of talent, quality, excellence, or giftedness by the various advocates of reform in science education discussed in this chapter. Almost every one of the scientists mentioned in this chapter, and every scientist who testified before the congressional committees on NDEA, invoked giftedness, talent, or high ability in students as a necessary focus for an adequate educational system, especially but not only in science, mathematics, and engineering. More productive than mention of numerous versions of the talent development argument, or the education of the gifted emphasis, is a look in depth at the argument as it was developed in specific cases in order to see what evidence there was behind it.

The thrust of the argument for stressing the education of the gifted and talented, whether offered by scientists or by others, was that there was a distressing gap between the numbers of gifted who went to college and the total number of gifted or talented students. Those who proffered this argument often did not refer to any data to back it up, but spoke always as if there were concrete data on which to base the argument. The PSAC Panel on Education, for example, began its treatment of educating the gifted with an obligatory mention of the democratic character of American education, which meant that all students needed to be served, and served well, by the educational system. After stating, and restating, this priority, the panel then moved to a different twist in argument for democratic education. It stated: "we recognize that in a democracy we should provide each individual with the opportunity to develop his talents to the fullest. It would be difficult to think of anything less democratic than a system that sacrifices in any way the stimulation of the bright student, either to learn more or to progress faster through prescribed work." The panel went on to applaud the offering of Advanced Placement (AP) courses in high schools as an effective way of challenging the talented, and to decry the various circumstances that prevented some high schools from offering those courses and the gifted students in those high schools from being able to take AP courses in other high schools where they were offered.[61]

The panel called the situation to the attention of foundations, corporations, and individuals who were interested in investing in the scholarly improvement of American society. This plea for philanthropic support for expanding opportunity for gifted students stuck in ungifted high schools, an awkward but accurate term that no formal study group would ever use to describe a high school, addressed only a subset of what the panel considered the most acute problem in the education of the gifted in the United States.[62] That problem was the financial handicaps that often caused gifted students at any level of education to circumscribe their development by not going on to the next level of the educational system. The panel critiqued the high school explicitly for poor service to the gifted, though its analysis of the problem called into question post-high-school education as well.

The panel indicated the high priority it put on the issue of appropriate educational opportunity for the gifted: "under no conditions should able young people be forced to discontinue their education at any level for economic reasons. They are the nation's most valuable, and its ultimate, asset. The nation as a whole should take the responsibility for seeing that they are permitted to make themselves as useful as they can become." Failing to meet this challenge was not an option for the panel. They concluded the section on the gifted as follows: "It is scarcely possible to put the matter too strongly. The potentially great scientist or engineer, scholar, physician, or educator who ends up, through no fault of his own, as an underling at a task below his native endowment, represents an indefensible national loss."[63]

Of course, the fact that the panel sought help only from private sources as a solution to the situation meant that the national loss they feared had already taken place. Recall that the NDEA as passed by Congress did not contain the scholarship program that was designed to address the need for financial support for the gifted identified by the panel, and vigorously supported by NDEA's main congressional sponsors as well as by the Eisenhower administration. Asking foundations, corporations, or individual donors to respond to this acute crisis after the scholarships were not approved in federal educational legislation meant that the need far outpaced the private sector remedies being sought. Before considering the consequences of this, however, a look at the data behind the insufficient educational opportunity for the gifted argument is in order.

James Bryant Conant provided a set of recommendations for educational policy in the United States in a book he published in 1964 titled *Shaping Educational Policy.*[64] This work, published after two of Conant's volumes on the high school and on education in impoverished urban areas, presented Conant's idea of structural and administrative reforms to solve the educational problems of the United States. Conant indicated the core of his idea when he stressed cooperation between state educational agencies and state chief education officers who would work together in search of a "nationwide" rather than a national educational policy.[65]

The term *nationwide* allowed Conant to avoid the brickbats that would be thrown at his, or any, analysis that advocated national, or federal, intrusion into state educational affairs. For purposes of my analysis, however, it is more important that Conant, in listing issues to be addressed in this nationwide educational policy, chose to concentrate on the problem of able students. This should not be surprising, since the able, or talented, or gifted had been a subject of concern for Conant in most, if not all, of his published work on education. Conant's discussion of the need for nationwide policies such as accommodation of the gifted required that they be based on solid research. While data-driven is the contemporary term for this type of work, Conant's wording was "More facts, fewer slogans." As a perfect example of this approach, Conant mentioned a study sponsored by the NSF on high ability youth. He remarked that the study indicated "that on a national basis an alarmingly small percentage of able boys and girls go on to education in college and finish college."[66]

This notion of an inappropriately small representation of the gifted or talented in college was a staple of the arguments of most scientists, and of others, who believed that American education was woefully lacking in serving this group. It is important, therefore, for purposes of evaluating the acuity of the argument for the gifted, to look at the data that lay behind it. When one studies the NSF report on the education of high ability youth carefully, one comes away with as many questions about the argument as one does with answers to the problem it chose to address. The report offered the argument that there was a substantial loss in enrollment of able high school students between high school graduation and enrollment in college. More specifically, in considering the top 30 percent of a high school graduating class, as chosen by test scores, it noted that while the group graduated from high school at a rate of 89 percent, it enrolled in college only at a rate of 69 percent. Considering the top 10 percent of the class, the situation was even more disturbing: while 91 percent of this group graduated from high school, only 77 percent entered college. The report then considered a variety of evidence offered to explain this disturbing gap and concluded that, according to the studies it considered, "financial difficulty appears to be the largest single reason why high-ability high school graduates do not go on to college."[67]

To reach its conclusions the report relied first on data from a national study by Dale Wolfle, chief executive officer of the American Association for the Advancement of Science, published in 1954 and based on data from the 1952–53 high school graduating class.[68] Additionally, it considered evidence from several other national and state studies completed after Wolfle's that confirmed his results. While the extent of the gap between high ability student graduation from high school and entrance to college varied from study to study, the variance was slight enough in the size of the gap to allow for the conclusion to be drawn that it existed, and was sizable, amounting to one-third of high ability students (students in the top 30 percent of a graduating class) across the studies.[69]

Just as importantly, the finding of financial need as the single most important barrier to enrollment in college for high ability students was consistent from study to study. For example, in discussing a study of Merit Scholarship semifinalists who did not go on to college, the NSF report noted that "85 percent said they would have done so if financial assistance had been available." While the evidence was limited on the details of financial need, the report concluded that financial difficulties were the cause of lack of enrollment for "roughly one-half of those students who did not enter" and that a higher proportion of the group said "they would have gone if scholarship assistance had been offered.[70]

It must be said that, given the vagaries of social science research, in the 1950s and 1960s as well as in our own time, this report was a formidable effort. Its data were copious and were presented in a fashion that allowed the reader to see how the conclusions offered in its pages were reached, and, more importantly, how counterconclusions could be reached. Yet nowhere in any of the studies reported in this NSF report was there strong evidence that supports the argument of scientists and most other academic critics of the American high school that the high school curriculum, or in the case of able students dropping out from college, that the college curriculum, was a major part of the problem. The report came close to acknowledging this in the conclusions section of its initial chapter but, instead, chose to restate the unsubstantiated argument voiced by scientists about the inadequacy of the curriculum. There the report noted that although expense was the "most important deterrent to college entrance" of high ability students, and to a lesser extent for the "withdrawal of many of those who did enter," other factors such as lack of interest in study or lack of goal orientation and determination to reach a goal were significant. In this statement, however, nothing specific about the curriculum was mentioned. Yet the introductory chapter went on to conclude, with absolutely no evidence offered, that although losses of high ability young people in enrolling and completing college were "traceable to certain basic values and attitudes within our society, the failure to stimulate and challenge high-ability students early in their educational experience *must often be responsible.*"[71]

In addition to drawing conclusions seemingly unrelated to the evidence presented in the text, the report was inconsistent in its argument about standardized test scores. In its methodological chapter, the report noted "the imperfection of objective tests as devices for measuring ability is fully recognized."[72] In the rest of the report, however, though other data such as class rank were occasionally mentioned, test scores were the essential means used to measure ability, talent, or giftedness, in spite of the admonition quoted above. Stating the problematic nature of the use of test scores as an index of talent did not, therefore, stop the NSF from proceeding as if test scores were the most important, and the most reliable, criterion of talent. The report represented, then, a rigorous but seriously flawed analysis of the talent at various levels of the educational system. Any decisions taken based on its evidence and analysis, however, whether by parents, schools, or policymakers, too often ignored the flaws and proceeded as if they did not exist.

Science and Education: A Conclusion

This lengthy excursion into the scientists' position on the educational situation during and after NDEA reveals a powerful, politically astute group that acted effectively to protect, and to enhance, gains it had recently won through war-related research. Whether through lobbying, a presidential advisory committee, its own government agency the NSF, or through empirical research, the scientists devoted themselves to their agenda of pursuing their research and taking steps to deflect questions about that agenda raised from any quarter, whether it be the public, its representatives in the Congress, other academic specialists, or educators. Most astutely, the scientists were able to use the turmoil surrounding Soviet science that had preceded Sputnik, but intensified after the launch of the Soviet satellite, as an occasion to call into question science education in the high schools. This allowed scientists to pursue their own approach to science education reform, independent of any input from the school people. More importantly, the attention paid to the high school helped avoid any rigorous or critical analysis of the programs and actions of the scientists in their laboratories or in their classrooms.

A few other weaknesses in the program of the scientists deserve mention here. First, in the long run, the scientists did little to reform the high school curriculum, in spite of the efforts of the PSSC and other disciplinary attempts at high school course revision. A definitive study of these curriculum revisions by John Rudolph concludes that the scientists, who had critiqued progressive education for its functionality, produced a set of courses that were also functional, though in a different way. The functionality of the progressives was geared to trying to help students understand, and live in, their society. The functionality of the scientists was geared to understanding, or at the least to appreciating, the work of scientists in that society.[73] Neither approach paid particular attention to the intellectual issues involved in the proper instruction of high school students in the principles of science.

Next, the inadequacies of the work that scientists produced about science itself deserve brief attention. Importantly, the same disdain of school people that scientists exhibited in their campaigns for subject matter reform in the high school characterized their other activities. In a letter to the president about publication of the report of the Panel on Education of the President's Science Advisory Committee, a prominent science educator began with an appreciation for the task of improving science education addressed in the report. The science educator, however, criticized the confining of the effort in the report to only "certain narrow selected segments" of the enterprise and not to science education generally. He added that the panel lacked representation from secondary school people such as a science teacher or supervisor, or a state or local school administrator. Such representation, he concluded, might have prevented unfortunate references in the report such as one that insinuated that the schools acted as if all students were equal intellectually, and another that condescended to vocational students and vocational studies as activities and individuals below the proper reach of educational effort.[74]

Presidential science advisor James Killian was not overly impressed with the report of the PSAC on education. Killian remarked that "the education report was not as good as it might have been" even though its release by the White House garnered front-page stories in the nation's newspapers. What the report didn't do, however, was address seriously the prospects for sound science education in the nation's educational institutions. In spite of this, it contained many self-congratulatory references that, in turn, formed the base for its advocacy of more financial support of science from the federal government. Killian added that this was one occasion on which the president's admiration for scientists outran his good judgment. Eisenhower's implied endorsement of the report overlooked its inadequacies and its special pleading for federal financial support, with little solid evidence to justify it. The president thus overrode his own budgetary convictions about the careful investment of federal dollars to endorse a plea for funds made without serious consideration of what was to be funded and why.[75]

The agency within the federal government that spoke for science, the National Science Foundation (NSF), survived the enhancement of the Office of Education (OE) from the NDEA. While NSF funding increases did not match the OE increases caused by NDEA, the science body protected its core mission of support for basic science research and received substantial increases in funding for that effort. Also, it continued to pursue its educational activities that were geared to radical changes in school science at the same time that its official position on educational affairs was nonconfrontational with both OE and the school systems and officials in them that were supported by OE.

The NDEA era for science and scientists, then, represented a time of accomplishment. Scientists, unlike educators, managed to protect and even to enhance their public position and their material prospects. Few people looked down on scientists after NDEA, though many continued to criticize educators, in spite of, or perhaps because of, NDEA. Let us return now to direct consideration of the legislation, as put into practice during the first decade after its passage.

6
NDEA, 1958 to 1965

The enactment of NDEA in September 1958 initiated a period of markedly increased federal activity in education, in elementary and secondary schools as well as in colleges and universities. For the first time, the federal government became directly involved in improving the provision of services to schools such as counseling and guidance programs (though the service was mainly through support of college and university programs and fellowships for counselors and teachers who wanted to help students), and in the provision of equipment and other support for instruction in science subjects in all schools that requested it.[1] It was not until 1965, however, that the Elementary and Secondary Education Act (ESEA) institutionalized the principle of much more massive federal aid to education, this time for new purposes, most notably the improvement of educational opportunity for the poor. Until ESEA, NDEA was the major legislative achievement in the federal aid to education campaign. The forerunner of ESEA, NDEA was dwarfed both in amount of funding and in the reach of its educational programs by its successor.

The amount of federal funds expended on elementary and secondary education increased dramatically with NDEA. Precise figures are difficult to obtain, and amounts vary considerably considering whether authorizations, allotments, or appropriations are considered. The main point to be made, however, as illustrated in the chart of authorized amounts for NDEA's first four years, is that the federal funding for NDEA dwarfed prior programs. As noted, the authorizations for the first four years of $890 million neared the billion dollar threshold.

More particularly, in the first three years of NDEA's existence, a total of over $115 million was spent on K-12 classroom equipment, $53 million was allotted to state educational agencies and colleges for testing and guidance programs and institutes, and $2.8 million was provided to state agencies for improvements in statistical services provided to public schools.[2] This increase

Table 1. NDEA funds authorized for education for its first four years, 1958–59 to 1961–62

Category	1958–59	1959–60	1960–61	1961–62	Total (in millions)
Student Loans (Title II)	$47.5	$75	$82.5	$90	$295
Aid to Schools and States for Science, Mathematics, Foreign Language (Title III)	$75	$75	$75	$75	$300
Graduate Fellowships (Title IV)	$5.3	$13.45	$21.9	$24.75	$65.4
Guidance, Counseling and Testing (Title V)	$21.25	$22.25	$22.25	$22.25	$88
Language Development (Title VI)	$15.25	$15.25	$15.25	$15.25	$61
Media Research (Title VII)	$3	$5	$5	$5	$18
Vocational Education (Title VIII)	$15	$15	$15	$15	$60
State Statistics* (Title X)	$.4	$.4	$.4	$.4	$1.6
Total Federal Funds authorized					$890

Source: *School Life: Official Journal of the Office of Education* (October–November 1958): 5, 14 (copy in Lister Hill Papers, Box 238, Folder 90).

*Amount appropriated depended on requests from states. 1958–59 total is the actual appropriation; I simply used the 1958–59 appropriated amount for the next three years also.

continued in the years up to 1965, a period in which total federal elementary and secondary aid to education almost tripled from $2.1 billion in 1959 to $5.7 billion in 1965. While NDEA funds were only a part of these larger amounts, they increased from nearly $170 million in 1959 to $310 million in 1965.[3]

The conclusion of one analyst of educational policy, writing ten years after passage of NDEA, was, "the National Defense Education Act shows that special-purpose aid, carefully designed, could be enacted at a time when general-purpose aid could not be."[4] This evaluation was both correct and incomplete. It was correct in the sense that it was a literal description of what NDEA was when it was passed: an attempt to improve education in specific ways, such as the upgrading of science, mathematics, and foreign language education; the enhancement in numbers of high ability students, and others, going to college; and a significant increase in the number of college teachers in all subjects. The evaluation was incomplete, however, in the sense that it did not consider the future of NDEA as envisioned by its two congressional sponsors and the opposing view of much of the Eisenhower administration. Lister Hill and Carl Elliott understood quite well that it was likely NDEA would be far more than the temporary bill envisioned by President Eisenhower and that its provisions could, and likely would, be expanded to include fields other than those specified in the original bill. It is also significant to recall that, even in the original NDEA, the graduate fellowships provided in Title VI were not confined to particular academic fields, but rather were designed to address a general shortage of college teachers.

Elliott and Hill worked assiduously to make sure that NDEA lasted longer than its initial authorization period of four years, though their work had to be filtered through the local and national political climates in which they operated. The issues of race and religion that had bedeviled federal aid to education did not disappear in the period after NDEA was enacted. In fact, both issues intensified, though for different reasons. The election of John Kennedy, a Roman Catholic, to the presidency in 1960 meant that the religious school problem became even more controversial in national politics. The significance of religious schools as an issue was also increased by the election of more Democratic congressmen, mostly in large cities, particularly in the 1964 Democratic landslide that also resulted in Lyndon Johnson's reelection. Many of these new congressmen were Catholics and all of them knew that responsiveness to those who elected them, especially the white working-class Catholics in American cities, meant that inclusion of Catholic schools in federal aid provisions was an issue that needed to be addressed. In Alabama, though, the largely conservative Protestant electorate remained steadfast in its belief that aid to Catholic schools was a violation of the constitutional separation of church and state, a belief that was invigorated by a visceral anti-Catholicism that saw Catholics, especially but not only immigrant Catholics, as less than complete Americans.

Race also was a constant thorn in the side of advocates of general federal aid in the early 1960s, because of the threat of Powell or Powell-like amendments to legislation that prohibited funds from going to districts that were not desegregated. After 1964, when a powerful Civil Rights Act was passed, race played a lesser role in the debates over federal aid to education. Title VI of this act authorized the withholding of federal funds from school districts that did not desegregate and thus removed the necessity for amendments like those that had often accompanied federal aid bills prior to 1964.

In the years between 1958 and 1964, several attempts were made to pass general federal aid to education; they all foundered on the shoals of race and/or religion. For example, President Kennedy's general federal aid bill of 1961 was defeated in the House of Representatives by "a coalition of Republicans who opposed general aid, Catholics who resented fellow-Catholic Kennedy's exclusion of aid to parochial schools, and southerners who feared the civil rights wedge of federal school funds."[5] Kennedy, a Roman Catholic whose potential occupancy of the White House alarmed many Protestant Americans, had promised during his campaign for the presidency not to aid parochial schools. When he kept that promise by excluding Catholic and other religious schools from his general federal aid proposed program, he alienated many of his fellow Catholics.

Yet Kennedy was never a committed supporter of public schools. He had never attended a public school or a public institution of higher education and his appointments to the highest position in the Office of Education were made with little cognizance of public school interests. Neither his first appointee as OE commissioner, Sterling McMurrin, a professor of philosophy from the University of Utah, nor his second, Francis Keppel, dean of the Graduate School of Education at Harvard University, had a public school background or orientation. Kennedy's ineffectiveness in passing general federal aid to education was due at least in part, then, to deficiencies in his grasp of the situation as well as to his convictions about public and parochial schools.[6] While Congress was clearly an impediment to passage of Kennedy's proposed educational legislation, the president failed to master either the politics or the substance of the federal aid to education controversy, and his failure harmed the effort to pass general federal aid.

Kennedy faced continued difficulties on educational aid through the rest of his presidency. He failed to pass a higher education bill in 1962 and failed on another general aid to education bill in 1963. As a solution to the political blockage of general federal aid in 1963, as had happened in 1961, NDEA was renewed, each time with some increase in funding. Thus NDEA served as a vehicle through which to renew the national commitment to aid to education and to increase funding for various federal aid programs, without extending the reach of federal legislation into different realms. Since the NDEA title providing funds to schools for equipment in science classrooms allowed loans to private schools for this purpose, religious school supporters could favor its continuation and renewal and try to increase the funds for loans as part of that renewal. New educational federal aid programs, however, were stymied.

NDEA saw regular increases in its funding, beginning in the first year after its enactment, though not without continued work by its supporters. Conservatives in the Eisenhower administration threatened the prospects for NDEA when it came up for an early renewal a year after its passage, and opposition to renewal continued in the early years of the Kennedy administration. In the latter case, Arthur S. Flemming, then a former secretary of the Department of Health, Education, and Welfare (HEW), helped the publisher of *Parents* magazine, who had spearheaded a citizens' committee for NDEA in 1958, to reestablish the group as the Citizens' Committee for Extension of the National Defense Education Act as NDEA renewal was floundering in 1961.[7] The work of supporters of renewal and NDEA supporters in Congress and the administration succeeded not only in gaining renewal when it became an issue but also in gaining some increases in funding.

For example, in June of 1959, the commissioner of education announced an allocation for 842 graduate fellowships under NDEA, in addition to the initial allotment approved less than one year earlier. This addition was accomplished through an authorization by the president on May 20. The addition meant that a total of 1,000 graduate fellowships had been authorized during NDEA's first year.[8] The press release announcing the new authorization also noted that the fields in which the fellowships were approved varied widely, including "such studies as Far Eastern and Slavic Language and Literature, Child Development, American Studies, Quantitative Economics, Biochemistry and Solid State Physics." The release also noted that one-fifth of the fellowships were in the humanities, a slightly higher portion was in the social sciences, smaller portions (5 and 6 percent respectively) were in education and engineering, more than one-fourth were in the physical sciences and mathematics, and slightly less than one-fifth were in the biological sciences.[9] Thus, almost from its very beginnings, the graduate fellowship program, while ostensibly stressing the sciences, also provided almost one-half of its support to the humanities, the social sciences, and education.

By September of 1963, five years after the initial passage of NDEA and one year after its second renewal, $181 million had been spent on equipment and other measures for strengthening school instruction in science, mathematics, and foreign languages. These funds had allowed the number of language laboratories in public schools to increase from forty-six in 1958 to almost six thousand. Also, more than 180,000 local public school projects for equipment and other instructional improvement had been approved. Academic institutes for foreign language teachers had enrolled almost 14,000 teachers in over three hundred programs. The total spent on these programs was over $25 million. Over $65 million had been spent on guidance programs, with the result that the number of guidance counselors had increased from 12,000 in 1958 to 27,000 five years later. Also, $30 million had been spent on special institutes to improve the counseling abilities of high school teachers and counselors. In the 1963–64 academic year, over $7 million was spent on seventy-six NDEA Guidance and Counseling Training Institutes with over 2,200 students enrolled in them. Additionally, large expenditures through the vocational education title had been made for the education of technical specialists. Close to $20 million had been spent on research on the effective use of various educational media in enhancing instruction, with 227 research projects undertaken and 159 contracts awarded for disseminating results of the research. And finally, forty-eight state educational agencies had taken advantage of NDEA funds to improve and expand their statistical services to local school systems, with over $5 million spent on this aspect of NDEA since 1958.[10]

At the same time that appropriation increases and congressional renewals of NDEA were taking place, groups in areas far afield from science, mathematics, and foreign languages sought inclusion in NDEA funding for equipment and other instructional improvement. In the summer of 1964, for example, the executive director of the American Political Science Association wrote to Congressman Carl Elliott seeking the inclusion of civics and government as subjects eligible for federal assistance in equipment and teacher training. At the same time, school librarians in Alabama and throughout the nation sought inclusion in the funding available through NDEA for equipment and instruction.[11]

In October of 1964, these and other efforts proved successful when Congress added several amendments in its renewal of NDEA. The amendments included provision for training institutes for school librarians, media specialists, teachers of the disadvantaged, and teachers of English, reading, history, and geography. Equipment purchases and other instructional improvements in these fields were also approved. The number of graduate fellowships for college teachers was set to increase from its 1964 figure of 1,500 to 7,500 by 1967, and the number of fields in which those fellowships were to be offered was again expanded. The 1964 authorization for these fellowships was $7 million. Other amendments extended NDEA loans to half-time college students, doubled the appropriations for state supervisors in instructional fields, and extended the reach of the guidance and counseling provisions of NDEA to include elementary schools and junior colleges, along with high schools. The total authorization of the 1964 amendments was $1.8 billion, and their purpose was specified: to "broaden the coverage to more learners, more teachers, and more programs." The student loan program, which will be discussed extensively in the next section of this chapter, was also expanded in terms of the amount available for loans and of the academic background of students eligible for a loan.[12]

The total 1965 appropriation for NDEA activities was almost $350 million, with loans making up the largest single portion of that amount ($145 million), followed by instructional equipment ($70.5 million), guidance, counseling, and testing institutes ($56 million), graduate fellowships ($32.75 million), and smaller amounts to language and area centers, media research, and grants to states for statistical services. The same document that summarized the 1965 NDEA expenditures indicated that over $80 million more was in the request for the next year.[13]

Before the passage of ESEA in 1964, NDEA was therefore the signature program of federal aid to public education, a program that provided enough aid to private schools to prevent them from opposing it, and a measure that allowed Congress to make good on its declared interest in the improvement of American education. Congress and the administration, in addition to increasing the funding of NDEA, increased the reach of its various programs to serve students in an amazing variety of fields, without, however, crossing the boundary into aid for the poor and disadvantaged, which would be crossed with ESEA.

NDEA Title II: The Student Loan Program

The largest single program in NDEA, in the amount of funds expended and in the number of individuals reached, was Title II, the Student Loan Program. This program was the last to get underway, beginning in February of 1959, but it quickly exceeded all other programs in its institutional reach, number of participants, and dollars spent. While the repayment provision meant that funds expended would be partially replaced in future years, repayment did not begin until after graduation and was forgiven up to 50 percent over a five year period for students who taught full time in public elementary or secondary schools. The February authorization and a supplemental appropriation proposed at that same time were intended to provide over 30,000 loans, if students sought the maximum amount of $1,000 per year for each loan. The indications were, however, that more than 30,000 students would be helped since students were typically not seeking the full amount of support available. The first authorized sum of over $30 million for loans provided for only half of the $62 million that had been sought by the 1,227 educational institutions that initially applied for NDEA loan funds.[14]

In administering the student loan program, the Office of Education (OE) provided access to loans for students who applied for and received funding through a college or other similar institution. Ninety percent of the loan funds for each college came from the federal government, and institutions could borrow even their required 10 percent share of loan funds if necessary. Institutions applied to the Office of Education for their loan funds. To administer the program, OE employed the director of the New York State Regents' Scholarship and Examinations Program, who was granted a leave of absence to assume his Washington duties. While only half of the amount requested by students for loans was available initially, the process of granting the loans allowed every institution that applied to receive at least some of the funds it sought. Specific allocations were made on the basis of individual institutional requests in each state in proportion to the total number of institutional requests in the state and nationally. The release announcing the loan program was accompanied by a table indicating the amounts granted initially to each state and to individual institutions within that state. This information was valuable especially for members of Congress who could then report to their constituents how much money had been loaned to colleges and students in their states and districts.[15]

Shortly after the announcement of the specifics of Title II in February of 1959, Representative Carl Elliott testified before a subcommittee of the House of Representatives Appropriations Committee in support of additional funding for all titles of NDEA, but especially for Title II. For Elliott, this was the one program of NDEA that stood out "as facing a crucial shortage of funds." He noted that the $30 million requested by the administration for Title II was dwarfed by the documented demand for loans. Specifically, he added that "there will be a cumulative discrepancy of $62.5 million between the authorizations and the appropriations in the first two years of this four year program." He went on to recommend a program of more, but smaller, loans to meet the demand, but even in this case, he remarked, "it will be necessary to appropriate at least $40 million for next year," an amount that was

"$10 million more than the Administration has requested." Elliott concluded his testimony by noting that it had been "one of the most gratifying experiences of my Congressional career to be able to participate . . . in bringing to fruition this great dream we have had for education."[16]

In August of 1959, OE announced the provisions for the loan program for the next academic year. Both the number of institutions seeking loan funds and the amount authorized for loans increased by 25 percent, according to the announcement.[17] One year later, OE announced that the loan program had increased again, with the provision of loan funds for 1,400 additional students. This announcement was contained in a lengthy report on the students who had received NDEA loans from February 1959 through the summer of 1960. The bulk of the eighty-page document contained a series of tables on borrowers, broken down by a plethora of factors such as age, state, major subject, intention with regard to teaching school, and numerous others. Not surprisingly, the document declared that the data showed convincingly that the loan program was meeting the talent development rationale by granting loans to students in education, engineering, mathematics, science, and foreign language. Interestingly, however, the data showed that well over one-half of the students qualifying for NDEA loans were enrolled in fields other than science, mathematics, and foreign languages and that the 37 percent of borrowers who were in the field of education equaled the combined percentage of borrowers in science, engineering, mathematics, and foreign languages.[18]

Additionally, the document commended colleges for their careful administration of the loan program, which helped to achieve the talent development objective that was its rationale, at least for the Eisenhower administration. The increasing numbers and amounts available for student loans meant, however, that something beyond talent development was going on with the NDEA student loan program. The greater availability of loan funds extended opportunity to large numbers of students, of varying abilities, who either had not planned on going to college or whose plans to attend were greatly facilitated by the availability of the loans. Thus Carl Elliott's expansive desires for the loan program were also bearing fruit.

While OE was surely aware of the educational opportunity accomplishments of NDEA student loans, its published material on the loan program explicitly lauded the talent development aspects of the program. Members of Congress, however, were more closely attuned to the large number of students served and the amount of funds expended on those students. Thus, the student loan program that had been not too much more than an afterthought for many in the process of consideration and passage of NDEA became the most politically popular provision of the legislation. Carl Elliott wrote to Marion Folsom, former secretary of Health, Education, and Welfare, in August of 1963, about the student loan program. With renewal of NDEA looming on the horizon, Elliott reminisced about the genesis of the loan program, recalling that the impetus for a loan provision had come out of hearings his Special Education Subcommittee had held in the Midwest. Loans were advocated by conservatives who opposed the scholarship provision of NDEA as a federal giveaway of money. Folsom, according to Elliott, had sold the loan program to President Eisenhower on these grounds. When Republicans on the house committee heard that the president supported the loans, they were ecstatic. Elliott opined that "the popularity of the loan provision pulled the other very worthwhile provisions of the bill through the legislative mill." He feared that any attempt to separate the titles of the bill, while not harmful to the loan program, might well jeopardize the other programs. Elliott here either forgot or deliberately downplayed his devotion to a scholarship program, which was excised from NDEA just before its passage, to celebrate the loan program that had replaced the scholarships and pay homage to the Republican congresspersons and administrative officials who had persuaded the president to support it.[19]

Although he was not the developer of Title II, Carl Elliott saw how it could achieve much of what he had hoped to accomplish through federal scholarships. In fact, Stewart McClure, Lister Hill's chief clerk in the Senate, believed that Elliott was fully aware that loans would substitute well for scholarships to achieve his own goal of expanded opportunity for students who needed financial help to go to college. More specifically, McClure described Elliott's willingness to forego scholarships, in deference to the powerful political tide in the House of Representatives that wanted their removal from NDEA, as "another clever ploy. . . . Carl Elliott and his guys narrowed the issue to whether we should have the federal government hand out scholarships or loans. . . . And the minute the damn scholarship was done for, dead, the bill swooped through. I don't think anybody had read any other title in it. Oh that was clever stuff. Carl Elliott was a brilliant strategist."[20] Thus it should be no surprise that Elliott adopted the student loan title as his cherished favorite of the various programs of NDEA. In April of 1959, he told Elliot Richardson that Title II was alive and well in Texas, where Elliott had just spoken to a higher education group. He urged the administration to interest national media in the NDEA student loan program. He told Richardson that the "'exploding' college population of the 1960s will demand more, not less, Federal aid, and it is about time that the matter" was "presented to the American people in a way less dispassionate" than that which had characterized the discussion during the legislative process.[21]

Elliott took a special interest in the way Title II of NDEA unfolded in Alabama. He corresponded with administrators at many campuses in his state, seeking data on the amount expended on student loans as well as the names of students who received them. Campus officials responded with lists of names of all Alabama students as well as names of students from Carl Elliott's congressional district who had received student loans. From 1959 through 1965, Elliott requested and received names and addresses of students who were loan recipients from institutions such as The University of Alabama, Jacksonville State University, and Alabama Agricultural and Mechanical College, one of the two public black colleges in the state. Elliott and his staff went through the various lists, inserting the county where the student resided alongside of the address and paying special attention to the counties in his district.[22]

Soon after Elliott was appointed to chair a House of Representatives Select Committee on Government Research, he initiated a study of federal student assistance that was conducted by sending a two-page "Questionnaire on National Defense Education Act Student Loan Program" to students who had received a loan. The questionnaire, in addition to seeking demographic information, college attendance record, work experience, and amount and duration of loan, asked for an estimate of the value of the loan program to the recipient. Copies of completed questionnaires fill a large box of the Carl Elliott Papers. One returned questionnaire voiced opinions sure to please the congressman. The recipient remarked: "The student loan program has been very important to me because had it not been for the loan, I could not have finished college. My success in life to a great extent came about as a result of me being able to borrow this money from the government."[23]

Elliott no doubt gloried in responses such as this one. He also was not afraid to use the loan program to his political advantage. As noted in chapter 2, he distributed loan materials widely in his district and put recipients of the materials on a list to receive his political reports. In May of 1965, as he was leaving Congress and preparing a possible run for governor of Alabama, Elliott sent out a copy of a pamphlet on NDEA student loans to Alabama educators. In a cover letter, he stated that "the most important thing I did in my 16 years in Congress was to get a law passed setting up the National Student Loan Program. Under that law ambitious high school graduates can attend college if they really want to do so." He added that he hoped recipients of his pamphlet "might have some worthy student whose hands you would like to place it in—someone who might be benefitted by it." Elliott concluded that Alabama was enriched every time a student graduated from high school and even richer when "one of our sons or daughters finish college."[24] In addition to marking the end of Elliott's career in Congress, 1965 proved to be a banner year for NDEA college student loans. In August of that year, a supplemental allocation of close to $1 million brought the total funding for loans in the 1965–66 academic year to over $177 million.[25] Another accounting of the amount of money spent on the student loan program, given in 1969, would no doubt have pleased Carl Elliott. By that year, according to Hugh Davis Graham, "1.5 million men and women had gone to college on NDEA's student loan program."[26]

Thus, in the six years after the inception of the student loan program, the amount spent on loans grew almost six times greater than its initial $30 million allocation. In December of 1965, a new version of student loans, the Guaranteed Student Loan Program, was announced by the Lyndon Johnson administration as a supplement to the NDEA loan program. Rather than have the loans come from the federal government itself, as provided for in NDEA, the government was now a guarantor of a loan program to be conducted by private banks under the supervision of state governments. The federal government guaranteed the loans against the possibility of default and was a payer of interest on them while the recipients were still in college.

This changed government role was undertaken to increase the reach of the loan program. According to Francis Keppel, commissioner of OE, the new program was "an educational reformation." A partnership between federal and state government and private banks, the plan, according to Keppel, "was motivated from the start by the desire to send every qualified student to college regardless of his economic background." Keppel added that it was tragic whenever any "boy or girl turns away from higher education . . . because of a lack of money." The loan guarantee program was intended to help not just the poor but the middle-income family as well. "It is the intent of the Guaranteed Student Loan program to lessen the burden of higher education on family income and . . . to put college within the reach of every qualified boy or girl, whether he or she be an only child or the thirteenth of a baker's dozen."[27]

Keppel added that the loan guarantee program, initially proposed as a radical extension of the existing direct loan program in Title II of NDEA, had been vetted originally in January and considered carefully throughout 1965. Its institutionalization in the Higher Education Act of 1965 was not as a direct loan program but as a federal loan guarantee program. This change was adopted, according to Keppel, "because of the convincing arguments" of representatives of state governments and bankers' associations.[28] While Keppel's address on the loan guarantee program is in the Carl Elliott Papers, there is no record of Elliott's reaction to this supplement to the NDEA student loan program. Perhaps on the one hand he was delighted in that the change dramatically increased the number of student loans offered. On the other hand, perhaps he understood, or at least worried, that taking control of the program away from government and lodging it in private banks would result in college graduates being burdened by large repayment obligations with terms set by private sector rules at the same time that they were beginning their careers and starting families. What seems clear is that Carl Elliott and his fellow congressmen could, and did, take credit for the Title II student loan program and the increase it provided in educational opportunity. The permutations of the student loan program since 1965, however, were the responsibility of others, especially the private bankers and the state and federal politicians who supported private involvement in the loan program.

Loyalty Oath

I have not yet discussed the loyalty oath provision of the NDEA in this book. The reason is that it was not a prominent concern in the minds of any of those who developed the legislation, either on the congressional side or in the administration. Rather, the loyalty oath was inserted during congressional discussion of the final version of the bill. The insertion was made on the initiative of Senator Karl Mundt, conservative Republican from South Dakota.[29] Loyalty oaths were a mainstay of the McCarthy era, though the rabid anticommunism of the Wisconsin senator was beginning to decline in the late 1950s. Nevertheless, an insertion at the eleventh hour of a proviso that was present in many other federal policies requiring an oath of allegiance from recipients of federal funds did not provoke effective opposition. NDEA advocates were convinced that passage of the bill in the summer of 1958 was essential. Further delay, either through another conference committee or reconsideration in both houses of Congress would likely doom the effort to failure. Thus, advocates of NDEA like Carl Elliott saw the loyalty oath, like the demise of the scholarship provision, as an unfortunate, but necessary, cost of the give and take of the legislative process.

The loyalty measure in the National Defense Education Act contained two major provisions. The first mandated that any recipient of loans or other funds appropriated in NDEA must file with the commissioner of education "an affidavit that he does not believe in, and is not a member of and does not support any organization that believes in or teaches, the overthrow of the United State Government by force or violence or by any illegal or constitutional methods." This language resembled the formula that had long been popular with Senator McCarthy, J. Edgar Hoover, and other professed anticommunists. The second loyalty provision mandated that all recipients of NDEA loans or other funds take the following oath: "I do solemnly swear (or affirm) that I will bear true faith and allegiance to the United States of America and will support and defend the Constitution and laws of the United States against all its enemies, foreign and domestic."[30]

Members of Congress drastically underestimated the furor the loyalty provisions of NDEA would cause on many campuses. Almost immediately after passage of NDEA, opposition to the loyalty proviso arose. In April of 1959, for example, a college official from Hampton University told one of Carl Elliott's staff members that there was widespread resentment in colleges throughout the nation over the loyalty oath provision. This official added that she knew of one college, Mills College in California, that had declined to participate in the NDEA loan program because of the loyalty oath. Mills was a private women's college, and thus perhaps not as likely to take as much advantage of NDEA loans as other colleges. Mills officials argued, however, that they were in favor of loans and that their students would take advantage of loans, but not loans like NDEA loans, which required a loyalty pledge.[31]

The objection to the NDEA loyalty oath provisions was centered not in colleges like Mills College, however, but in the nation's most prestigious universities. Nathan M. Pusey, president of Harvard University, circulated his objections to the measures to his fellow presidents of the Association of American Universities (AAU), a federation of the nation's leading private and public research universities. Pusey argued that the affidavit requirement was the more pernicious of the two loyalty provisions. He specified nearly twenty objections to the affidavit—including that it was "superfluous and unnecessary," "ineffective," "self-defeating," and "discriminatory"; that it represented "interference on the part of Congress in an area of administration which belongs properly to the colleges and universities"; and that it was "open to administrative and legal abuse," was "deeply un-American," was "contrary to the kind of educational practice the Act seeks to promote," and was "wasteful of time and energy . . . a nuisance . . . [and] distasteful." Additionally, Pusey noted that the affidavit "cheapens the value of oaths and vulgarizes and perverts the use of affidavits"; "comes very close to being class legislation" [in that it required an affidavit from students who needed funds for college but not from those who didn't]; and that "it establishes a dangerous precedent" of inappropriate federal intervention in higher education. Pusey concluded his objections to the affidavit provision by noting that "the public must come to see why educators oppose requirements of this kind, how such requirements work against true education, and how, far from adding to our security, in the long run they can only help to lose it."[32]

Pusey made two other important points in his criticism of the affidavit requirement in NDEA. First he recounted that NDEA affidavit and oath provisions were modeled on Taft-Hartley Act provisions pertaining to labor leaders that had been adopted almost verbatim in the National Science Foundation (NSF) Act of 1950. In fact, the NDEA language had been drawn explicitly from the NSF legislation. Higher education leaders had not been directly involved in administering NSF aid to students, since it went to the students themselves and not to them through their institutions. With NDEA, however, Pusey noted that colleges and universities were full partners with the federal government in that they had to administer the demand for compliance with these odious restrictions by recipients. Additionally, Pusey noted that the affidavit requirement was far more objectionable than the oath, stating that although "we do believe the oath to be unnecessary and ineffective, we do not have any militant objection to it." Pusey concluded his memorandum by urging AAU members to continue their campaign with members of Congress to repeal the affidavit.[33]

As president of Harvard University, Pusey was one of the most visible and effective opponents of the affidavit provision of NDEA. In addition to communicating with other college and university administrators such as members of the Association of American Universities, he made the round of congressional officers to register his objections to the affidavit, as well as his support of the oath provision. For example, in December of 1959, he visited Carl Elliott's Washington office and discussed the matter with one of Elliott's chief aides. In reporting to Elliott on the visit, the aide was impressed by Pusey, noting that the Harvard president was "an amiable man," that he was "of humble origin, having been born in Iowa," and adding that Pusey did not have the financial wherewithal to attend the public university in Iowa City but had won a scholarship to Harvard. Pusey had argued to Elliott's staff person that Harvard was not a school of the "idle rich" and remarked that the over half of Harvard students who might qualify for NDEA aid would not get it until repeal of the affidavit, since the Harvard faculty had voted "by a large margin . . . against the use of the funds so long as the disclaimer provision is in the Act." Further discussion of Pusey's views by Elliott's assistant noted that the Harvard leader talked "with ease and conviction, yet not as a rabid liberal," and that he was the first Harvard president not from New England. This description surely was intended to place Pusey in a favorable light in the mind of the Alabama congressman, who had been schooled at all levels in public institutions in Alabama, though the discussion of the Harvard president's finances as a student preventing access to the University of Iowa and a scholarship providing for successful matriculation at Harvard ignored the New England background of Pusey's family and its long-standing ties to Harvard.[34]

Pusey, according to Elliott's aide, was generous in his praise of the NDEA, though he had firm reservations about the affidavit requirement. The Harvard president reiterated many of the criticisms he had made in the memorandum to his fellow college presidents, stressing the drastic difference in the positive oath of the loyalty provision and the negative disclaimer about not having been a member of unspecified organizations. He was happy with the former and dismayed by the latter. For Pusey, the affidavit was deeply un-American, probably unconstitutional, and singled out students as the only recipients of federal funds who were treated in this fashion. Farmers and others who received federal funds had no loyalty requirements, while students faced both the oath and the affidavit. Pusey added that many student groups, as well as his Harvard faculty and other faculty bodies, were against the affidavit provision of NDEA.[35]

Harvard was not the only institution that formally objected to the affidavit provision of NDEA. Joining Harvard and Mills in filing "provisional" applications for NDEA loan or grant funds, applications that would become active only on repeal of the affidavit, were the following institutions: Amherst, Antioch, Bennington, Brandeis, Brown, Colby, Mt. Holyoke, Oberlin, Pacific Oaks, Princeton, Reed, Sarah Lawrence, Smith, Swarthmore, Chicago, Vassar, Wesleyan (CT), Wilmington (OH), and Yale. Institutions not filing provisional applications but declining participation in NDEA included Beloit, Bryn Mawr, Colby Junior College, Goucher, Grinnell, Haverford, a black theological seminary in Georgia, New School for Social Research, Newton College, Radcliffe, and St. John's (Maryland).[36] The geographical preponderance of New England and West Coast institutions and the dominance of elite private colleges among these institutions likely told congressmen from southern, midwestern, and western states that they had not as much to fear politically from affidavit opponents as did their colleagues in the other regions of the nation.

Carl Elliott's legislative assistant acknowledged this reality in his report on Nathan Pusey's visit to discuss the affidavit requirement. Elliott's aide remarked: "We can live with the disclaimer affidavit, I feel sure. And I feel sure a vast majority of colleges and universities will continue to participate in the loan program even if the disclaimer affidavit is retained." Elliott's assistant added that the real issue was larger. It was not a case of simply living with something but rather a situation in which it was necessary "to encourage a partnership of trust, confidence, and cooperation between the academic world and the government."[37]

It is not clear that Elliott saw the situation in the same way his staff member did. Elliott's papers are full of letters from individuals and groups opposed to the disclaimer affidavit and, to a lesser extent, the loyalty oath. In a letter of response he composed, Elliott noted first that his main objective in writing the NDEA had been "to make it possible for worthy students to get a college education where they otherwise could not obtain one" and that "over 100,000 students are now in college because they have been able to get loans under the Act." He added that the loan program was working well in accomplishing its purpose. He stated that he had "no strong personal feelings about taking the oath as required by the Act" and noted further that he regretted "exceedingly that the loyalty and disclaimer provisions have caused some colleges to withdraw entirely from the program." He concluded the letter by assuring his continued "deep interest in the student loan program" and adding that he would "take whatever action that I can to see that it accomplishes the purposes for which it was established."[38]

It is hard to read any principled objection to the loyalty oath or to the disclaimer affidavit into Carl Elliott's sentiments. Some reasons for his lack of fervor for repeal were outlined in a letter to his fellow congressman, Al Ullman of Oregon, who had forwarded a statement of opposition to the disclaimer affidavit from the president and faculty of the University of Oregon. Elliott told Ullman that the loyalty provisions were not in the original NDEA bill that Elliott had steered through the House of Representatives and noted that a great many of the schools objecting to the NDEA provisions had been participating for ten years in an NSF program from which the language of the oaths was drawn. He added that "oaths similar to that in the National Defense Education Act are required of members of the armed forces," of many federal employees, of teachers in many states, and of applicants to the bar in several states. He concluded by noting that several bills repealing the oaths had been introduced in the House of Representatives and added that his Subcommittee on Special Education, though it had not scheduled any actions on these bills, would "probably be able to hold hearings on the progress of the National Defense Education Act before the end of this session [of Congress]."[39]

Elliott may have had reason to modify his position, somewhat, in the next year. In June of 1962, his Senate colleague Lister Hill received a letter from the Auburn University chapter of the American Association of University Professors (AAUP) objecting to the disclaimer affidavit provision of NDEA. In addition to the objections to the affidavit that had been voiced by others, the Auburn professors added one that was intended to reflect views that would be received favorably in the South. They noted that the disclaimer affidavit implied "a measure of federal control on higher education in this country." The professors concluded by noting their long appreciation for Hill's efforts on behalf of education and asking him to lend his leadership "to the efforts of those members of the Congress who are seeking to repeal the 'disclaimer affidavit provision' of NDEA." Hill replied that the "Education Subcommittee of the [Senate] Committee on Labor and Public Welfare . . . has tentatively approved the removal of the disclaimer requirement" and added that he expected that final removal was on the horizon. He made a handwritten addition to the letter, to the effect that "I favor this."[40] Although no record of the Auburn AAUP action was found in the Elliott Papers, it seems likely he was aware of the actions of a prominent faculty group at one of his state's two major institutions of higher education. Whatever the case, Lister Hill, and Carl Elliott as well, were relieved when the disclaimer affidavit provision was finally removed from the NDEA by Congress late in 1962.[41]

Congressional leadership in the repeal effort came from Senator John Kennedy of Massachusetts. Given Kennedy's Harvard degree and his coming campaign for the presidency of the United States, it was not surprising to see him take a prominent role in gaining repeal of the affidavit requirement. Neither Carl Elliott nor Lister Hill, nor most other members of Congress, had as much to gain politically from repeal as did Kennedy. Pursuing, and attaining, repeal furthered his image as responsive to the wishes of Harvard University and other institutions of higher education in his state, and the nation.

Strengthening Alabama Schools, Colleges, and Universities

A very real accomplishment of the National Defense Education Act was the enhancement of public schools and many of the colleges and universities throughout the United States. Especially significant beneficiaries of NDEA included public universities in the South and the West, institutions that were outside the ranks of the leading research institutions that dotted the two coasts and a few places in the Midwest. Rather than try to characterize the institutional enrichment nationally, I will confine myself to developments in the state of Alabama, in the public schools and at The University of Alabama in Tuscaloosa, and other higher education institutions in that state. Given Alabama's relative poverty and lack of educational distinction in relation to other states, one can reasonably assume that improvements in Alabama were at the least matched, if not exceeded, in most other states.

NDEA fellowships were one of the means used to build the Graduate School at The University of Alabama, at a time when graduate education was in its infancy at this institution. In 1961–62, for example, thirty-five fellows were supported in various graduate programs at the Tuscaloosa university. Of these thirty-five, thirteen were in the sciences and allied fields, three in physics, eight in biology, and two in mathematics; another eight were in the Department of Spanish and French; five were enrolled in a program in Hispanic history in the History Department; and ten were in the education area, with six in the field of guidance and educational psychology and four in curriculum study and research. Thus roughly one-half the graduate fellows were enrolled in the sciences and the other half in professional education or in the humanities.[42] This is a testimony to the wide reach of the NDEA fellowships and to the diversity of fields that entered into graduate work at the university through NDEA support.

The University of Alabama official mainly responsible for Washington contacts was Alex Pow, who in 1961 held the position of director for contract and grant development. In this capacity, he often wrote to Carl Elliott or Lister Hill, indicating the specific progress the university was making through NDEA. In January of 1961, for example, Pow informed Elliott of the number of fellowships granted through NDEA for the next three years, as well as of the impending sponsorship by the university of a summer foreign language institute for secondary teachers of French and Spanish and a year-long institute for counseling and guidance to train high school counselors. He closed his letter to Elliott as follows: "We continue to be grateful for the opportunities which have been afforded us for service to Alabama and this region under the National Defense Education Act and for the support you have given our applications under this legislation."[43]

The University of Alabama continued to receive a significant number of NDEA graduate fellowships well into the 1960s, and notification of these positive results was often forwarded to either Senator Hill or Congressman Elliott from university officials or, on occasion, from Office of Education leaders. In March of 1965, however, for the first time since the passage of

NDEA, The University of Alabama received no allocation of fellowships for the next academic year, 1965–66. Alex Pow, who had become vice president for institutional development, informed Carl Elliott of this result and the university's disappointment in it.[44]

Elliott was aware of this development before he heard about it from Pow, and the congressman sought immediately to find out what was behind this change in treatment of his home-state university. In a memo to him from one of his staff dated the same day as Alex Pow's letter, Elliott learned of a change in the allocation of NDEA fellowships, negating the original stipulation that mandated that fellowships be used to expand existing programs and create new graduate programs. The Office of Education now was establishing new criteria for the awards, and those criteria were applied to almost all of the new applications. For the 1,300 fellowships available for award in 1965–66, Elliott was told that 157 institutions had applied for them. Of the 157, however, only forty-four were successful in obtaining fellowships. In the South, the successful applicants were "Duke, Tulane, Vanderbilt, University of North Carolina, and University of Virginia." Elliott then learned that applications were now being reviewed with a process that rated the quality of the department from whence they came, and no credit was given for being a new or developing graduate department or program. Among the southern universities eliminated from consideration through this process, in addition to The University of Alabama, were the universities of Florida, "Georgia, Tennessee, Mississippi, and . . . South Carolina." These institutions, according to the OE official in charge of administering the fellowship program, had failed to recognize the "new" approach to the fellowships, one that required substantial development in an institution's graduate school and its graduate programs that would indicate progress toward the establishment of a "first class graduate school."[45]

The preponderance of first class status in private universities receiving support with the new administration of the graduate fellowship procedures, in the South and elsewhere, indicated that whatever expansion of opportunity that had taken place since the beginning of the NDEA fellowship program was in danger of being compromised. One would find it hard to believe the private schools mentioned in the preceding paragraph drew their students, graduate or undergraduate, from the same social strata that populated the southern state universities. A similar social stratification likely characterized other states as well.

Elliott's aide suggested that The University of Alabama try to do something about fellowships in the upcoming academic year through contact with the director of the fellowship program and invite him, or one of his staff, to come to Tuscaloosa and discuss the new situation and how the university might address it. Additionally, the aide suggested that the university seek to have Alex Pow, or some other official, named to the advisory panel that approved the awards each year. While such membership would mean recusal in the case of deciding on applications from Alabama, understanding the priorities and procedures in the program would outweigh the negative consequences. These two steps could help the university obtain a better result in the ensuing graduate fellowship competition.[46] While this strategy seems plausible, it ignored the changing reality in the OE that meant the federal agency would look less favorably on institutions in states like Alabama that struggled within a political atmosphere that sought, first, to keep taxes low rather than to support its public educational institutions. I will have more to say about this change in the final chapter of this book. For present purposes, suffice it to say that the OE fellowship program, until this change, had been the mainstay in the development of graduate education at The University of Alabama, and that university leaders cooperated with Alabama's congressional delegation to try to protect any gains made in graduate education and to improve on them, if possible.

Graduate fellowships, of course, were not the only federal funds received by The University of Alabama. Alex Pow regularly apprised Carl Elliott of the total federal funding that came to the university from NDEA titles. In May of 1960, for example, Pow told Elliott the university had to that point received over $800,000 from various NDEA provisions. While graduate fellowships made up the largest portion of that amount, almost one half, student loans were responsible for almost as much as graduate fellowships, with counseling and guidance, foreign language, and educational television programs accounting for the rest of the funds received. Pow's cover letter indicated that he himself had compiled the summary for the congressman in gratitude for Elliott's constant activity on behalf of the university as well as for a recent speech he had made on campus. Needless to say, both the university and the congressman intended to continue their cooperative efforts on behalf of the financial interests of The University of Alabama, through tapping the funds available in the various NDEA titles.[47]

Alex Pow and Carl Elliott were not the only ones interested in pursuing the advancement of The University of Alabama through NDEA and other federal funding opportunities. On several occasions, the president of the university, Frank A. Rose, contacted Carl Elliott or Lister Hill on behalf of the university, as well as on behalf of the larger cause of public education in the state. In May of 1956, for example, Rose sent a telegram to Senator Hill alerting him to the threat of a cut of over 25 percent of Alabama's current allotment of two million dollars of NDEA Title III funds for improving science, mathematics, and language instruction in the state's public schools. Hill quickly responded that he was aware of the potential danger for the state and intent on heading off the cuts in his role as chair of a powerful Senate committee that considered educational finance.[48]

As president of The University of Alabama, Rose took seriously his leadership role in educational affairs in the state and pursued his institution's interests, often in contacts with Senator Lister Hill. A little less than a year after the exchange with Senator Hill regarding Title III of NDEA, Rose sought help from Senator Hill again, this time in pursuit of funding under a recently passed International Education Act, which would provide funds to build graduate programs and centers in international affairs at selected universities. Rose was intent on obtaining funds for such a center at his university and contacted Hill for suggestions on ways to be successful in lobbying officials in the Johnson administration on behalf of this effort. A White House official indicated to Hill that Rose had contacted the White House in pursuit of international education expenditures. Hill acknowledged his awareness of this interaction and vowed to help in whatever way he could the general cause of federal support of international education and the successful participation in that cause by The University of Alabama. Hill made good on his promise by soon sponsoring a luncheon at which President Rose was able to make his case for funds for international education to a group of influential senators and administration officials.[49]

Like Carl Elliott, Hill worked assiduously on behalf of the educational interests of the school people in his state, as well as on behalf of its colleges and universities. In May of 1967, for example, correspondence between Hill and various education officials discussed an impending appropriation for Title III NDEA funds that would fail to increase the amount going to Alabama schools. Hill promised to do what he could to address the situation and a few months later was able to tell a school leader that his own Senate committee had managed to increase substantially the total amount for Title III funds in the upcoming year.[50]

All of this is to say that Carl Elliott and Lister Hill saw themselves as protectors of their state's public schools and of its colleges and universities, particularly the state university in Tuscaloosa where they both had been student leaders. These two congressmen helped Alabama public schools to obtain funding through NDEA, to avoid cuts in the funds they were receiving, and to increase that funding wherever possible. In the case of The University of Alabama, NDEA and its two congressional sponsors were major forces in the development of graduate education. Alas, the pace of that development failed to satisfy federal officials who in the mid-1960s changed an equity-oriented objective of spreading graduate fellowships to have-not institutions to a more meritocratic policy of locating the support in places with the "best" programs. That shift is considered in the next, and final, chapter of this volume, where I attempt to evaluate NDEA with a long-term perspective. Before that effort, however, discussion of one more topic is in order, the ways in which NDEA affected the size, funding, and influence of the U.S. Office of Education.

Strengthening the Office of Education

The U.S. Office of Education (OE) was the name of the federal educational agency in 1958 when NDEA was passed. As discussed in an earlier chapter, it was the successor to the U.S. Department of Education, founded in the mid-nineteenth century and downgraded rapidly to bureau status in the Department of the Interior.[51] By the middle of the twentieth century, OE had been transferred twice within the federal government and had become an office within the recently created Department of Health, Education, and Welfare (HEW). Whatever its title and wherever it was housed, prior to the National Defense Education Act the federal educational agency was a minor player in the federal administrative apparatus and in American education. The one consistent role OE and its predecessors had played was that of data gatherer and disseminator. That role was enhanced significantly by Title IX of the National Defense Education Act, which authorized federal dollars to help state departments of education to improve their data and statistical services. More importantly, however, the other titles of NDEA provoked a near explosion in the responsibilities of the OE and in the staff needed to carry them out. It was this enormous enhancement of OE by NDEA that, though not necessarily intended, proved to be a major outcome of the legislation.

The commissioner of OE at the time of enactment of NDEA was L. G. Derthick, a former public school administrator who had served most recently as a school administrator in Nashville, Tennessee. Derthick and his colleagues were aware at the time of passage of NDEA of the enormous responsibilities the legislation thrust on the federal educational agency. They set out to make sure that Congress, professional educators, and the public knew that OE was taking its new roles and responsibilities seriously. By the end of September 1958, the month in which President Eisenhower had signed NDEA into law, OE officials were in contact with staff representing the congresspersons who had oversight responsibility for the administration of NDEA. They informed the congressional staffers that new directors had been hired to administer the student loan program of NDEA (Title II) and the foreign language programs of Titles III and VI of the law. These hires and others anticipated at top levels had been difficult to accomplish, according to OE officials, because of the relatively poor salaries available for federal employees, salaries that were well below those in private business as well as below administrative salaries in public education and in higher education. In addition to new leadership positions in several program areas, OE noted that it anticipated the hiring of 150 new staff people within the next six months and another 150 two months later, if an anticipated supplemental NDEA authorization was approved by Congress.[52] This army of new staff members was to prepare and disseminate calls for proposals for programs under the various NDEA titles, to develop and implement procedures for considering the proposals submitted under those titles, and to make sure that the awards granted under the titles were made equitably and within the guidelines of the legislation.[53]

In addition to the new staff positions, OE needed to set up a series of advisory committees for NDEA and its various titles, as mandated by the legislation. These committees were cumbersome to OE, which had its own apparatus for obtaining advice for its operations and, again, were constrained by the paltry financial payments designated for committee members and the even more paltry OE funds available for the payments. Commissioner Derthick and his staff had named 150 people to these various panels by October of 1958.[54] An absolute necessity for OE, for political reasons and for the smooth initiation and operation of NDEA, was good relations with state school officials. In pursuit of this goal, a series of meetings was set up between OE leaders and the Chief State School Officers at which regulations and relations, including the financial strictures put on advisory committee members, were seriously discussed.

The immediate organizational additions to OE caused by all these changes were massive. A new financial aid branch was added to the Division of Higher Education to administer student loans and graduate fellowships. A Financial Aid to State and Local Schools Branch was added to the Division of State and Local School Systems, which had a Guidance Counseling, and Testing section, a Mathematics, Science, and Foreign Language section, and a Plans and Report section. New branches devoted to NDEA titles were also added to the Division of Statistics and Research and to the Division of Vocational Education. Accompanying these organizational additions was a flurry of activities to implement all the programs called for in the various NDEA titles. While the graduate fellowship and student loan programs were still in the planning stage, the programs called for in most of the other titles were much closer to implementation within thirty days of passage of the legislation.[55]

These initial additions and alterations to OE because of NDEA were followed by a systematic reorganization of the office in 1961. Stimulated by NDEA, the commissioner appointed a committee that, in turn, laid out a reorganization plan that was successfully implemented. That plan called for dividing the OE commissioner's operation into four separate offices: Information, Administration, Program and Legislative Planning, and Field Services. Specifically because of the reach of NDEA into state and local schools, the Field Services office set up its own regional offices under the Department of Health, Education, and Welfare, to help state and local school administrators understand and take advantage of the legislation.[56]

In addition to administrative subunits, the reorganization of OE provided for three bureaus relating to the operating functions of the office: Educational Research and Development, International Education, and Educational Assistance Programs. The first and third of these bureaus were enormously affected by NDEA. The Educational Research and Development Bureau's Division of Research became responsible for the research programs and the dissemination of results of these programs under the media research title of NDEA. The Bureau of Educational Assistance Programs boasted two divisions created specifically to administer NDEA programs: the Division of State Grants and the Division of College and University Assistance. The state grants division administered Title III NDEA grant programs for equipment and services to improve instruction and supervision in mathematics, science, and foreign language education and Title V programs in testing, guidance, and counseling. The college and university assistance division took on the activities of four titles of NDEA that provided assistance to colleges and universities. The student loan program of Title II was a special responsibility of this division and was housed in a new Student Financial Aid Branch. The other branches in this division were Counseling and Guidance Institutes, Graduate Fellowships, and Language Development.[57]

Relatively rapid development of administrative procedures relating to NDEA took place in every area. The situation in the New Educational Media Branch of OE provides one example. Within a few months of the passage of NDEA, OE had disseminated a complex but relatively short set of instructions for applying for grants under Title VII, the media title of the legislation. The instructions covered general matters such as proposal length, content, design or method, budget, and the abstract. Additionally, the criteria for evaluation of proposals accompanied the instructions as well as a final addendum of questions and answers related to applying for a grant. The resulting ten-page document seems mundane in the twenty-first century, when applicants for federal grants in education and elsewhere face much more complicated, and lengthy, requirements. What seems worthy of mention here, however, is that OE was able to get this title and other titles in operation quickly and relatively effectively.[58]

In addition to reorganization, OE had to drastically increase communications with congressional overseers and with grant seekers. The OE also moved effectively to publicize quickly its NDEA activities in professional forums. In a journal it published for K-12 school people, the Office of Education devoted a full issue to NDEA, one month after the law was enacted. The October–November 1958 issue of *School Life* devoted all of its pages to the National Defense Education Act. Its title-by-title description of the act was supplemented by a more general discussion of the significance and reach of NDEA. This focus was justified in the first paragraph of the publication, where Commissioner L. G. Derthick cautioned against a title-by-title perspective, arguing, "We will do the Act justice only if we see it as a mighty complex, in which each part reinforces the other, and all parts join to strengthen education across the board." Derthick added that the act provided "an occasion for reaching, in education, a new high level of shared responsibility and creative cooperation—among public and private agencies, individuals, and institutions, wherever and whatever they may be."[59] This language no doubt was intended to reassure those who feared the law would result in more federal control of education and less autonomy for states and schools and colleges. That fear was also addressed by Arthur S. Flemming, secretary of the Department of Health, Education, and Welfare, who noted that NDEA continued "a historic partnership which has demonstrated its value to the American people . . . in the past—a partnership in which the Federal Government assists States, communities, and private institutions to pioneer in new educational programs and to strengthen others that have proved their worth." Flemming added that the legislation stood to increase support for education from states, local communities, and private interests and that it also offered an opportunity for "teachers, school administrators, and public officials to enlarge their services to our free society."[60]

After these reassuring comments from the top administrator of OE and the cabinet secretary in which the office was housed, the magazine informed school people of the benefits to be reaped from NDEA. It noted that over one billion dollars would be made available for improvements at every level of education "from the elementary through the graduate." About three-fourths of the funds, it added, would be "grants to the state educational agencies" for strengthening instruction in elementary and secondary schools, testing and counseling, statistical services, and vocational programs. Thanks to NDEA, "every young person, from the day he first enters school, should have the opportunity to develop his gifts to the fullest." This objective was appropriate for an education defense act, according to the OE publication, for it recognized "that in a free society the individual is the first line of defense."[61] The rest of the document included a title-by-title summary of the act, an accounting of the actions that had been undertaken to get it started, and a four-page listing of individuals and groups who had been or would soon be consulted to advise in implementation.

In September of 1959, OE commissioner Derthick wrote an article in the National Education Association magazine in which he reported the large amount of funds that had gone to individuals for loans and fellowships and to school systems for instructional improvement in the past year. Appropriations for the coming year promised an increased expenditure of federal dollars on NDEA provisions, the commissioner concluded. He also noted that increased enthusiasm for NDEA was being detected in reports from the field in educational institutions and that "this enthusiasm will also prevail at the grass roots as the people there begin to witness and to feel . . . the full force of the expanded opportunities under these programs that extend our educational horizons on many fronts."[62]

In September of 1959, a year after passage of NDEA and less than a year after consultation with members of Congress and their staffs, and communication with elementary and secondary educators, the federal educational agency addressed directly the interest group not included in earlier efforts, higher education officials. In a publication devoted to higher education, the September 1959 issue contained two feature articles on NDEA. The first, written by HEW assistant secretary Elliot Richardson, addressed the larger issue of a national policy for higher education. Richardson began the article by noting significant federal financial commitment to higher education before NDEA, but also by adding that this commitment was focused on professional training and applied research in health, science, child welfare, vocational rehabilitation, and agriculture. NDEA, in contrast, was focused on what Richardson called the "main tent" of basic research and pure education, the "strengthening of the teaching and research institution itself." For Richardson, this new focus acknowledged "the vital dependence of our Nation's future on the development of its best brains in every field of advanced study." Richardson saw NDEA as the beginning of federal expenditures in higher education, which would have to double in the next decade to keep up with the demographic boom that would envelop colleges and universities.[63] Fortunately, according to Richardson, economic growth meant that a doubling could be accomplished without increasing the proportion of federal dollars going to higher education. He concluded by noting that of "all the prospects of American life, none holds richer promise than that of higher education constantly advancing," and adding that such advance was based on the recognition of "the supreme position of the university as the citadel of freedom and the treasury of knowledge."[64]

In an article following Richardson's, the new leader of the Financial Aid Branch of the Division of Higher Education in OE, whose position had been added to account for and administer most of the higher education support programs in the law, described those programs and detailed the expenditures on them. He discussed the student loan program, the graduate fellowship program, the counseling and guidance training institutes, and the language development programs of NDEA. He dealt with each program in some detail, and identified the amounts spent in the past year and increases announced for the forthcoming year (in all but one area). While explicitly defense-oriented areas such as science and mathematics were mentioned, the article also noted that increases had gone to the social sciences and humanities and to the field of education. The focus of all the programs, according to the new OE official, was on the development of educational talent, at the high school, undergraduate, and graduate levels. Such a focus "was an expression of public awareness of the need to bring the resources of all the Nation to bear on problems which ultimately affect the strength and security of the American people as a whole."[65]

In addition to communication and publications geared to Congress, to elementary and secondary schools, and to higher education, the Office of Education and Department of Health, Education, and Welfare made sure the message of benefits from NDEA reached an audience wider than school and college and university leaders. In this effort, the *Congressional Quarterly* marked the first anniversary of NDEA with a report detailing the total amount spent on NDEA, on each of its titles, and the amount spent in each state.[66]

In another new initiative, OE impaneled a prestigious group of consultants prior to the campaign for renewal of NDEA near the end of 1960. This group included, among others, James B. Conant, former HEW secretary Marion Folsom, several college presidents and other administrators, and local and state school leaders. Its report not surprisingly called for renewal of all titles of the legislation, increased funding for many, and implementation of the scholarship program that had been removed by Congress just before it passed the final version of NDEA in August of 1958. While scholarships were not reinstated in the renewal, OE astutely used its consultants to persuade Congress, and the public, of the need for renewal of NDEA, with increased funding.[67]

OE and its parent HEW were successful at sustaining the drumbeat of approbation of NDEA well into the 1960s, as the national administration and the staff of the two agencies underwent substantial shifts. While the Kennedy and Johnson administrations leaned toward federal aid that addressed issues and categories different from those in NDEA, they understood that politically, NDEA had broken the opposition to federal aid and opened the way for the further development of federal educational programs that would take place in the 1960s.

For the Office of Education in particular, NDEA meant a coming of age as a federal agency with substantial responsibility and a professionally qualified staff large enough to meet that responsibility. At the tenth anniversary celebration of NDEA, OE commissioner Harold Howe acknowledged the importance of NDEA for the development of OE. He remarked that with NDEA, Congress "in a stroke changed the Office from the 97 pound weakling of the world of education into a robust organization whose importance to the country could not be overlooked and whose potential for leadership could not be ignored." Specifically, Howe noted that NDEA increased OE employment "from 589 in 1958 to 9,000 the following year and finally to today's [1968] total of more than 30,000 men and women." Howe added that OE and the educational enterprise it served had come a long way, though education in America was still far from where it should be. He concluded by acknowledging that every student who was cheated of educational opportunity diminished the total American educational achievement, but added that "starting with the National Defense Education Act 10 years ago, this country determined to reverse our educational decline and to commence building the schooling needed for the development of our people and the progress of our country."[68]

While Howe's remarks contained a good bit of boosterism appropriate for an institutional anniversary, they also recognized the increased significance of OE because of the National Defense Education Act. OE and HEW understood the opportunity presented to federal educational officials by NDEA and they moved astutely to consolidate the benefits presented to the agency by the legislation. There is little doubt that NDEA, and ESEA also, gave the federal educational agency a position of institutional strength it developed even further in the ensuing years. We turn now to those years, from 1965 to the present, for a final evaluation of NDEA.

7
NDEA in Perspective

I begin this chapter with a summary of my conclusions about NDEA. One major theme of my work is that NDEA was about science education and about much else besides science education. The primacy of science in the conception of NDEA was not adhered to by any of the major players discussed in my book—not by Lister Hill, Carl Elliott, Dwight D. Eisenhower, or Elliot Richardson. Similarly, primacy for science was not advocated by the educators discussed in chapter 4 or, for that matter, even by the scientists discussed in chapter 5. Educators wanted federal aid to education that reached far beyond science and the other categorical areas targeted for support in the titles of NDEA; they sought an expansive federal aid program that would provide general aid funds to meet acute needs in the schools such as construction and higher teacher salaries. Scientists endorsed the NDEA involvement with fields other than science more for strategic reasons related as much to their relations with nonscience colleagues on their campuses than for any real openness to equality among fields in higher education or between educators in secondary schools and scientists in research universities. Thus, NDEA, though it was much more than a science education measure, can also be judged to have enhanced scientists' dominance over their academic colleagues in nonscience fields and elementary and secondary educators.

I also argued that NDEA was produced by a combination of the political liberalism of Carl Elliott and Lister Hill in Congress and the moderate Republicanism of Dwight Eisenhower and Elliot Richardson in the executive branch. The legislation that emerged, as was usually the case, mixed the desires of the proponents as well as extraneous elements acquired through legislative give and take. While both the liberalism of Elliott and Hill and the moderate commitment of Eisenhower and Richardson supported federal aid to education, as embodied in NDEA, the two ideologies had different conceptions of and expectations for the measure. Most obviously, the time frame of four years in the initial NDEA accorded with the moderates' notion that federal aid was a temporary measure appropriate to meet a crisis symbolized by the Russian launch of Sputnik. The rapid extensions of NDEA in the decade after 1958, along with the expansions of its titles to include more individuals and fields within their reach, however, fulfilled the desires of Elliott and Hill for a long-term federal aid to education policy commitment that was destined to extend higher education to more students. NDEA also provided educational funds that would help all states, but especially those, like Alabama, that were disadvantaged economically. Increased educational opportunity for students was evidenced in the student loan title and in the graduate fellowship title, which expanded the chances for undergraduate and graduate studies respectively. Extension of the reach of the fellowship title to new or expanding programs encouraged the institutional enhancement of relatively undeveloped colleges and universities, particularly in states like Alabama where the new programs were often centered and where such development was desperately needed. Each of these results conformed to the expectations of Elliott and Hill.

In terms of the privileged position of high status institutions and high status programs within those institutions, I argued that NDEA threatened these institutions and programs through its loan and fellowship policies, but that the threat did not dislodge these institutions or programs from their lofty perch. I noted a number of developments in the administration of NDEA in its first decade that reinforced the primacy of some academic fields over others, particularly the prominence of the sciences, and of prestigious research universities over other institutions of higher education. More importantly, NDEA reinforced the enhancement of values such as quality, ability, or giftedness in education at the expense of competing values such as equity or equality. The NDEA title on testing, guidance, and counseling epitomized this development, and its strong support from scientists, from psychometrists, and from educational testing agencies, as well as a lack of sustained and rigorous criticism of its commitments from school people or from opportunity advocates such as Carl Elliott, guaranteed that its advocacy for service for elite individuals in education would become a more important focus of the educational enterprise, in higher education as well as in secondary schools.[1]

NDEA can be said then to have represented some success for advocates of the liberal values of extended and more extensive educational opportunity as well as considerable success for the scientists and others who valued standards, excellence, ability, and giftedness as protections against negative, leveling consequences of increased educational opportunity. Before considering the relationships between equity and excellence in the rest of the twentieth century and into the current decade, I want to offer a brief comment on the political fate of the major actors in developing NDEA, and of the ideologies they espoused.

Lister Hill and Carl Elliott, as noted at the end of the chapters on each man, left politics in the 1960s when their liberalism foundered on the shoals of race, as the overt racism developed and intensified by Alabama governor George Wallace precipitated Elliott's defeat and Hill's refusal to run for re-election in a situation where defeat seemed inevitable. During and after the 1960s the southern liberalism espoused by Hill and Elliott literally disappeared from Alabama politics, more precisely from white Alabama politics. Resurrection of white liberal politics in Alabama, as elsewhere in much of the South, is a process that seems unlikely to happen, though less unlikely in 2008 when the Obama candidacy energized southern black voters and the candidacy of John Edwards brought at least one southern white liberal to the forefront of the national political scene.

The moderate Republicanism championed by Elliot Richardson and subscribed to often by Dwight Eisenhower became perhaps even scarcer than white southern liberalism. Eisenhower retired to his golf game and Richardson, after serving in two of the subsequent Republican administrations, including a term as secretary of Health, Education, and Welfare, became almost invisible in the wake of the victory of Republican conservatism. Ronald Reagan in the 1980s, Newt Gingrich in the 1990s, and the efforts of George W. Bush and the political henchmen in his administration in the first decade of the twenty-first century drove the Republican Party to the right, almost to the extreme right. The party that had formally adopted the positions proffered by Barry Goldwater in 1964, positions that were rejected as extreme by the American electorate at that time, eventually made those policies a large part of the political mainstream. In a year like 2008, when John McCain, whose conservative credentials seem impeccable on many issues, is seen as too moderate by many of the influential Republican constituencies such as the Christian right, one wonders if Republicans will ever recover any breadth in their outlook. Perhaps the calamities inflicted on the United States by the Bush administration may push Republicans back to the middle of the political spectrum.

Educators and Scientists

In addition to the political fate of the sponsors of NDEA, I would also like to briefly characterize what I think happened to the two major interest groups involved with NDEA, educators and scientists. The elementary and secondary educators discussed in chapter 4, and more particularly their institutional representation through the National Education Association (NEA), have survived the aftermath of NDEA, though the NEA has been radically altered and somewhat weakened politically by its unionization. While NEA is now arguably the largest labor union in the nation, and while its dues fuel a substantial enterprise in its national office, the association in the twenty-first century cannot be said to have the political influence over Congress and the executive branch that it enjoyed in the years before and at the time of passage of NDEA. NEA's militant advocacy of teachers and their welfare has borne some political fruit in Washington, such as the enactment of legislation creating the U.S. Department of Education in 1979. Yet NEA has also become identified as a teachers' union and thereby lost its earlier claim of being the representative of the entire educational profession. In fact, NEA has become a teachers' union limited to representing teachers in public schools, though it has some representation from higher education faculty. What NEA does not now possess is any high visibility or significant influence in higher education policy circles in Washington, a position taken over by the organizations represented at and around One Dupont Circle. Similarly, NEA no longer speaks for school administrators, for school boards, or for parents, all of which were in NEA-affiliated organizations in the mid-twentieth century.

Development of the Office of Education (OE) after NDEA did not live up to the high expectations created by the legislation. While OE after NDEA grew enormously, it failed to gain the stature of a competent federal agency. Hugh Davis Graham's description of OE during the Kennedy and Johnson years is most unflattering. While Congress ultimately built on NDEA and funded education at the federal level even more generously through ESEA and the Higher Education Acts of the 1960s, Graham argued that OE languished as a bureaucratic backwater unable to provide firm direction to the federal educational effort. His explanation for OE's plight centered on its too strong ties to education interest groups such as NEA, which by the mid- to late 1960s was seen mainly as an elementary-secondary teachers' group, the American Council on Education, which represented higher education, and groups representing school administrators and the land grant colleges. Additionally, OE was hampered, according to Graham, by the low federal civil service rank of its commissioner, which came with pay well below that of many school administrators. He also argued that a lack of staff from the higher ranks of the federal classification system meant that OE employees were not as competent as comparable employees in other federal agencies with similar responsibilities. Although Graham exempted OE commissioner Francis Keppel from his negative evaluation, he also noted that Keppel's major reorganization of OE in 1966 did not garner sufficient funding or personnel policies to accomplish the upgrade that was desperately needed.[2] In spite of this, OE continued to be charged with the administration of a raft of federal programs, NDEA, ESEA, and two higher education acts. What this all meant was that while the federal education effort was increasing enormously in terms of programs and personnel, the federal educational agency languished organizationally.

One proposal to improve the stature and efficiency of OE during this period was to join it with the National Science Foundation (NSF), a group with a more direct relationship to the president and a better reputation for organizational efficiency. The eventual rejection of this proposal was due, in part, according to Graham, to the fear that the environment OE characterized could harm NSF programs.[3]

The favorable image of NSF within the federal government has continued up to the present time. Science and scientists have also continued to enjoy a positive image in the minds of the American public. Putting a man on the moon encouraged appreciation for science and scientists, as did the positive press often given to developments in medical research. Scientists, however, seemed to lose the interest in education that had characterized much of their activity during and immediately after the passage of NDEA. Similarly, scientists receded in importance within the administration under presidents Kennedy and Johnson, as symbolized by the eventual demise of the President's Science Advisory Committee (PSAC). Even so, science's public positive image continued to justify significant expenditures on research sponsored by NSF and other federal agencies such as the National Institutes of Health.

Yet, in educational policy, the influence of scientists receded as their treasured high school curriculum reforms such as the Physical Science Study Committee (PSSC) were institutionalized in high schools with decreasing input from the scientists who seemed no longer to care about them.[4] Even within higher education and, more particularly, graduate higher education where research scientists could still claim significant influence, the enrollment in science programs came to be dominated by non-American students clearly capable of the work though not necessarily oriented first to the nation in which they worked. Scientists such as those in the PSAC under Eisenhower would have surely been concerned, if not appalled, by this increasing absence of homegrown talent in their fields, even though many of them were not American born. However, the next generation of scientists failed to voice such concern effectively, if at all, seemingly content to have competent graduate assistants for their own research, even if they were not from the United States.

NDEA in an Era of Educational Excellence

Thus far, I have argued that NDEA, a liberal-moderate measure, was a breakthrough in the federal aid to education arena, a breakthrough extended by ESEA and two higher education acts in the 1960s. This development was not accompanied, however, by a similar alteration in the federal educational agency that guaranteed an administration of federal aid that was as effective as the policies were ambitious. Added to this failure, a decline in the success of the liberal and moderate political orientations that had sparked the federal aid accomplishments, a fragmenting of the educational interests that had long cooperated in the advocacy of federal aid into a set of interests that often opposed each other, and the retirement from the educational arena of scientists who had exerted substantial influence over the passage of NDEA all led to a situation in which the NDEA-ESEA thrust spent its force. While the Carter administration in the late 1970s managed to replace OE with a cabinet level U.S. Department of Education, this action turned out to be the last real accomplishment of the equity-oriented federal aid to education groups, though not involving all of them. The NEA was the acknowledged leader of the lobbying for the Department of Education, though it could not even enroll all teachers in the effort, especially those represented by its small but visible rival teachers' union, the American Federation of Teachers.[5] Similarly, the higher education interest groups failed to participate unanimously and enthusiastically in the effort to establish the new department. The tendency of the Carter administration to let its organizational reform substitute for new and significant federal funds for education also meant that meaningful enhancement of federal aid was not on the administration's agenda.

Carter's diffidence over federal aid was followed by a wrenching change in federal educational policy initiated by Ronald Reagan. The election of Reagan in 1980 convincingly ended the era of equity-oriented federal aid to education, though little innovation in that direction had been accomplished for a decade or more before the election. Reagan did not accomplish his goals of dismantling the Department of Education, or of reestablishing prayer in the public schools and gaining tuition tax credits for private (religious) school parents. He did succeed, however, in displacing the equity agenda in education, not just in federal education policy but also in education policy in many states and localities. The gradual replacement of the free spending equity agenda of NDEA-ESEA with an excellence agenda began with the 1983 publication of the pamphlet produced by a presidentially appointed committee on education, "A Nation at Risk."[6]

Using a language of fear of economic competitors such as Japan that was just as apocalyptic as much of the post-Sputnik, anti-Soviet rhetoric that framed the political climate within which NDEA was developed, "A Nation at Risk" helped to inaugurate an educational excellence agenda at the federal level that came to be seen as anti–public school by many within the elementary, secondary, and college and university teacher education universe. Certainly the advocacy of school choice by every administration starting with Ronald Reagan and proceeding to the two Bush administrations of the twenty-first century connoted dissatisfaction with public education. Only the Clinton administration, by limiting its choice advocacy to charters and other public sector applications, was not openly questioning of public schools. The increasing embrace of private schools, especially private religious schools, as well as the public interest in and the increasing advocacy of home schools by interests associated with the Christian right, meant that public schools no longer assumed good will in the views of the executive branch. Politicians of both parties scrutinized public schools for their presumed deficiencies in producing academic achievement.

Ronald Reagan in his attack on federal educational activism moved the focus for educational affairs firmly back to the states and local school districts. Subsequent development of federal-state cooperative programs under

George H. W. Bush and Bill Clinton, calling for testing of students in core subjects and the setting of high standards of achievement for those tests, was endorsed enthusiastically by the nation's governors from both parties. This federal-state cooperation in turn resulted in the return of federal power in education, but not in the interest of equity or equality. Rather, George W. Bush's successful implementation of No Child Left Behind (NCLB) in 2002 invoked equity rhetorically in its title but adhered to an excellence agenda that often intimidated students preparing to take the tests, threatened the viability of schools that failed, and endangered the jobs of teachers who were deemed to be responsible for that failure. Thus the movement for educational excellence begun, or at least impelled, by "A Nation at Risk" in 1983 turned into a federal juggernaut mandating more and more curriculum change, systematic pedagogy to teach the changed curriculum, and a rigorous measurement system to assess the results.[7]

In a very real sense, the excellence movement turned on its head the equity-oriented federal aid to education movement that was prominent in several titles of NDEA and dominant in federal educational activity for twenty or so years after its passage. While many in public elementary and secondary education had advocated substantial federal aid to education in the interest of decreasing the funding inequity among states and among school districts within states, and tried to design that assistance carefully not to increase federal control of education, what was realized with No Child Left Behind was the opposite, a massive increase in federal control of education in terms of curriculum and testing procedures, with little if any increase in federal funding.

Comprehensive discussion of the excellence movement and its role in the development of NCLB is beyond the scope of this work. To link it directly with NDEA, however, is quite possible. I would note that the educational excellence movement continued the emphasis on academics, academic achievement, and measurable quality in education that were all promoted in Title V of NDEA, the testing, guidance, and counseling title. These emphases were also espoused by scientists and other academics critical of high schools and supportive of NDEA. Henry Chauncey, a member of the Panel on Education of the President's Science Advisory Committee, described public secondary education in the most unflattering terms in a memo to the education panel in June of 1958. He argued that secondary education, in its rush to become open to all students, had allowed "many able students to duck the tough courses and take the new courses instead." He added that attempts to make education more interesting meant "not holding all students taking a course to standards, to real achievement of the objectives." As a solution for these and other problems of high schools compromised as vehicles for obtaining quality education, Chauncey advocated national standards in the most important courses, tests of student achievement in relation to those standards, and "federal support for testing and guidance" as in the proposed NDEA.[8] As the head of the Educational Testing Service, a group that clearly had much to gain from Title V, particularly its testing provisions and its orientation to identifying gifted and talented students, Chauncey had both a personal and professional interest in NDEA and its Title V. He advocated, however, only national standards that were voluntary standards, adopted in the interest of attaining valid benchmarks that states and school districts might emulate, and of establishing qualifications for scholarships, prizes, or other forms of federal aid to students.

The most recent historical work on federal educational policy has made

1980 the dividing year, marking a clear shift away from federal policy and funding to implement an equity agenda to a direction oriented to standardized academic achievement. Carl Kaestle has attributed the change to the evolution of a more complex environment in which policy developed. The complexity included a proliferation of and shift in the nature of interest groups, increasing ideological diversity symbolized by the rise of conservative think tanks often devoted to questioning the legitimacy of public education, and technological development that has resulted in a proliferation of information and opinion. It also involved a reconstitution of the educational polity, in part due to federal court decisions that have devolved the resolution of educational controversies relating to race and religion to state and local contexts, and a discussion among policy scholars and policy makers about how ready and able states are to tackle issues related to educational excellence and achievement.[9]

To modify what I have said so far about NDEA, then, I would repeat that it was both a science education and a much-more-than-science education measure, and it broke the dam against federal aid to education through astute use of a national defense metaphor by all of its proponents. Further, it had liberal democratic provisions pointing toward equity in some of its titles and excellence oriented policies and practice in other titles. The liberal aspects of NDEA pointed toward its immediate successor measures such as ESEA and two higher education acts, but its excellence titles pointed toward the repudiation of equity in the interests of educational excellence that would be the goal of federal educational policy after 1980. If this description is correct, NDEA then was both liberal and conservative, equity and excellence oriented, and it resulted in both a breakthrough in the amount of federal funding for education that resulted in a strong equity emphasis in federal educational policy and a prefiguring of the direction that federal educational policy would take as it broke away from the equity orientation and the emphasis on federal funds without abandoning either completely.

A New NDEA?

I write these words in the late spring of 2008, a few months before the fiftieth anniversary of the enactment of NDEA on September 2 of this year. In the past two or three years, there has been a minor flurry of action directed toward passage of a new NDEA. A brief consideration of that action is in order here to see how the new NDEA compares with, and differs from, its ancestor.

On February 16, 2005 the Council of Graduate Schools, an agency representing the graduate schools and colleges of the nation's research universities, issued a press statement endorsing recommendations for increasing the support of graduate education to respond to a pending crisis described in *The Knowledge Economy: Is the United States Losing Its Competitive Edge.* The president of the graduate school organization sought the solution of the crisis as follows: "A new NDEA for the 21st Century is needed to make the investments in our future workforce to continue the American's leadership role in science and research innovation."[10]

Further impetus for a new NDEA came from the Department of Defense (DOD), which, in its budget proposal for fiscal 2006, requested $10.3 million for a new National Defense Education Program. The proposed program included scholarships and fellowships in the fields of science, mathematics, engineering, and languages. The DOD proposal was quickly endorsed by the Association of American Universities (AAU), a group of elite institutions of higher education. AAU this time endorsed the DOD proposal and recommended that further effort on this initiative be undertaken in conjunction with the National Science Foundation, the Department of Education, and the White House Office of Science and Technology Policy.[11]

These two initiatives, coming from within the government and from two groups with a major interest in graduate education, were followed up with a congressional initiative. On June 13, 2006, senators Edward M. Kennedy, John Kerry, and Hillary Clinton introduced a new National Defense Education Act to "ensure education standards, strengthen math and science teaching and education, expand college access and encourage the study of math, science, and critical need foreign languages, and improve job training for those currently in the workforce." In pursuit of these objectives, the proposed NDEA would be responsible for "providing incentives and resources for States and schools to develop and implement more rigorous standards in math, science, and reading; . . . providing grants and incentives . . . to recruit and retain highly qualified math, science, and critical-need foreign language teachers to teach in high poverty schools: . . . increasing investment in education programs at the National Science Foundation." Further, it would involve "Creating a program that guarantees students that if they work hard and get into college, their unmet need will be met through additional state and federal aid; Making college and graduate school tuition free for low-income students studying math, science, technology, engineering, or critical need foreign languages; . . . and . . . Providing competitive grants for job training to support innovative strategies to meet emerging labor market needs."[12]

There is little doubt that the senators added a few new wrinkles to what the DOD envisioned for its program. The new NDEA, as developed and refined before appearing on the legislative docket, shares much with its predecessor. It has become an omnibus measure, containing many things for many people—fellowships, loans, special financial incentives for economically needy students, workforce development, all based on a notion of international competitive need, especially in science, mathematics, engineering, and foreign languages. Reference in the proposals to the NSF and the Department of Education, successor to the Office of Education that administered almost all of NDEA, also resembles the earlier legislation. Missing from the contemporary proposal is the testing, guidance, and counseling emphasis that was in the legislation to ensure that the gifted would no longer be neglected by public schools too concerned with equality and equity. That omission may well be due to the fact that many public schools have downplayed, if they have not abandoned, that concern, as they have had to respond to the requirements for increased achievement and tests administered to assure that result.

More important than the resemblance of the twenty-first-century NDEA proposal with its predecessor are the differences between the measures and the climates in which they were produced. First, the sense of emergency referred to in the contemporary proposals has not reached the American public, at least not to the extent that Sputnik swept the public mind and created the opportunity to act that Congress and the administration capitalized on in 1958. Unless and until it does, the proposal will likely remain a proposal, which it still is in 2008, three years after it first surfaced. Next, the thinness of the forces involved in the presentation of the new NDEA deserves mention. The Department of Defense, graduate school interests, and three liberal senators, two from Massachusetts and one from New York, do not represent a wide-ranging political coalition. Where are the moderates, the southerners, the elementary and secondary educators, the scientists, and the journalists and other public media agencies that felt at least an interest in, if not a devotion to, the old NDEA? Unless these or other interests surface, in addition to graduate educators and liberal senators, the new NDEA faces enormous obstacles to its passage, obstacles that are unlikely to be overcome absent a new political climate. And finally, the fundamentally flawed nature of the discussion of American education in the contemporary era deserves mention. This is an era of wall charts in which achievements that can be measured are trotted out and used by politicians to make hay in one way or another for a variety, perhaps even a hodgepodge, of proposals and practices. It is also an era in which educational policy, while it has certainly been enhanced as a scholarly enterprise by a host of new practitioners and agencies devoted to the field, seems largely bereft of any intellectual, dare I say ideological, commitments related to the enhancement of equity in the educational enterprise. Educational policy analysts are expert at providing data to policy makers. What they do not seem able to do is to interpret those data in any way other than offering their versions of what policy makers want them to mean. Until these situations are all addressed, I think it is safe to conclude that there will be no new NDEA. The one we had in 1958 was an astute piece of legislation that met a wide variety of interests and served the purposes of a variety of proponents for much of the half-century since its passage.

Notes

Preface

1. Wayne Flynt, *Alabama in the Twentieth Century* (Tuscaloosa: The University of Alabama Press, 2004), 69.

Introduction

1. Barbara Barksdale Clowse, *Brainpower for the Cold War: The Sputnik Crisis and National Defense Education Act of 1958* (Westport, CT: Greenwood Press, 1983).

2. This summary of NDEA is based on the act itself, and on summaries provided by Clowse in *Brainpower for the Cold War,* 162–67 and William Stanley Hoole, The National Defense Education Act of 1958: A Brief Chronology, Box 4 Office of Education Records, Record Group 12: Records of the Office of Education, Records of the Commissioner of Education Relating to the National Defense Education Act; National Archives, Steny Hoyer Building, College Park, MD.

3. Clowse, *Brainpower for the Cold War.*

4. Joel H. Spring, *The Sorting Machine: National Educational Policy, 1945–1976* (New York: Longman, 1984).

5. Diane Ravitch, *The Troubled Crusade: American Education, 1945–1980* (New York: Basic Books, 1983).

6. Carl F. Kaestle and Marshall S. Smith, "The Federal Role in Increasing Equality of Educational Opportunity," *Harvard Educational Review* 52 (November 1982): 384–408.

7. Carl F. Kaestle, "Federal Aid to Education since World War II: Purposes and Politics," in *The Future of the Federal Role in Elementary and Secondary Education,* ed. Jack Jennings (Washington, DC: Center on Education Policy, 2001), 13–35.

Chapter 1

1. On the liberal character of Alabama's congressmen, see Wayne Flynt, *Alabama in the Twentieth Century* (Tuscaloosa: The University of Alabama Press, 2004), 68–69.

2. Stewart E. McClure, oral history interview (December 8, 1982 to May 3, 1983), 84, Eisenhower Library, Abilene, KS.

3. Ibid., 76, 101.

4. Ibid., 74.

5. Hill's racial views will be discussed more completely later in this chapter.

6. Virginia Van der Veer Hamilton, *Lister Hill: Statesman from the South* (Chapel Hill: University of North Carolina Press, 1987), 146.

7. Ibid., passim.

8. Ibid., 39. Hamilton's comprehensive and judicious biography was reprinted in a paperback edition by The University of Alabama Press in The Library of Alabama Classics. This account of Hill's early career is based on Hamilton.

9. Ibid., 45.

10. Ibid., chap. 3.

11. Lister Hill, "Nation's Responsibility for Education," *National Education Association Journal* 30 (September 1941): 30.

12. For example, see Notes for an address by Senator Hill (n.d., February 1951?) by William G. Carr. Carr, then Assistant Executive Secretary of the National Education and Secretary of its prestigious Educational Policies Commission, prepared these notes, which were more like an actual speech, for use by the senator. William Carr Papers, Folder 494–497, Box 3058, National Education Association Archives, Washington, DC.

13. A copy of the speech that was read into the Congressional Record on March 28, 1947 is found in Folder 47, Box 462 of the Lister Hill Papers, hereafter cited as the Hill Papers, at the Archives in the Special Collections Library of The University of Alabama in Tuscaloosa.

14. Lister Hill to Eleanor Cook (February 5, 1946), in which Hill discussed his speech to the Farm Bureau group of December 17, 1945. Hill Papers, Box 461, Folder 23.

15. Hamilton, *Lister Hill,* 74.

16. J. L. Crigler to Hill (January 16, 1946) and Hill to Crigler (January 22, 1946), Hill Papers, Box 461, Folder 22.

17. Elizabeth H. Wier to Hill (March 30, 1946), Hill to Wier (April 3, 1946), quotation, Hill Papers, Box 461, Folder 24.

18. W. Mims Jones to Hill (April 18, 1947) and Hill to Jones (April 21, 1947), Hill Papers, Box 461, Folder 37.

19. Resolution Adopted by Moundville Post #174 American Legion (February 19, 1948) and Hill to Manly Hall (February 29, 1948), Hill Papers, Box 462, Folder 57.

20. Willard Givens to Hill (November 4, 1947), Hill to Givens (November 7, 1947), Hill Papers, Box 236, Folder 1.

21. C. L. Scarborough to Hill (February 17, 1948) and Hill to Scarborough (February 23, 1948), Hill Papers, Box 462, Folder 55. Hill to forty-one radio stations (April 1, 1948), Hill Papers, Box 462, Folder 64.

22. W. A. Lovvorn to Hill (March 13, 1950), resolution included, Hill to Lovvorn (March 17, 1950), Hill Papers, Box 463, Folder 105.

23. Earl McGrath to Hill (July 14, 1952), Hill Papers, Box 236, Folder 5. Public

Law 815 provided for school construction aid, and this letter enumerated the particular projects, and the amounts, slated for Alabama. Public Law 874 provided non-construction aid to schools and districts impacted by federal activity.

24. John C. Carter to Hill (September 4, 1951) and Hill to Carter (September 6, 1951), Hill Papers, Box 463, Folder 116. On the school lunch program, see Susan Levine, *School Lunch Politics: The Surprising History of America's Favorite Welfare Program* (Princeton, NJ: Princeton University Press, 2008).

25. Ralph McDonald to Hill (March 23, 1951) and Hill to McDonald (March 26, 1951), Hill Papers, Box 463, Folder 114. There are thirteen folders in Box 464 of the Hill Papers, folders 140–52, containing correspondence and other materials relevant to extending the G.I. Bill from 1950 to 1966.

26. Hamilton, *Lister Hill,* 181. Stuart Symington to Hill (March 29, 1957), Paul H. Douglas to Hill (April 4, 1957), and Pat McNamara to Hill (April 4, 1957), Hill Papers, Box 464, Folder 138.

27. Hamilton, *Lister Hill,* 136–39.

28. M. D. Mobley, "A Review of Federal Vocational Education Legislation, 1862–1963," *Theory into Practice* 3 (December 1964): 167–70.

29. Ibid.

30. R. E. Cammack to Hill (February 2, 1951) and Hill to Cammack (February 10, 1951), Hill Papers, Box 463, Folder 111. Cammack, Director of Vocational Education for the State of Alabama was a frequent correspondent of Hill's.

31. Memorandum to Lister Hill from John E. Campbell (April 22, 1953), Hill Papers, Box 430, Folder 5.

32. Lister Hill to Dear Friend (July 12, 1954), Hill Papers, Box 463, Folder 126.

33. Telegram (July 20, 1955) and list of recipients designated, Hill Papers, Box 430, Folder 17.

34. Catherine Dennis to Hill (March 14, 1956), Hill Papers, Box 430, Folder 24.

35. Alice Davidson [President, National Council of Parents and Teachers] to Hill (August 17, 1956) and John E. Campbell to Davidson (August 21, 1956), Hill Papers, Box 465, Folder 207.

36. Lister Hill to M. D. Mobley (May 11, 1957); Hill to J. E. Speight (June 10, 1957); and R. E. Cammack to Hill (June 25, 1957) and Hill to Cammack (June 27, 1957), all in Hill Papers, Box 431, Folders 47, 39, and 42.

37. R. E. Cammack to Hill (January 6, 1958), Hill to Cammack (January 11, 1958), Hill Papers, Box 461, Folder 4.

38. Box 461, Folder 11, and Box 519, Folder 12 of the Hill Papers are full of letters from vocational leaders imploring Hill to protect the vocational title in NDEA. Ibid. also contains the *Montgomery Advertiser* editorial (July 25, 1958) praising NDEA but questioning the inclusion of vocational education.

39. John S. Forsythe to Hill (December 12, 1958), Hill Papers, Box 461, Folder 21.

40. Hill to Jesse A. Duke (May 14, 1963) and Hill to Selby Hanssen (May 28, 1963), Hill Papers. Box 520, Folder 60.

41. J. F. Ingram to Hill (September 30, 1966) and Hill to Ingram (October 3, 1966), Hill Papers, Box 433, Folder 112.

42. Hamilton, *Lister Hill,* 101. For a citation to the speech, see Hamilton's note 5.

43. Hill Papers, Box 463, Folder 119, Senate Bill S 138 (January 17, 1953).

44. J. R. Cudworth to Hill (June 4, 1956) and Hill to Cudworth (June 12, 1956), Hill Papers, Box 519, Folder 3.

45. George H. Smathers to Hill (October 10, 1957), Ibid., Folder 9.

46. Stewart E. McClure to Hill (December 27, 1957), Hill Papers, Box 461, Folder 2.

47. Robert A. Divine, *The Sputnik Challenge: Eisenhower's Response to the Soviet Satellite* (New York: Oxford University Press, 1993), vii.

48. Hill to R. E. Cammack (January 11, 1958), Hill Papers, Box 461, Folder 4.

49. George Land to Hill (February 8, 1958) and Hill to Land (February 18, 1958), Hill Papers, Box 461, Folder 7.

50. Ibid., Folder 8.

51. As I will show in chapter 3, the Eisenhower effort also involved more than aid to science education.

52. National Defense Education Act, A Full Report, United States Department of Health Education and Welfare, *School Life: Official Journal of the United States Office of Education* (October–November, 1958), quotation, 13, copy in Hill Papers, Box 238, Folder 90.

53. Flynt, *Alabama in the Twentieth Century,* 69.

54. Department of Health, Education, and Welfare, United States Office of Education Release (June 4, 1959), Hill Papers, Box 238, Folder 92.

55. Report of the Consultants to the Secretary, Department of Health, Education, and Welfare on areas related to the National Defense Education Act of 1958 (n.d. [panel met in September and November of 1960]), quotation, ii, Hill Papers, Box 238, Folder 98.

56. U.S. Department of Health, Education, and Welfare, Office of Education, Fact Sheet on the 1964 Amendments to the National Defense Education Act (October 16, 1964), quotation, 2, Hill Papers, Box 238, Folder 106.

57. Hill to Merril M. Collins (September 3, 1959), Hill Papers, Box 519, Folder 16.

58. Letters in Hill Papers, Box 520, Folder 76.

59. Letters in Hill Papers, Box 521, Folder 98.

60. Harriet Miller to Mike Mansfield (March 7, 1967), Mansfield to Hill (March 20, 1967), and Hill to Mansfield (April 3, 1967), Hill Papers, Box 521, Folder 101.

61. Hill to Hurst R. Anderson (February 16, 1968), Hill Papers. Box 521, Folder 107. Five other letters in that same folder related to language and area studies centers.

62. Meet Mr. NDEA, *NEA Washi:ngton Outlook on Education* (March 17, 1967), Hill Papers, Box 645, Folder 78.

63. Ibid. (March 6, 1967).

64. C. M. Dannelly to Hill (April 25, 2947) and Hill to Dannelly (April 28, 1947), Hill Papers, Box 461, Folder 39. Dannelly was the superintendent of the Montgomery public schools who objected to aid for parochial schools. Hill explained how his bill allowed federal funds to follow state funding patterns.

65. *Everson v. Board of Education of the Township of Ewing Et Al.* 330 U.S. 1 (1947).

66. Hill to Dannelly (April 28, 1947), Hill Papers, Box 461, Folder 39.

67. Chicago Region, I.C.P.T. [Illinois Congress of Parents and Teachers] to Dear Sir (February 4, 1948), Hill Papers, Box 462, Folder 47.

68. A. L. Meadows to Public School Officials (April 38, 1948), Hill Papers, Box 462, Folder 66.

69. Msgr. Leo M. Byrnes to Hill (March 27, 1948) and Hill to Byrnes (March 29, 1948), Hill Papers, Box 462, Folder 63.

70. Hill to Austin Meadows (March 23, 1949), Hill Papers, Box 462, Folder 76. Hill recounted in this letter to the Alabama superintendent the contents of the letter that the Bishop of Mobile had sent that invoked the child benefit theory.

71. Rose Mary Norville to Hill (August 3, 1949) and Hill to Norville (August 8, 1949), Hill Papers, Box 462, Folder 86.

72. Father Ralph to Hill (February 7, 1950), Hill to Father Ralph (February 11, 1950), and an exchange of letters between the two in February of 1949, all in Hill Papers, Box 463, Folder 93.

73. Lee Callman to Hill (February 15, 1950) and Hill to Callman (February 26, 1950), ibid., Folder 97.

74. A. H. Reid to Hill (April 20, 1949), Hill to Reid (April 22, 1949 [not sent]), Hill Papers, Box 462, Folder 78. Hill to Reid (April 30, 1949), ibid., Folder 78.

75. Hamilton, *Lister Hill,* 23–24.

76. Ibid., 88.

77. Ibid., 123, 148.

78. Ibid., 147.

79. Ibid., 115, 124, 127.

80. Joseph A. Berry to Hill (May 18, 1948), Hill Papers, Box 462, Folder 67.

81. John E. Bryan to Hill (January 11, 1950), ibid., Folder 88.

82. L. H. Scott to Hill (November 11, 1954); Hill to Scott (November 11, 1954), Hill Papers, Box 463, Folder 128.

83. Clowse, *Brainpower for the Cold War,* 47.

84. Hamilton, *Lister Hill,* 213.

85. Ibid., 216.

86. Hubert Humphrey to Hill (May 26, 1956), Hill Papers, Box 464, Folder 136.

87. Hamilton, *Lister Hill,* 221.

88. Roger W. Newman, *Hugo Black: A Biography* (New York: Pantheon, 1994), 690n16.

Chapter 2

1. Barney Weeks to Curtis W. Ellison (March 24, 1965), Carl Elliott Papers, Box 196, Folder 7915, Archives, Hoole Special Collections Library, The University of Alabama, hereafter cited as Elliott Papers.

2. Ibid.

3. Carl Elliott Sr. and Michael D'Orso, *The Cost of Courage: The Journey of an American Congressman* (New York: Doubleday, 1992), 32. A paperback edition of *The Cost of Courage* was published by The University of Alabama Press in 2001.

4. Ibid., 12. We will deal in depth with Elliott's racial views later in this chapter.

5. Carl Elliott, *Annals of Northwest Alabama* (Tuscaloosa, AL). This five-volume series was privately printed. Copies of each volume are in The University of Alabama Library.

6. Elliott and D'Orso, *Cost of Courage,* 51, 59.

7. Ibid., 62–65.

8. Ibid., 75, 76.

9. Ibid., 86, 89.

10. Ibid., 99.

11. Ibid., 101, 108.

12. Ibid., 66.

13. Ibid., 89.

14. Carl Elliott, "After Civil Rights—What's Next?" Speech to Young Men's Business Club of Birmingham, Alabama (July 26, 1965), Elliott Papers, Box 196, Folder Elliott, Carl, After Civil Rights, What's Next. The topic will be considered at length later in this chapter.

15. Elliott and D'Orso, "After Civil Rights—What's Next?"

16. Elliott and D'Orso, *Cost of Courage*, 124, 129.

17. Ibid., 130–32. The Elliott papers are filled with correspondence from veterans in Elliott's congressional district, elsewhere in the state, and from other states. He meticulously answered each veteran and did his best to respond to their needs, even after focusing on his work on the Education and Labor Committee.

18. Stewart E. McClure, Oral History Interview (December 8, 1982 to May 3, 1983), 95.

19. Elliott to J. D. Jardeman (February 7, 1952), Elliott Papers, Box 52, Folder 1966.

20. Frank L. Grove to Elliott (February 22, 1952), ibid., and Elliott to Mitchell Drake (April 21, 1952), Elliott Papers, Box 52, Folder 1967.

21. Elliott and D'Orso, *Cost of Courage,* 132.

22. Elliott to W. T. McKee (February 3, 1953), Elliott Papers, Box 59, Folder 2451.

23. Elliott to Mary Ruth Holleman (July 20, 1953), Elliott Papers, Box 59, Folder 2454.

24. R. E. Cammack to Elliott (January 21, 1953), Elliott Papers, Box 59, Folder 2351.

25. Elliott to Dora Fuller (May 26, 1955), Elliott Papers, Box 66, Folder 3098.

26. Elliott to Walter M. Jackson (July 25, 1955) and Jackson to Elliott (July 27, 1955), Elliott Papers, Box 68. Folder 3172.

27. Elliott to Frank E. Karleson (May 9, 1956), and Elliott to W. M. Gardner (July 7, 1956), Elliott Papers, Box 75, Folder 3629.

28. William Frank Banks to Elliott (July 8, 1955) and Elliott to Banks (July 12, 1955), Elliott Papers, Box 68, Folder 3172.

29. Representative Elliott on school study group, the *Birmingham News* (June 26, 1976), clipping in Elliott Papers, Box 73, Folder 3582.

30. Elliott to Graham Barden (n.d. [ca. December, 1956]), Elliott Papers, Box 80, Folder 3914.

31. Elliott and D'Orso, *Cost of Courage,* 142.

32. Committee Roster, Committee on Education and Labor (n.d. [January, 1957]), Elliott Papers, Box 80, Folder 3914.

33. J. F. Ingram to Elliott (February 1, 1957), Elliott Papers, Box 81, Folder 3969.

34. Carl Elliott's Week in Washington (August 12, 1957), Elliott Papers, Box 81, Folder 3934.

35. Statement of Dr. Kenneth J. Little, Director of Institutional Studies and Professor of Education, University of Wisconsin (October 28, 1957), Elliott Papers, Box 81, Folder 3934. Little's study was one of several summarized in a 1964 National Science Foundation study of educational opportunity, which will be discussed in chapter 5.

36. Harold Enarson to Elliott (October 30, 1957) and List of Questions for subcommittee hearing in Salt Lake City, Utah (November 1, 1957), Elliott Papers, Box 81, Folder 3934.

37. Oral History Interview, Stewart McClure (December 8, 1982 to May 3, 1983), 116; Eisenhower Library.

38. M. H. Trytten, Critical Days in Higher Education (May 17, 1956), Elliott Papers, Box 73, Folder 3581. I will discuss this speech at length in chapter 5.

39. Trytten, Critical Days in Higher Education, 21.

40. Education—Your Investment in Freedom: An Address Prepared for The Honorable Carl Elliott in accordance with his instructions by Charles A. Quattlebaum, Specialist in Education and Herman A. Sieber, Research Assistant in Education and American Government (October 30, 1957), 3, 4, 5, Elliott Papers, Box 5503, Folder Education. The copy contains both the printed text from the Legislative Reference Service and Elliott's handwritten insertions.

41. Ibid., 6, 7.

42. Ibid., 7, 8.

43. Ibid., my emphasis.

44. Ibid., 9, 10.

45. Ibid., 10.

46. R. E. Cammack to Elliott (January 6, 1958) and Cammack to Elliott (January 22, 1958), Elliott Papers Box 88, Folder 4345; and Elliott to Cammack (February 6, 1958), Elliott Papers, Box 88, Folder 4346.

47. Abstract by Dr. W. S. Hoole, Hearings House Committee on Education and Labor (February 6, 1958): Statement of L. S. DuBridge, President, Cal Tech., Elliott Papers, Box 88, Folder 4346.

48. Ibid., my emphasis.

49. For Congressman Carl Elliott (February 26, 1958), Elliott Papers, Box 85, Folder 4346.

50. For a consideration of Chauncey and his effectiveness, see Nicholas Lemann, *The Big Test* (New York: Farrar, Straus and Giroux, 1999).

51. Pitrim A. Sorokin to Ralph Gwynn (February 20, 1958), Elliott Papers, Box 85, Folder 4347.

52. Benjamin Shimberg to Elliott (June 20, 1958), Elliott Papers, Box 91, Folder 4411.

53. Provisions of the Hill-Elliott Bill Relating to Guidance and Counseling, Memorandum Prepared at the request of Hon. Carl Elliott—by Mary Allen (December 4, 1958), Elliott Papers, Box 89, Folder 4353.

54. History of the Hill-Elliott Act (n.d. [1958]), 15, passim, Elliott Papers, Box 89, Folder 4353; Elliott and D'Orso, *Cost of Courage,* 170.

55. The Student Loan Program in the Proposed National Defense Education Act Prepared at the Request of the Honorable Carl Elliott by Helen A. Miller and Vivian v. Gordon, Education and Public Welfare Division [USOE] (July 29, 1958), Elliott Papers, Box 92, Folder 4416.

56. Committee on Education and Labor, U.S. House of Representatives, Memorandum [for] Television (July 18, 1958), Elliott Papers, Box 92, Folder 4415.

57. See Education—Your Investment in Freedom, Elliott Papers, Box 5503, Folder Education.

58. Elliott and D'Orso, *Cost of Courage,* 166.

59. *Baptist Newsletter* [Baptist State Executive Board of the Alabama Baptist State Convention] (March 13, 1957) and Elliott to Aloysius Pleasance (March 14, 1957), Elliott Papers, Box 82, Folder 3970.

60. Elliott to Leslie Wright (February 26, 1960), Elliott Papers, Box 300, Folder 12F.

61. Aloysius Pleasance to Elliott (September 25, 1962), Elliott to Pleasance (October 2, 1962), and Elliott to Leslie S. Wright (September 28, 1962), ibid.

62. Leslie Wright to Edith Green (September 28, 1962), Green to Wright (October 4, 1962), both in ibid.

63. Elliott to Charles E. Creel (February 11, 1963) and Elliott to Brian J. Egan (August 8, 1963), Elliott Papers, Box 158, Folders 6765, 6768. Elliott received numerous letters on this issue throughout the early 1960s.

64. Bobby Nunn to Elliott (August 19, 1963) and Elliott to Nunn (February 4, 1963), Elliott Papers, Folder 6771; Elliott to J. M. Partain (September 12, 1963), Elliott Papers, Box 159, Folder 6772.

65. Elliott to Frank E. Karelsen (May 9, 1956) and Elliott to W. M. Gardner (July 7, 1956) Elliott Papers, Box 75, Folder 3629.

66. Elliott to George Meany (July 7, 1957), Elliott Papers, Box 82, Folder 3973; Bettye Rushing to Elliott (March 1, 1957) and Elliott to Rushing (March 7, 1957), Elliott Papers, Box 79, Folder 3890.

67. Speech of Carl Elliott, Member of Congress, at the Russellville High School Graduating Exercises (May 31, 1957), 14, Elliott Papers, Box 84, Folder 4036.

68. Speech of Carl Elliott, M.C. at Carson Mill High School Homecoming Exercises (October 11, 1957), Elliott Papers, Box 84, Folder 4036.

69. Dan T. Carter, *The Politics of Rage: George Wallace, the Origins of the New Conservatism, and the Transformation of American Politics* (Baton Rouge: Louisiana State University Press, 2000).

70. Carl Elliott, "After Civil Rights—What's Next?"

71. Elliott and D'Orso, *Cost of Courage,* 283.

72. Ibid., 281, 285.

73. Carl Elliott to Albert Brewer (June 3, 1970), Elliott Papers, Box 5503, Folder Political.

74. Elliott and D'Orso, *Cost of Courage,* 179, 180, 181.

75. Ibid., 182, 306–7.

Chapter 3

1. Chester J. Pach Jr. and Elmo Richardson, *The Presidency of Dwight D. Eisenhower,* rev. ed. (Lawrence: University Press of Kansas, 1991).

2. On the EPC, see Wayne J. Urban, "The Educational Policies Commission, 1936–1968: Notes for an Autopsy," *Sophist's Bane* 3 (Fall 2005): 15–30.

3. James L. Sundquist, *Politics and Policy: The Eisenhower, Kennedy, and Johnson Years* (Washington, DC: Brookings Institution, 1968), 155.

4. William Stanley Hoole, *The National Defense Education Act of 1958: A Brief Chronology,* 5: Box 4, Office of Education Records, Record Group 12; Records of the Office of Education, Records of the Commissioner of Education Relating to the National Defense Education Act; National Archives, Steny Hoyer Building, College Park, MD; hereafter cited as OE Records. William G. Carr, NEA Official Evaluates White House Conference Committee Report (April 6, 1956), Carr Papers, NEA Archives, Box 3059, Folder 619–623.

5. Financial Aid to College and University Students. A Statement Prepared by The Division of Higher Education, Office of Education, Federal Security Agency (June 1, 1949), OE Records, Box 5, Folder OE Position Paper on Scholarships, Foreword.

6. *New York Times,* November 11, 1954, 20.

7. Hoole, *The National Defense Education Act of 1958,* 17.

8. Sundquist, *Politics and Policy,* 175.

9. Ibid., 9; Hoole, *The National Defense Education Act of 1958,* 39–40.

10. Hoole, *The National Defense Education Act of 1958,* 40.

11. On Richardson, see Geoffrey Kabaservice, *The Guardians: Kingman Brewster, His Circle, and the Rise of the Liberal Establishment* (New York: Henry Holt, 2004), 5–6 and passim. Also see "Elliot Lee Richardson: Lawyer and Public Servant, 1920–1999," *Notable American Unitarians,* retrieved from www.harvardsquarelibrary.org/unitarians/richardson.html on May 26, 2006.

12. "Elliot Lee Richardson: Lawyer and Public Servant, 1920–1999," *Notable American Unitarians.*

13. Robert A. Divine, *The Sputnik Challenge: Eisenhower's Response to the Soviet Satellite* (New York: Oxford University Press, 1993), vii.

14. Ibid., 12. The Science Advisory Committee will be discussed at length in chapter 5.

15. Divine, *The Sputnik Challenge,* 15.

16. Ibid., 165.

17. Elliot L. Richardson to Dr. Derthick (May 21, 1957), OE Records, Box 5, Folder OE Position Paper on Scholarships.

18. Financial Aid to College and University Students. A Statement Prepared by the Division of Higher Education, Office of Education, Department of Health, Education, and Welfare (May 31, 1957), OE Records, Box 5, Folder Position Paper on Scholarships.

19. Melvin W. Sneed to Elliot L. Richardson (November 14, 1957), OE Papers, Box 7, Folder 1957 October–December (Flynt).

20. Federal Aid to Students for Higher Education: Arguments Pro and Con, The Library of Congress Legislative Reference Service (November 12, 1957), OE Papers, Box 7, Folder 1957 October–December (Flynt). This is the same body that prepared a speech on education for Carl Elliott, as noted in chapter 2.

21. James P. [*sic*] Conant to Sherman Adams (November 10, 1957), OE Papers, Box 10, Folder Elliot Richardson Files re NDEA November 1957 (1).

22. Sherman Adams to James B. Conant (November 12, 1957), OE Papers, Box 10, Folder Elliot Richardson Files re NDEA November 1957 (1).

23. Elliot L. Richardson, Memorandum for the Files (November 15, 1957), OE Papers, Box 10, Folder Elliot Richardson Files re NDEA November, 1957 (2).

24. Elliot L. Richardson, Memorandum for Files (November 26, 1957), Subject: Telephone Call from Dr. Wells of Indiana University, OE Papers, Box 10, Folder Elliot Richardson Files re NDEA November, 1957 (2).

25. Reginald G. Conley to Elliot Richardson, Friday Meeting with National Science Foundation Officials (November 21, 1957), OE Papers, Box 10, Folder Elliot Richardson Files re NDEA November, 1957 (2). NSF is discussed in detail in chapter 5.

26. James R. Killian, *Sputnik, Scientists, and Eisenhower* (Cambridge, MA: MIT Press, 1977), 12–30. The educational activities of scientists and NSF will be discussed more in this chapter and will be discussed in detail in chapter 5.

27. Elliot L. Richardson to the Secretary (December 11, 1957), OE Papers, Box 10, Folder Elliot Richardson Papers re NDEA December 1957 (1).

28. Rufus Miles to Assistant Secretary Richardson (November 24, 1957), OE Papers, Box 10, Folder Elliot Richardson Files re NDEA December 1957 (2).

29. Wendell Godwin [Superintendent, Topeka, KS Schools] to Finis Engleman [American Association of School Administrators Executive Officer] (December 4, 1957), OE Papers, Box 10, Folder Elliot Richardson Papers re NDEA December 1957 (1).

30. Elliot L. Richardson to McGeorge Bundy (December 5, 1957), Bundy to Richardson (December 9, 1957), Richardson to Bundy (December 12, 1957), OE

Papers, Box 10, Folder Elliot Richardson Files re NDEA December, 1957 (1). Richardson had heard the same objection to the stricture for new or expanded programs from the president of Indiana University; see the document identified in note 23. This issue in microcosm represented a tension between a more populist and a more elitist approach to education that would surface in a variety of arenas. Chapter 5 discusses it within the scientific community. For more on Richardson and Bundy, see Kabaservice, *The Guardians,* passim.

31. Message from the President of the United States Transmitting Recommendations Relative to our Educational System, To the House of Representatives (January 27, 1958), OE Papers, Box 7, Folder 1958 (Flynt).

32. Press Release (January 29, 1958), From the Offices of Senator Lister Hill and Congressman Carl Elliott, Hill and Elliott Propose $3 Billion National Defense Program, OE Papers, Box 7, Folder 1958—February—(Flynt).

33. OE Papers, Box 8 contain the briefing materials and sample testimony prepared by OE staff.

34. Excerpt from Testimony of Elliot L. Richardson before the Subcommittee on Special Education of the Committee on Education and Labor, House of Representatives (February 5, 1958), OE Papers, Box 7, Folder 1958—February—(Flynt).

35. Elliot Richardson to John Graham (February 4, 1958), OE Papers, Box 11, Folder Elliot Richardson Files re NDEA Jan.–March, 1958 (2).

36. Elliot Richardson to The Secretary (March 5, 1958), Compromise with the Hill Elliott Bill, OE Papers, Box 11, Folder Elliot Richardson Files re NDEA Jan.–March, 1958 (2).

37. Ibid., and S. A. Saperstein to Elliot Richardson (April 4, 1958), OE Papers, Box 11, Folder Elliot Richardson Files re NDEA April–Oct., 1958. The eventual proposal for vocational education, arrived at with the consent of the vocational education lobby, was for a $20 million increase in existing vocational education monies, justified with language proclaiming that it was for technical specialists needed for national defense. See Parke M. Banta to Elliot Richardson (April 30, 1958), OE Papers, Box 11, Folder Elliot Richardson Files re NDEA April–Oct. 1958.

38. Marion Folsom to Jacob Javits (February 10, 1958), OE Papers, Box 11, Folder Loans, Student Legis. 1958 Educ.

39. Reginald Conley to Harry G. Haskill (May 1, 1958) and Elliot L. Richardson to Mr. Aughenbaugh (March 28, 1958), OE Papers, Box 11, Folder Loans, Student Legis. 1958 Educ.

40. Ibid., and Elliot L. Richardson Memorandum for James R. Killian (April 10, 1958), OE Papers, Box 11, Folder Loans, Student Legis. 1958 Educ.

41. Reginald Conley to Elliot L. Richardson (June 27, 1958), OE Papers, Box 11, Folder Elliot Richardson Files re NDEA April–Oct. 1958.

42. Robert E. Ansheles to Asst. Secretary Richardson (June 27, 1958), OE Papers, Box 11, Folder Elliot Richardson Files re NDEA June 1958.

43. Robert E. Ansheles to Asst. Sec. Richardson (July 11, 1958), OE Papers, Box 11, Folder Elliot Richardson Files re NDEA April–Oct. 1958.

44. Mr. Richardson (August 18, 1958), report of a phone conversation with Carl

Elliott; J. R. Killian to Mr. Elliott (August 21, 1958); and William J. Hoff [General Counsel, NSF] to Carl Elliott (August 19, 1958) with supporting letter from Alan Waterman [Director, NSF] to Lindsey Buckworth (August 16, 1958), OE Papers, Box 11, Folder Elliot Richardson Files re NDEA April–October 1958 (2).

45. Dwight D. Eisenhower to Mr. Wainwright (July 7, 1958) and Stuyvesant Wainwright to Mr. President (July 2, 1958), Copies in OE Papers, Box 8, Folder 1958—March–July—(Flynt).

46. Stuart McClure, Oral History Interview (December 8, 1982 to May 3, 1983), 118, Eisenhower Library.

47. Clowse, *Brainpower for the Cold War,* 133–34.

48. Ibid., 162–63.

49. Ibid., 133.

50. "Conant Seeks Reform of High School System," *Washington Post.* April 2, 1958, clipping in OE Papers, Box 11, Folder Elliot Richardson Files re NDEA April–October 1958.

51. Ralph C. M. Flynt to Lindley Beckworth (August 20, 1958), emphasis in document, OE Papers, Box 6, Folder 1958 August–September (USOE File).

52. Elliot L. Richardson Memo For the File (August 7, 1958), attached Cross Reference Sheet; and Elliot Richardson to Mr. Elliott (August 19, 1957), all in OE Papers, Box 11, Folder Elliot Richardson Files re NDEA April–October 1958 (2). On Powell amendments, see chapter 2.

53. Elliot Richardson Memorandum to the Committee on Education and Labor (August 19, 1958) and Statement of Justification for Ten Supergrade Positions in the Office of Education As Provided in S 4237 (n.d.), both in OE Papers, Box 11, Folder Elliot Richardson Files re NDEA April–October 1958 (2).

54. Divine, *The Sputnik Challenge,* 165–66.

55. Clowse, *Brainpower for the Cold War,* 137.

56. More will be said about this in chapter 6.

57. Elliot Richardson to Mr. Elliott (August 23, 1958); Richardson to Senator Hill (August 23, 1958); Carl Elliott to Richardson (August 26, 1958) and Lister Hill to Richardson (August 26, 1958), all in OE Papers, Box 11, Folder Elliot Richardson Files re NDEA April–October 1958 (2).

58. Handwritten notes and partial text of Harold Howe's Welcoming Remarks (September 10, 1968), OE Papers, Box 344, Folder AO 6-2 Tenth Anniversary.

59. Program Outline (September 10, 1968) and Elliot L. Richardson to Wilbur J. Cohen (August 28, 1968), OE Papers, Box 344, Folder AO 6-2 Tenth Anniversary.

60. Marion Folsom Oral History Interview (January 1968), 47, Eisenhower Library.

61. Daniel P. Moynihan, "A Second Look at the School Panic," *The Reporter,* June 11, 1959, 16.

62. Elliot L. Richardson, "The NDEA Idea," *The Reporter,* July 23, 1959. There is a manuscript draft misfiled in the OE Papers, Box 10, Folder Elliot Richardson Files re NDEA November 1957 (2). I will use the draft in this explanation.

63. Ibid.

64. Ibid.

65. Elliot L. Richardson, *The Creative Balance: Government, Politics, and the Individual in America's Third Century* (New York: Holt Rinehart and Winston, 1976), xxvi, 122. The juxtaposition of conservatism and compassion was echoed, though not acknowledged, by George W. Bush in his 2000 presidential campaign.

66. Ibid., 68, 122, 123, 124.

67. Ibid., 342.

68. Elliot Richardson, *Reflections of a Radical Moderate* (New York: Pantheon, 1996), 88. 96. 206.

69. Ibid., 7–8, 27.

70. Ibid., 27.

71. Ibid., 245.

Chapter 4

1. On the early NEA, see Paul Mattingly, *The Classless Profession: American Schoolmen of the Nineteenth Century* (New York: New York University Press, 1975).

2. On the NEA remodeling, see Wayne J. Urban, *Gender, Race, and the National Education Association: Professionalization and Its Limitations* (New York: Routledge/Falmer, 2000), chap. 1.

3. Ibid., chap. 2.

4. On the EPC, see Wayne J. Urban, "The Educational Policies Commission, 1936–1968: Notes Toward an Autopsy," *Sophist's Bane* (Fall 2005).

5. "Youth Being Neglected Says Eisenhower," News and Trends, *NEA Journal* (February 1954); "HEW Secretary States Views on Education," News and Trends, *NEA Journal* (December 1954): 531.

6. "Carr Testifies on Education Bills," News and Trends, *NEA Journal* (May 1954); 259.

7. "NEA Federal Legislative Agenda," *NEA Journal* (October 1954): 436.

8. News and Trends, *NEA Journal* (January 1955): 3, 4.

9. "NEA Federal Legislative Policy," *NEA Journal* (October 1954): 436–37.

10. "Highlights of Senate Hearings on the Administration's School-Aid Plan [S 968]," *NEA Journal* (April 1955): 206.

11. William G. Carr, "The Opportunity of the White House Conference," *NEA Journal* (November 1955): 473.

12. William G. Carr, "The Achievement of the White House Conference," *NEA Journal* (January 1956): 9.

13. "NEA Official Evaluates White House Conference Committee Report," NEA Press Release (April 6, 1956), William G. Carr Papers, NEA Archives, Box 3059, Folder 638–642.

14. James L. McCaskill, "How The Kelly Bill Was Lost—And Why," *NEA Journal* (September 1956): 363–66; quotations 363, 366.

15. "Party Platforms on Education," *NEA Journal* (October 1956): 409 and "A Legislative Balance Sheet," ibid., 437. "A Follow-Up Report on The White House Conference," *NEA Journal* (December 1956): 572.

16. Dwight D. Eisenhower, "Education, The Most Important Subject," *NEA Journal* (May 1957): 300–302.

17. "NEA and the Federal Government—Legislative Policy, 1957–58," *NEA Journal* (October 1957): 466.

18. William G. Carr, "Statement concerning President Eisenhower's Address," (November 14, 1957), Carr Papers, Box 3060, Folder 687–691 and Press Release from NEA Statement of William G. Carr regarding President Eisenhower's Special Message on Education (January 27, 1958), ibid., Folder 707–12, NEA Archives.

19. Arthur E. Bestor Jr., *Educational Wastelands: The Retreat from Learning in Our Public Schools* (Urbana: University of Illinois Press, 1953).

20. Somewhat dated but still the "classic" treatment of progressive education is Lawrence A. Cremin, *The Transformation of the School: Progressivism in American Education, 1976–1967* (New York: Alfred A. Knopf, 1967).

21. We will consider the testimony of scientists before Congress at length in the next chapter.

22. Hyman G. Rickover, *Education and Freedom,* Foreword by Edward R. Murrow, Preface by Charles Van Doren (New York: Dutton, 1959).

23. Proceedings of the Special Called Meeting of the Educational Policies Commission, New York, NY (December 14–15, 1957), Educational Policies Commission Papers, Box 958, NEA Archives, 1.

24. Ibid., 15–16.

25. Ibid., 43–45, 102–7.

26. Educational Polices Commission, *The Contemporary Challenge to American Education* (Washington, DC: The National Education Association, 1958), 5.

27. Ibid., 9.

28. Ibid., 20, 23.

29. "The Contemporary Challenge to American Education," *NEA Journal* (March 1958): 188, 192, 194–200; insert p. 197.

30. NEA Executive Secretary Testifies Before U. S. Senate Committee on Education's Needs, Press Release (2/20/58), Carr Papers, Box 3060, Folder 713–17, NEA Archives.

31. Ibid.

32. Ibid.

33. "A Matter of Deduction," *NEA Journal* (February 1958): 103, 141; and J. L. McCaskill, "NEA Scores a Tax Victory," *NEA Journal* (May 1958): 284–85.

34. The platform actions are described in Irving F. Pearson, "Charting a Course: Education and the Federal Government," *NEA* Journal (September 1958): 429. Carr chose to address the delegates to the convention about an expansion in NEA programs and dues that had recently been adopted. See his address, "The First Year of the Expanded NEA Program," NEA Addresses and Proceedings (June 29, July 4, 1958) [hereafter NEA Proceedings], 85. In contrast, both U.S. OE commissioner

Lawrence Derthick and James B. Conant spoke to the delegates about educational concerns related to NDEA. Derthick discussed Russian education, commenting on a recent visit to the Soviet Union that he and colleagues from U.S. OE had undertaken. Conant spoke of his ongoing study of high schools, commenting on education for the gifted and adequate testing, counseling, and guidance services as areas of need. See Lawrence G. Derthick, "Greetings from the Office of Education," and James B. Conant, "The Unique Characteristics of American Public Education," NEA Proceedings (1958), 36–40 and 77–85.

35. Ibid., 144.

36. Ibid., 140–44; quotation 143–44.

37. Ibid., 144–47.

38. *New York Times,* July 4, 1958.

39. Ruth Stout, "The 85th Congress: A Milestone in American Education," *NEA Journal* (October 1958): 461–64, quotations 460, 461.

40. William G. Carr, "Not in Our Stars, But in Ourselves," *NEA Journal* (October, 1958), 490–95; quotation 490.

41. For the details of the Office of Education's history, see Harry Kursh, *The United States Office of Education: A Century of Service* (Philadelphia: Chilton Books, 1965), especially chap. 1 and Appendix A.

42. The best treatment of the early federal educational agency is Donald R. Warren, *To Enforce Education: A History of the Founding Years of the United States Office of Education* (Detroit, MI: Wayne State University Press, 1974).

43. Kursh, *The United States Office of Education,* 28.

44. On taking the schools out of politics, see David B. Tyack, *The One Best System: A History of Urban Education* (Cambridge, MA: Harvard University Press, 1974).

45. "NEA Federal Legislative Policy: As Defined in the NEA Platform and the Resolutions of 1954," *NEA Journal* (October 1954): 437.

46. Derthick's background in the NEA is outlined in NEA Proceedings (1958), 129.

47. Lawrence G. Derthick, "Greetings from the U.S. Office of Education," NEA Proceedings (1958), 36–40; quotation, 40. Also, Lawrence G. Derthick, "Whose Future," *NEA Journal* (October 1958): 457.

48. Kursh, *The United States Office of Education,* 37.

49. Ibid., 101, 103.

50. On NEA and higher education historically, see Wayne J. Urban, "Higher Education and the National Education Association: A Sesquicentennial Review," *NEA 2007 Almanac of Higher Education* (Washington, DC: National Education Association, 2007), 27–40.

51. Harrison Saucer, "New Federal Programs Promote Testing and Guidance," *NEA Journal* (January 1959): 29.

52. J. L. McCaskill, "Prospects for 1959: Education and the Congress," and Mary Jo Tregilgas, "I'm for Federal Support of Education," *NEA Journal* (January 1959): 66, 67; "Fact Sheet on the Murray-Metcalf Bill," *NEA Journal* (February 1959): 49; and "News and Trends," *NEA Journal* (May 1959): 3.

53. Proceedings of the Educational Policies Commission (April, 29, 1963), 15–16; EPC Papers, Box 963, NEA Archives.

54. Hugh Davis Graham, *The Uncertain Triumph: Federal Education Policy in the Kennedy and Johnson Years* (Chapel Hill: University of North Carolina Press, 1984), 43.

55. Ibid.

56. "McMurrin Insists He Quit to Teach: But Former Education Chief Admits Rift with N.E.A.," *New York Times,* October 22, 1962, clipping in Carr Papers, Box 3062, Folder 860–864, NEA Archives.

57. William G. Carr to Sterling McMurrin (October 24, 1962), Carr to McMurrin (October 29, 1962), McMurrin to Carr (October 31, 1962); all in Carr Papers, Box 3062, Folder 860–864, NEA Archives.

58. Carr to McMurrin (November 17, 1962), Carr Papers, Box 3062, Folder 860–864, NEA Archives.

59. James B. Conant, *My Several Lives* (New York: Harper and Row, 1970), 394–97. On Keppel's appointment, see also Arthur G. Powell, *The Uncertain Profession: Harvard and the Search for Educational Authority* (Cambridge, MA: Harvard University Press, 1980), 235–36.

60. On this matter, see Urban, *Gender, Race, and the National Education Association,* chap. 5.

Chapter 5

1. James Phinney Baxter, *Scientists against Time* (Boston: Little, Brown, 1948), 15 and J. Merton England, *A Patron for Pure Science: The National Science Foundation's Formative Years, 1945–1957* (Washington, DC: National Science Foundation, 1982), 4.

2. James G. Hershberg, *James B. Conant: Harvard to Hiroshima and the Making of the Nuclear Age* (New York: Alfred A. Knopf, 1992), chap. 8. Kistiakowsky, as noted later in this chapter, served as the president's science advisor, replacing James Killian in that position shortly after NDEA was passed.

3. Conant, as quoted in Hershberg, *James B. Conant,* 134.

4. Paul Boyer, *By the Bomb's Early Light: American Thought and Culture at the Dawn of the Atomic Age* (Chapel Hill: University of North Carolina Press, 1992), 60.

5. John L. Rudolph, *Scientists in the Classroom: The Cold War Reconstruction of American Science Education* (New York: Palgrave, 2002), 37.

6. England, *A Patron for Pure Science,* 9–10.

7. *Science: the Endless Frontier: A Report to the President by Vannevar Bush, Director of the Office of Scientific Research and Development, July, 1945* (Washington, DC: U.S. Government Printing Office, 1945). Quotations are from England, *A Patron for Pure Science,* 21–22.

8. England, *A Patron for Pure Science,* 21–22.

9. Ibid., 61–81.

10. Ibid., 109.

11. Rudolph, *Scientists in the Classroom,* 42.

12. England, *Patron for Pure Science,* 100–104. The NDEA loyalty oath is discussed in the next chapter.

13. Waterman could not name the Wisconsin senator, but readers of the article did not have too much trouble reading between its lines. See Alan Waterman, "Acceptance of Science," *Scientific Monthly* 80 (January 1955): 10–14.

14. Rudolph, *Scientists in the Classroom,* 54.

15. Ibid., chap. 5.

16. (Washington, DC: National Science Foundation, 1982).

17. Daniel Kevles, *The Physicists: The History of a Scientific Community in Modern America* (Cambridge, MA: Harvard University Press, 1987), 349.

18. As quoted in England, *A Patron for Pure Science,* 227.

19. For a thorough review of the universities and Sputnik, see Roger Geiger, *Research and Relevant Knowledge: Research Universities since World War II* (New York: Oxford University Press, 1993), chap. 6.

20. James R. Killian Jr., The Challenge of Soviet Science (April 8, 1957), Eisenhower Library, Fred A. Seaton Papers, Ewald Research File, Box 7, Folder Education (3).

21. M. H. Trytten, "Critical Days in Higher Education," Speech at the Annual Meeting of the Alabama Association of Colleges (May 17, 1956). I found a copy of this speech in the Carl Elliott Papers, Special Collections, The University of Alabama Library, Box 73, Folder 3581.

22. Trytten, "Critical Days in Higher Education," 17.

23. Ibid., 18.

24. Ibid., 21.

25. Ibid., 20.

26. Hyman G. Rickover, *Education and Freedom* (New York: E. P. Dutton, 1959). Rickover was developing his ideas at the same time Trytten was making his speech; see H. G. Rickover, "The Situation in American Science and Engineering Education," *School and Society* (May 26, 1956): 75–79. James B. Conant, *The American High School Today: A First Report to Interested Citizens* (New York: McGraw-Hill, 1959).

27. Trytten, "Critical Days in Higher Education," 2, 3.

28. Ibid., 20.

29. Ibid., 21.

30. Howard A. Meyerhoff, "The Plight of Science Education," *Bulletin of the Atomic Scientists* (November 1956): 333–37.

31. Ellliot Tozer, "What the Engineering Shortage Means," *Aviation Age* (July 1956): 20–24.

32. Oral History Interview, James R. Killian (1969, 1970), Eisenhower Library, 104.

33. Ibid., 47.

34. Ibid., 101, 108, 125.

35. George Kistiakowsky Oral History Interview (November 17, 1976), Eisenhower Library, 20.

36. Killian Interview, 47, 53–54.

37. James Rhyne Killian, 1904–1948, Papers, 1923–1948, Manuscript Collection—MC 423, Institute Archives and Special Collections, Massachusetts Institute of Technology, 4; hereafter Killian Papers. Also see James R. Killian Jr., *The Education of a College President: A Memoir* (Cambridge, MA: MIT Press, 1985).

38. Killian Papers, 4.

39. Killian Interview, 44 (my emphasis).

40. Ibid., 45–46.

41. There also may have been security reasons for ignoring discussions of American scientific development. While, as noted in chapter 3, Eisenhower believed strongly that American technology was not in danger of being surpassed by Soviet accomplishments, revealing the particulars of American technological development as would happen in an open comparison of Soviet and U.S. scientific accomplishment was seen as possibly compromising U.S. science by making the particulars of its accomplishments available to the nation's chief rival.

42. James R. Killian, Science and Public Policy (December 29, 1957), Eisenhower Library, Fred A. Seaton Papers, Ewald Research File, Box 7, Folder Education (1).

43. Killian, Memorandum for Dr. Lee A. DuBridge (May 23, 1958), Eisenhower Library, White House Office Files, Office of the Special Assistant for Science and Technology Box 8, Folder Education Panel (1957–1960) (2); and Lee A. DuBridge to Dr. Killian (December 17, 1957), White House Office Files, Office of the Special Assistant for Science and Technology, Box 8, Folder Education Panel (1957–1960) (1).

44. Killian Interview, 274–75, 360.

45. Ibid., 303, 304.

46. Ibid., 306.

47. Eisenhower to Killian (May 28, 1959) and Killian to Eisenhower (May 27, 1959), Eisenhower Library, Whitman Administration, Box 23, Folder Killian, James R. 1957 (1).

48. Minutes of Cabinet Meeting (December 2, 1957), Eisenhower Library, Whitman Collection, Cabinet Series, Box 10.

49. Folsom Interview, 78, 87. Folsom's successor as HEW secretary, Arthur Flemming, recalled that he was more directly involved with the president during his service in his role as director of Defense Mobilization, a position he held prior to becoming DHEW Secretary, than he was when he assumed the cabinet-level position. Oral History Interview, Flemming, Arthur S. (November 24, 1978), 27.

50. Arthur E. Burns, Science Education Program (November 25, 1957), Eisenhower Library, Price, Douglas R. Records, 1955–1960, Box 8, Folder Education (2).

51. Charles B. Ruttenberg to Philip S. Hughes (August 26, 1958), Eisenhower Library, White House Office, Box 143, Folder 9/2/58 National Defense Education Act HR 13247.

52. Lee A. DuBridge to Arthur S. Flemming (September 9, 1958), Eisenhower Library, White House Office, Office of the Special Assistant to the President for Science and Technology, Records, 1957–1961. Box 8, Folder Education Panel, 1957–1960 (3).

53. L. A. DuBridge to Caryl P.Haskins, Alan T. Waterman, Jerrold R. Zacharias (January 13, 1958), Eisenhower Library, White House Office, Office of the Special Assistant to the President for Science and Technology, Records, 1957–1961. Box 8, Folder Education Panel (2).

54. President's Science Advisory Committee, *Education for the Age of Science* (May 24, 1959), Washington, DC: The White House.

55. Ibid., v.

56. Ibid., 1–3.

57. Ibid., 10.

58. Ibid., 10–11.

59. Ibid., 18.

60. Ibid., 33.

61. Ibid., 13–14.

62. Ibid., 14.

63. Ibid., 14–15.

64. James B. Conant, *Shaping Educational Policy* (New York: McGraw-Hill, 1964).

65. Ibid., chap. 5, "Toward a Nationwide Educational Policy."

66. Ibid., 124. *The Duration of Formal Education for High-Ability Youth: A Study of Retention in the Educational System,* National Science Foundation 61-36 [for Select Committee on Government Research U.S. House of Representatives]. No doubt, Conant was also aware of other relevant studies, such as those mentioned in notes 67 and 68.

67. *The Duration of Formal Education for High-Ability Youths,* 2.

68. Dale Wolfle, *America's Resources of Specialized Talent* (New York: Harper and Brothers, 1954).

69. The major studies discussed in the report in addition to Wolfle included R. R. Iffert, "Retention and Withdrawal of College Students," *U.S. Office of Education Bulletin* (1958), 1, (Washington, DC: U.S. Government Printing Office, 1957); A. A. Daughtry, "A Report on the Post-Graduation Activities of the 1955 Kansas High School Graduates," *Emporia State Research Studies* 5 (1956): 38–41; and J. Kenneth Little, *A State-Wide Inquiry into Decisions of Youth about Education beyond High School* (University of Wisconsin, School of Education, 1958). For the statement of loss of one-third of high ability students, see *The Duration of Formal Education for High Ability Youth,* 31.

70. *The Duration of Formal Education for High Ability Youth,* 23, 24.

71. Ibid., 4, 7 (my emphasis).

72. Ibid., 9.

73. Rudolph, *Scientists in the Classroom,* 199.

74. Robert H. Carleton to the President of the United States (June 4, 1959),

Eisenhower Library, White House Office, Office of the Special Assistant for Science and Technology, Records, 1957–1961, Folder Education Panel, 1957–1960 (5).

75. Killian Interview, 311.

Chapter 6

1. The impacted aid program provided school construction aid and operations assistance to those districts deemed to be impacted by federal installations and programs. This aid began in 1950 and continued beyond the time of NDEA.

2. Congressional Quarterly Service, *Congress and the Nation, 1945–1964: A Review of Government and Politics in the Postwar Years* (Washington, DC: Congressional Quarterly, 1965), 1200–1201.

3. Ibid., 1199. The chart includes a breakdown of federal funds for education that includes NDEA funds in the column marked Other. This is one of three columns indicating various types of federal aid for elementary and secondary schools. The other two columns were for Federally Impacted Areas programs and for the school lunch–school milk programs.

4. James L. Sundquist, *Politics and Policy: The Eisenhower, Kennedy, and Johnson Years* (Washington, DC: Brookings Institution, 1968), 207.

5. Hugh Davis Graham, "The Transformation of Federal Educational Policy," in *Exploring the Johnson Years,* ed. Robert Divine (Austin: University of Texas Press, 1981), 156.

6. Ibid., and Graham, *The Uncertain Triumph: Federal Education Policy in the Kennedy and Johnson Years* (Chapel Hill: University of North Carolina Press, 1984), 3.

7. George J. Hecht to Arthur S. Flemming (September 25, 1961), Flemming, Arthur S. Papers, 1939–1975, Eisenhower Library, Box 11, Folder Hau-Hec; and Telegram to Mr. Hecht (n.d., [ca. September 1961]), Flemming Papers, Box 41, Folder Citizens' Committee for Extension of the National Defense Education Act.

8. U.S. Department of Health, Education, and Welfare, Office of Education, Advance Release for Thursday, June 4, 1959, Lister Hill Papers, Box 238, Folder 92.

9. Ibid.

10. U.S. Department of Health, Education, and Welfare, Office of Education, Release (September 1, 1963), in Elliott Papers, Box 154, Folder 6676.

11. Evron Kilpatrick to Carl Elliott (July 30, 1964) and Carl Elliott to Ruth Waldrop (August 7, 1964), Elliott Papers, Box 183, Folder 7494.

12. U.S. Department of Health, Education, and Welfare, Fact Sheet on the 1964 Amendments to the National Defense Education Act (October 16, 1964), Hill Papers, Box 238, Folder 106.

13. DHEW Legislative Notes (August 6, 1965), p. 2, Hill Papers, Box 237, Folder 50.

14. U.S. Department of Health, Education, and Welfare, Office of Education, Advance Release (February 3, 1959), Hill Papers, Box 238, Folder 91.

15. Ibid.

16. Statement of Carl Elliott, M.C., before the Subcommittee on Labor and

Health, Education, and Welfare, Committee on Appropriations, U.S. House of Representatives (April 10, 1959), Elliott Papers, Box 100, Folder 4792.

17. M. Allen to Mr. Elliott (August 5, 1959), Elliott Papers, Box 100, Folder 4787.

18. Robert C. Hall and Stanton Craigie, National Defense Student Loan Program: Student Borrowers, Their Needs and Resources (Washington, DC: U.S. Government Printing Office, 1962), in Elliott Papers, Box 140, Folder 6188.

19. Carl Elliott to Marion B. Folsom (August 1, 1963), Elliott Papers, Box 158, Folder 6771.

20. Stewart McClure Oral History Interview (December 8, 1982 to May 5, 1983), 118, Eisenhower Library.

21. Carl Elliott to Elliot Richardson (April 16, 1959), Elliott Papers, Box 100, Folder 4792.

22. For example, see Baskin Wright [Jacksonville State College] to Carl Elliott (November 10, 1959), Elliott Papers, Box 100, Folder 4787 and Leon Belcher [Alabama Agricultural and Mechanical College] to Carl Elliott (November 18, 1964), Elliott Papers, Box 181, Folder 7433. Elliott also received a twenty-page list of loan recipients for the 1962–63 academic year, with addresses and amount of the loan, from The University of Alabama; see Elliott Papers, Box 140, Folder 6188. Lister Hill also received information on Alabama loans, though not with names and addresses; see Hill Papers, Box 298, Folder 102.

23. Carl Elliott to Dear Friend (September 1964) and Questionnaire on National Defense Student Loan Program filled out by Miss Essimena Williams of Greenwood, Mississippi, in Elliott Papers Box 180, Folder 7361.

24. Carl Elliott to Dear Friend (May 15, 1965), Elliott Papers, Box 195, Folder 7893.

25. U.S. Department of Health, Education, and Welfare, August 23, 1965, Supplement No. 10 to June 14, 1965, Notification to Congress, Hill Papers, Box 237, Folder 571.

26. Graham, *The Uncertain Triumph*, 223.

27. Francis Keppel, "The Gleaming Promise of Guaranteed Student Loans" (December 16, 1965), Elliott Papers, Box 5503, Folder Education.

28. Ibid.

29. Clowse, *Brain Power for the Cold War*, 131.

30. The complete text of the oath provisions is found in a memorandum from Harvard president N. M. Pusey to the Members of the Association of American Universities (November 25, 1959). A copy of this memorandum is in the Elliott Papers, Box 100, Folder 4787. The oath is summarized in Clowse, *Brainpower for the Cold War*, 167.

31. Margaret B. Fisher to Mary Allen (April 10, 1959), Elliott Papers, Box 243, Folder XX.

32. N. M. Pusey to the Members of the Association of American Universities (November 25, 1959).

33. Ibid.

34. Harry V. Barnard to Carl Elliott (December 8, 1959), Elliott Papers, Box 100, Folder 4787. Barnard was an Alabamian, a high school teacher with a doctorate in education who became a faculty member at the University of Kentucky after leaving Carl Elliott's staff. On Nathan Pusey's background, see Morton Keller and Phyllis Keller, *Making Harvard Modern: The Rise of America's University* (New York: Oxford University Press, 2001), 173–75.

35. Barnard to Elliott (December 8, 1959).

36. The institutions were listed in an article discussing the repeal of the affidavit requirement; see John Walsh, "Compromise on Repeal Quiets One Controversy," *Science* 138 (December 28, 1962): 1381.

37. Barnard to Elliott (December 8, 1959).

38. Carl Elliott to Carol Anne Hollowell [and numerous others] (February 17, 1960), Elliott Papers, Box 244, Folder 20P.

39. Carl Elliott to Al Ullman (April 22, 1960), Elliott Papers, Box 244, Folder 20P.

40. David H. Malone to Lister Hill (June 19, 1961) and Hill to Malone (June 22, 1961), Hill Papers, Box 464, Folder 162.

41. John Walsh, "Loyalty Affidavit," *Science* (December 28, 1962).

42. NDEA Fellows 1961–1962, The University of Alabama Graduate School, in Elliott Papers, Box 124, Folder 5704. The significant addition to the ranks of American scholars pioneered by NDEA fellowships deserves special recognition here. As I have discussed this work with colleagues in history and history of education around the country, I learned often that one or another distinguished scholar in my field was supported by an NDEA fellowship in graduate work.

43. Alex S. Pow to Congressman Carl Elliott (January 17, 1961), Elliott Papers, Box 124, Folder 5704.

44. Alex S. Pow to Carl Elliott (March 2, 1965), Elliott Papers, Box 195, Folder 7892.

45. Mary Allen, Confidential Memorandum to Carl Elliott Re: The University of Alabama (3/2/65), Elliott Papers, Box 124, Folder 5704.

46. Ibid.

47. Alex S. Pow to Congressman Carl Elliott (May 3, 1960), Elliott Papers, Box 112, Folder 5254.

48. Frank Rose to Lister Hill (May 19, 1966) and Hill to Rose (May 19, 1966), Hill Papers, Box 433, Folder 109.

49. Lister Hill to Dear Senator (May 2, 1967), and Lister Hill to Douglas Cater (May 5, 1967), Hill Papers, Box 433, Folder 117; Frank Rose to Lister Hill (June 22, 1967), Hill Papers, Box 433, Folder 119.

50. V. C. Helms to George W. Andrews [Alabama Congressman] (May 22, 1967), copy; Lister Hill to V. C. Helms (May 25, 1967) and Hill to Helms (August 10, 1967), all in Hill Papers, Box 433, Folder 117.

51. On the founding and early years of the federal educational agency, see Donald R. Warren, *To Enforce Education: A History of the Founding Years of the United States Office of Education* (Detroit, MI: Wayne State University Press, 1974).

52. Administrative Actions Taken by the Office of Education under the National

Defense Education Act, as of October, 1, 1958) [Conference with Commissioner L. G. Derthick; Deputy Commissioner Wayne O. Reed, Director of Higher Education Ralph C. M. Flynt, and Budget Officer Jack Hughes, held at Department of Health, Education, and Welfare] (October 1, 1958), Elliott Papers, Box 92, Folder 4420.

53. Ibid.

54. Ibid.

55. Ibid., passim.

56. Harry Kursh, *The U.S. Office of Education: A Century of Service* (Philadelphia and New York: Chilton Books, 1965), 49–50.

57. Ibid., 50, 88, 100, 101.

58. U.S. Department of Health, Education, and Welfare, Office of Education, concerning Title VII, National Defense Education Act of 1958 (n.d.), Elliott Papers, Box 98, Folder 4757. While there is no date in the document, internal evidence in the document reveals that it was disseminated in late 1958 or early 1959.

59. Lawrence G. Derthick, "Perspective," *School Life: Official Journal of the Office of Education-National Defense Education Act, A Full Report* (October–November 1958), 2.

60. Arthur S. Flemming, "Partnership Continued," *School Life* (October–November 1958): 3.

61. Ibid.

62. Lawrence G. Derthick, "Box Score on the National Defense Education Act," *NEA Journal* (September 1959); 37–38.

63. Elliot L. Richardson, "Towards a National Policy for Higher Education," *Higher Education* (September 1959): 3–7; quotations 4, 6.

64. Ibid., 7.

65. Gerald W. Elbers, "The National Defense Education Act and Higher Education," *Higher Education* (September 1959): 8–16.

66. CQ Fact Sheet, On Aid to Education (August 28, 1959), in Hill Papers, Box 238, Folder 93.

67. U.S. Department of Health, Education, and Welfare, Report of the Consultants to the Secretary of Health, Education, and Welfare and the U.S. Commissioner of Education on areas related to The National Defense Education Act of 1958 (n.d. [January 1961]), Hill Papers, Box 238, Folder 98.

68. Handwritten notes and partial text of Harold Howe's Welcoming Remarks (September 10, 1968), OE Papers, Box 344, Folder AO 6-2 Tenth Anniversary.

Chapter 7

1. David Gamson, in a chapter in a book on federal policy edited by Carl Kaestle, argued that NDEA represented a continuation of a socially biased approach to public education invented by administrative progressives four decades prior to the 1950s. Basically, administrative progressivism attempted to streamline public schools, to make them more efficient, often at the cost of providing relevant services to minority populations represented by immigrants, minorities, and other members of the lower

classes. Concentrating on the counseling and guidance title of NDEA, Gamson argued that its emphasis on increasing testing programs in the high schools and, later in the elementary schools, fostered a concern for the academically gifted student that resulted in neglect of other students. NDEA-supported guidance institutes trained school counselors in the administration of various standardized tests, and in the ideology of a limited talent pool and a stress on its development, that had long animated the actions of many American school leaders. Gamson's argument is powerful, and seems appropriate in its analysis of Title V of NDEA. His claim that subject matter reforms in other NDEA titles, such as those covering science and mathematics, and foreign languages, were also involved in restricting educational opportunity in the same way that testing and counseling did, seems less well supported than his critique of Title V. Also, the student loan and the graduate fellowship titles stand in tension with, if not in contradiction to, Gamson's argument that NDEA limited equality of educational opportunity more than it enhanced it. See David Gamson, "From Progressivism to Federalism: The Pursuit of Equal Educational Opportunity, 1915–1965," in *To Educate a Nation: Federal and National Strategies of School Reform*, ed. Carl F. Kaestle and Alyssa Lodewick (Lawrence: University Press of Kansas, 2007), 177–201.

2. Hugh Davis Graham, *The Uncertain Triumph: Federal Education Policy in the Kennedy and Johnson Years* (Chapel Hill: University of North Carolina Press, 1984), 93–100.

3. Ibid., 93.

4. John Rudolph, *Scientists in the Classroom: The Cold War Reconstruction of American Science Education* (New York: Palgrave, 2002).

5. See Deanna Michael, *Jimmy Carter as Educational Policy Maker* (Albany: State University of New York Press, 2008).

6. National Commission on Excellence in Education, "A Nation at Risk" (Washington, DC: U.S. Department of Education, 1983).

7. It is the case that many of the equity initiatives from prior to 1983, including federal aid to schools and to college students, continued in existence after 1983.

8. Henry Chauncey Memorandum to the Education Panel (June 18, 1958), White House Office, Office of the Special Assistant for Science and Technology, Records, 1957–61, Box 8, Eisenhower Library.

9. Carl F. Kaestle, "Federal Education Policy and the Changing Polity for Education, 1957–2007," in *To Educate a Nation*, ed. Kaestle and Lodewick, 17–40. Jennings Wagoner Jr. and I have made a similar distinction in our textbook on educational history, *American Education: A History* (New York: Routledge, 2009), where we divide the last two chapters with the 1980 election and note the difference in emphasis by titling the pre-1980 chapter "The Pursuit of Equality" and the post-1980 chapter "From Equality to Excellence."

10. At www.cgsnet.org.portals/0/pdf/GR_CoReport_0205.pdf.

11. At www.aau.edu/education/ndeaop.pdf.

12. At http://Kerry.senate.gov/cfm/record.cfm?id=25738.

Index